THE
AMERICAN
AMBASSADOR

BOOKS BY WARD JUST

FICTION

A Soldier of the Revolution · *1970*
The Congressman Who Loved Flaubert · *1973*
Stringer · *1974*
Nicholson at Large · *1975*
A Family Trust · *1978*
*Honor, Power, Riches, Fame and
   the Love of Women* · *1979*
In the City of Fear · *1982*
The American Blues · *1984*
The American Ambassador · *1987*

NONFICTION

To What End · *1968*
Military Men · *1970*

THE
AMERICAN
AMBASSADOR

WARD JUST

HOUGHTON MIFFLIN COMPANY   BOSTON

A RICHARD TODD BOOK

Library of Congress Cataloging-in-Publication Data

Just, Ward S.
   The American ambassador.

   "A Richard Todd book" —
   I. Title.
PS3560.U75A79 1987   813'.54   86-20126
ISBN 0-395-42694-4

Printed in the United States of America

P 9 8 7 6 5 4 3 2

An excerpt from this book originally appeared in the Winter 1986 issue of *TriQuarterly*, a publication of Northwestern University.

The quotation from Dylan Thomas's "Do Not Go Gentle Into That Good Night" on page 92 is from *Poems of Dylan Thomas*. Copyright © 1952 by Dylan Thomas. Reprinted by permission of New Directions Publishing Corporation.

TO SARAH

THE
AMERICAN
AMBASSADOR

PROLOGUE

Y OU ASKED ME about their corruption. The occasions that
come most easily to mind are Thanksgivings. You don't
have them where you come from. They're an American
tradition begun, oh, three hundred and fifty years ago; more. A
feast to celebrate the harvest after the killer winter of 1621. Something about Thanksgiving brought out their decay, the utter care-
lessness and ignorance with which they view the world. Giving
thanks, they were at their most sentimental. Of course it was the
ambassador's favorite holiday. He always proposed the same toast,
a quotation from Lincoln's Second Inaugural. *It may seem strange
that any men should dare to ask a just God's assistance in wringing their
bread from the sweat of other men's faces.* . . .

Strange indeed, my angel.

Thanksgiving 1979, we were in Paris. Halfway through dinner
he had an inspiration. He thought we needed a history lesson,
mother and me. We'd take a couple of days and visit some of the
War One cemeteries and monuments. Mother looked at him in
surprise and said in her sarcastic way, Oh, great! Grrrreat! That
means she thinks it's a terrific idea; it's the way they talk to each
other, always have. He leaned across the table, his fat mouth full

of French turkey, and looked at me. I suppose he thought we could be boys together. But I looked back at him with no expression at all and shrugged, Whatever you say. Whenever I do that, it irritates the shit out of him. He thought for a minute and said that if we would bear with him for a couple of days, then he'd agree to stop for the night near Épernay and we could drink Champagne with dinner. Mother laughed and said, Right on! Their solution to everything is to have an expensive meal and drink Champagne.

We set out a few days later in an embassy car. I would have liked to beg off, but I didn't have any money; and he wouldn't give me any, even if I had asked, which of course I would never do. And in a way, I didn't mind going, to see how he would approach it. How the ambassador's moral vision would cope with the Western Front. Nothing's left to the imagination, and I wondered what he'd say, standing in the cold surrounded by gravestones. He has a theory about everything.

My angel, we are in your part of the world. So bring the killing grounds into your mind's eye: the low hills, the sudden valleys, the irregular woods, the milky sky. It's cold, you can see your breath. Observe him, a tallish American, slightly stooped. He thinks of himself as one of them, for he, too, has known battle, having been a casualty; an incident in Africa, years before. He was wounded then and as a result his back gives him trouble. His wife stands beside him. You know immediately that they are married, and have been married for many years. There is similarity in their postures: she, too, looks slightly stooped. He is talking and she is looking at him, her head cocked; she is smiling, even though nothing he is saying is amusing. She touches his arm and they walk off together, alone.

We went first to the Somme Cemetery, fourteen acres, 1837 dead. Then we went to the Aisne-Marne Cemetery, forty-two acres, 2288 dead. The Aisne-Marne is near Belleau Wood, and he insisted that we walk through that. He bought a guidebook so that we could understand the flow of the battle. "Flow of the battle," his words; the great river of Western civilization. On the way to the Oise-Aisne Cemetery — thirty-six acres, 6012 dead — we stopped at the Château-Thierry monument, built by the same firm that built Washington, D.C., chunks of marble piled one on top of the other.

2

It looked like a Roman ruin that you'd find in Palestine or Libya. All rectangles, except for an occasional pillar; imperialist realism. He was driving like a madman and near dark we got to the Meuse-Argonne Cemetery. Bow your heads, ladies and gentlemen. Say a prayer. This was the greatest boneyard of them all, one hundred and thirty acres! A grave every three and a half feet! 13,246 stiffs.

In ten hours we'd seen twenty-five thousand graves, an infantry division of dead. Superb. It was really superb. All those white crosses, and bones under each cross. No monuments to the civilians, however; this was exclusively for the soldiers, and the higher the rank, the gaudier the monument. One of them reminded me of the bell tower at my old school in Massachusetts, bought and paid for by an alumnus, a Boston banker, Banker's Tower, a hundred and fifty feet high; it looked like a one-hundred-and-fifty-foot hard-on. It was where we beat the shit out of that English teacher, that time I told you about, Mel's revenge. These reminded me of that. Same thing, same thing exactly. I looked at the plots and wondered if it was true that the hair and fingernails continue to grow, while the brain, testicles, liver, heart, and eyes become dust. There were people here and there at the Meuse-Argonne Cemetery, old people standing around at attention. A tableau vivant, the ambassador called it. I imagined the ground beginning to move, caving and splitting, releasing a gust of noxious gas, and the corpses rising in a great wail, all bones and hair and nails, and all of us dancing, a boogie of our own time; all of us locked in an embrace.

Can't you see it?

Back in the embassy car, she took the wheel. He was reading some book and quoting passages about how the British troops were playing cricket at Flanders while the shells flew overhead. They played cricket listening to the explosions and the screams of their comrades. Haw, haw, those English. Well bowled, Wilfred! Dinka-doo, baby. It was pathetic. And by then we'd gotten away from Épernay, so he didn't get his great meal with the wine of the region. That was the good part. They drank Champagne of course but it wasn't the same because it wasn't the wine of the region.

I said it sounded to me like blood was the wine of the region.

You have a point, son, the ambassador said.

They never shut up during dinner. They talked about the cem-

3

eteries and monuments we'd seen, and what the Great War meant. They talked as if it ought to have some great meaning, something beyond itself, an epiphany, boomlay boomlay boomlay boom. But I couldn't understand what they thought it was, except the simple fact that a couple of million sons of bitches died for empire. The ambassador said, The nineteenth century died, right here on the Western Front. Uh-huh. They are not very original people, the ambassador and his wife; the ambassador drops centuries the way other people drop names. The British upper crust, he said; their ruling class destroyed, a generation lost. I thought, What a darn shame. All those la-di-da peers, dead in the mud. Oh, dear. Well, it was their empire. Why shouldn't they die for it? No tears, please.

Well, I said, why *did* it happen?

I wanted him to explain it to me, as best he could. He'd read so much about it, it's like a hobby with him, stamp collecting, furniture making, the Great War. The library in the house on O Street is filled with books on the First War. A few of them discuss the economic causes, and I thought he might address those. Assign some weight, give them specific gravity. For instance, Who profited? But he didn't say anything about it. He seemed to feel that fate played a hand. He said, Arrogance, ignorance. Things went out of control.

And they wanted it so badly, he said.

I just looked at him. It was the only thing he'd said all day long that made any sense, though not the sense that he intended.

Next day, Verdun. A three-star graveyard, worth a journey. Six months of fighting, a quarter of a million dead. Cold as shit, north wind, rain, and fog, an ideal day to view the remains. We walked through the Ossuaire, then out again. They just looked, didn't say much. I kept the conversation going, determined to be light. I was reading from the guidebook, the circumstances of the legend of the Tranchée des Baionettes, an infantry regiment buried by German artillery, only the ends of their rifle barrels and bayonets visible at the end. You don't want to hear about it, French nostalgia. *La gloire.*

I was reading aloud, and suddenly saw myself in the trench. What would I have done? I continued to read automatically, but I was imagining the smoke and the flame, and the explosions, the officers' shouts. I was thinking of the Ukrainian Machno, Lenin's

4

friend. Everyone loved Machno. No one dared attack Machno, even in 1918 when the Russians were slaughtering each other, and no one was safe. Machno's austere slogan: "Kill all civil servants. Kill them without prejudice, no matter what party they belong to or what government gave them their posts." I closed the book and watched them walk away a little distance. He was more stooped than usual. Mother had her arm around his waist and was talking earnestly at him, her there-there now-now tone. His head was bowed and he kept nodding. When I approached, they walked off again; a classified conversation.

Of course I knew what it was about. He had been silent all morning, after seeing the paper. A new development in Teheran, the Revolutionary Guards were getting nasty. They were threatening the lives of Americans! Obviously he knew many of the people in the embassy, the ones taken hostage — though hostage is a strange term for people whose job it was to *spy*, no more and no less, who invented the tyrant Pahlevi, installed him as shah, paid him, armed him, and advised him, lawyer to client. I would call them prisoners of war. The idea seemed to be that they were neutrals, only carrying out the orders of the President via the Department of State, that they were somehow immune and not to be held responsible for their actions. They were *excused*. Weird. I watched them talk, muttering at each other. She had both hands on his chest, and then she kissed him. Her hair glistened with rain. Then I heard his deep voice, raised for a moment. Those *assholes*, he said. I turned away, laughing. Did he really think that was what they were? He could see no farther than the men's locker room, the perfect Bourbon prince. Nothing learned, nothing forgotten. Machno, Machno. I began to laugh again. Where are you now that we need you?

Verdun was the last of the battlefields, though naturally when you are touring in that part of Europe you cannot avoid them; they are as common as vineyards. But now he only noted the signs; we did not "go in." We moved easily from War One to War Two, meandering north. We passed within a few miles of Waterloo, but no one said anything. They talked in the front seat, I read or dozed in the rear. I remember one little bit of conversation regarding the great crisis.

She said, "What are they going to do?"

5

The ambassador said, "The time for doing something is past."

"Well, they can't do nothing."

He said, "Yes, they can. They let it get to a point where they can only play the cards they have. There won't be another deal. And it's a nothing hand."

D'accord, Ambassador.

At last we arrived in Hamburg. You know Hamburg in early December, the Alster frozen and the icy wind from the North Sea. They wanted to meet some friends in Hamburg. There was a fish house they liked in the harbor, so we drove there after checking into the Hotel Prem. You remember the harbor. We ran the gauntlet of whores. God knows what was in their veins, they stood on the cobblestones about twenty meters apart, black tights, red skirts. Quite young, most of them, and good-looking.

They were meeting embassy people. A German joined us later. Herr Kleust worked in the Foreign Ministry, and they'd known him in Africa. I vaguely remembered him, because I was very young at the time. He was with the ambassador during the incident in Africa. The ambassador always maintained that Herr Kleust saved his life. So when they meet they always throw their arms around each other. Grunts and backslapping, old comrades that they are. The ambassador wipes away a tear while his wife looks at them, shaking her head. They are speaking rapid German. The ambassador calls him my-dear-friend-who-came-in-at-the-end-of-everything. A reference to something in the past, I have no idea what it is.

There are the three of us, two embassy people, and, later, Kleust. I'm certain that one of the embassy people was the chief spy. I had his name, but who knows if it's his real one. They're interchangeable parts, the spies. This one looked about thirty years old, except you knew he was fifty. Smooth complexion, short hair, cleft chin, looked like he stepped out of the window of J. Press, a trust-fund English professor at Yale. Melville and the Lake Poets. He was one of the old boys, the new ones aren't so smooth. Southern accent, young wife. His German was perfect. They were talking about the great crisis, switching back and forth between English and German, using euphemisms, code words, metaphors, probably to confuse me.

"We had too many men on the ice," J. Press said. "There should have been a cut in the squad five, six months ago."

"Try three years," the ambassador said.

They were drinking a lot of wine and halfway through the entrée the ambassador began to talk about the White House, and how incompetent they were. *Assholes,* he said; and here I thought he'd meant the Revolutionary Guards. The ambassador is full of surprises. The spy took offense, only President we've got, give him our full support, tough decisions, hate to be in his shoes, oh bruthah. That plantation accent. The ambassador changed the subject, and then they were talking about the latest scandal, the one that hadn't gotten into the newspapers — not yet! Some FSO ran off with counterpart funds and his secretary and was in Brazil, where no one could get at him. They were talking about what a mild-mannered fellow he was, pussy-whipped all those years by his wife, and what a shame, etcetera etcetera. Class alliance. Foreign Service Protective Association.

Kleust walked in then and he and the ambassador went through their comrades-in-arms act. The German didn't say much, just sat and listened. He was almost bald, with a heavy, dour face. Herr Kleust displayed little on the surface, except to smile when the ambassador would reach over and punch him on the arm.

They began to talk about the difference between American and European scandals. Some of the scandals I'd never heard of, but the idea seemed to be that the Europeans were tempted by ideology and sex, the Americans by money. The Americans used to be tempted by ideology but ideology had no meaning for today's American. Uh-huh. They had a fine time talking about scandal. The great continuum of scandal, scandal through the ages. The spy, half drunk at the end of dinner, put a cigar in his tight little mouth and talked for fifteen minutes, his Yale lecture. How inevitable it all was. Scandal inevitable. War inevitable. Error inevitable. Life in the West. The imperfectability of man. The long twilight struggle, sigh. Oh, the spy was saying, we've seen it all. Nothing new under the sun for us, loyal civil servants. We've been around forever. Got to take the long view, ha-ha. It was a disorderly world, filled with troublemakers.

"Americans," I said.

He looked at me. "What?"

"Most of the trouble is made by Americans."

He looked at the ambassador, eyebrows elevating.

The ambassador said,"My son has the idea that his countrymen are not letter-perfect."

"Let us hear what he has to say." That was Herr Kleust, speaking in German.

"Vietnam, I suppose," J. Press said.

"Palestine and Iran," I said.

He continued as if he hadn't heard me; he probably hadn't. He was not the sort of spy who *listened*. He was too fond of his own theories. For Americans, especially young Americans, Vietnam stood in the way of the horizon. It stood in the way of history. It was a tumbril in Constitution Avenue. But you don't have to worry about it, he said; it won't ever happen again. "Americans won't ever again believe, the way those Americans believed. Two centuries of belief ended in Indochina. Of the people, by the people, and for the people; that all ended, too. Follow me. That ended. I thought a kind of class warfare would begin, but it didn't. So the belief in justice: that ended, too."

"Is that what you think?" Herr Kleust said.

"Absolutely," J. Press said.

"I meant the young man." The German smiled coldly at me. He had not taken his eyes off me and now he said softly, "The trouble in Palestine and Iran is caused by the Americans?"

Herr Kleust had no interest in Indochina; he had no more interest than I did, though for different reasons.

"Can we get off this?" the ambassador said, pulling a long face. He signaled the waiter for another round of schnapps.

"Yes," Mother said. "Let's, please."

But it was between Kleust and me. I said, "And the Germans."

He said, "I see."

"In Palestine," I added, in case he had failed to get the point. I knew he hadn't. He wasn't that kind of German.

"Of course," he said. "The Germans also."

"The German people . . ." J. Press said. He began to bluster again, his plantation accent thicker and more disgusting. Yet I listened to him; he was not a stupid man, obviously. The Americans are dangerous because they are so easily underestimated. They seem to skim over the surface of things, and their listeners forget that that is often where things *are*, on the surface. He was off now on a tour of twentieth-century horrors, and how the Germans were not responsible for all of them. Most talented people in Europe, etcetera. The hardest-working. The most dynamic economy, etcetera. I tuned out then. I think that Herr Kleust did, too. I watched them talk and said nothing further. Eventually they returned to their discussion, the great crisis, and scandal; sex, money, and ideology. World-weary Americans are amusing, in the way that an adolescent in a three-piece suit and a fedora is interesting. So: the corruption of sex, ideology, and money, and nothing to be done about it, human nature being what it is. Old as mankind, old as the hills. The secret, according to the spy, was not to be surprised. You couldn't allow yourself to be *surprised*.

And then this idea came to me. I began to smile, thinking of it — that if someone had said, Hey, baby, have you heard the news? The *Post* had a piece about it. They're burning folks out at Chevy Chase. Built a couple of ovens right next to the country club, eighth tee, going full-out, every day, every night, burning niggers! This asshole would listen and say, Well, waaaaaiiit a minute. We've heard all this before! That's nothing new! What about Belsen and Auschwitz? What about Dachau? Let's have a little perspective here!

We were the last ones out of the restaurant. It was midnight but the port was busy, the Germans being talented, hard-working, and dynamic. The whores were at their stations, but began to drift in our direction when we appeared on the street. I swear to God, angel, one of them was carrying a teddy bear. The ambassador and Herr Kleust were talking, their arms around each other's shoulders. My mother and the other embassy person stood huddled in the doorway. The whores came in closer. I was reminded of animals circling a garbage dump. The spy nudged me. He said, "Best-looking whores in the world, in Hamburg. Better'n Marseille or Singapore, or Saigon in the old days. You get a minute, you ought to go to Saint Pauli, just for the hell of it. Look, don't touch. There're fifty-seven varieties of clap in Hamburg." He laughed loudly and made a motion with his hands, and the whores were suddenly alert. I was sick of him, his arrogance and presumption, and was about to reply when he walked away, looking for the cars. One of the whores was staring at me and I smiled and shook my head. They began to back off, into the shadows. I could hear the clanking of gears behind me, a ship being off-loaded. The air was gummy with salt and oil.

They were standing together now, the ambassador and his wife and Herr Kleust. She was in the middle. They had their arms around each other, talking with animation, their breath pluming in the tart air. So happy to see each other again. She looked from one to the other, laughing. The ambassador had made a joke. Herr Kleust replied, the occasion for more laughter. She gave them each a peck on the cheek. Then they became grave, and I knew they were talking about the great crisis. I heard the ambassador say, God, sometimes he's so difficult. So it was me they were talking about. They moved off into the shadows, arms around each other.

You know the port of Hamburg, its noise and its energy, ships from every port in the world. Listening to it, I knew what I was going to do. I waved at them, and said I would walk back to the Prem. The ambassador said it was too far, and too cold. I said I needed the air, and did not mind the cold. I was very excited. I hurried away down the dark street. There was a whore in every doorway, sometimes I saw only a face or a flash of skirt. Naturally I heard their voices, harsh, coarse German. And I answered in kind, and heard their laughter.

I left the others standing on the sidewalk in front of the restaurant. Someone had brought the embassy car, its lights casting long shadows in front of me. I ducked into an alley and looked back at the ambassador and his wife. I thought they were suddenly frail, without substance or nerve. They were without force.

But as I told you, my parents are mediocre people.

In any case, I did not see them again for three years.

PART ONE

I

AMBASSADOR NORTH'S apprehension had begun with a pain in his wrist, noticed one afternoon while he was fishing off- shore on Middle Ground, the boat tipping gently in the chop where the Sound's floor dropped abruptly from six to sixty fathoms. He thought the pain was caused by the oppressive south- west wind, the prevailing wind at the end of summer, blowing for days, humid and unnerving; the fishing was terrible. It was a noisy, surly wind, putting everyone on edge, even Elinor, who was usu- ally unaffected by climate. He thought the wind was the New En- gland version of the mistral or the tramontana, hot northern winds that agitated livestock and drove people indoors, unbalanced. But as it came from the southwest, it was related to the sirocco, the North African wind that swept the Mediterranean to oppress southern Europe. The southwest wind brought the damp Gothic humors of the American South, altogether foreign to the bony New England coast, Tennessee Williams seducing Cotton Mather.

Disorienting and perverse, the wind was ample cause for psy- chosomatic complaint. But when the wind stopped — it took twenty- four hours to do so, a torrential rain in the evening, then a slow swing around the compass until the next afternoon when, centered in the Maritimes, it moderated, becoming chilly and dry — the pain did not go away. His wristwatch and wedding band were tight on his skin. He joked that the metal was contracting, along with his shirt collars and trouser waistbands. This continued for a week.

Then one night at dinner he turned to laugh at something Elinor said — "You know, sometimes I like you as Jules and sometimes I like you as Jim, and tonight I'm in a Jules mood, how about you?" — and his cigarette dropped to the rug. They were finishing a fine conversation, the one they had every now and then: how exceptionally lucky they were in their choice of each other, what fun they had, how well their lives fit. This home leave, spent entirely at their cottage on Lambert's Cove, had been particularly tranquil and playful. The undertow was less charitable: and we haven't needed anyone else. How nice it's been, just us two. She'd said, "I can feel it coming on, another attack of the smugs. It's just as well we've only got a week left. Our home leave. Except it seems less and less like home. Is something burning?" He found himself staring at his two naked fingers poised comically half an inch from his mouth. His left hand was numb, inert as a piece of sculpture. The absence of pain was alarming and he drew back, the laughter dying, and put his hand in his lap, out of sight. Deep within him, something turned over but he forced his WASP's smile; his mother's smile, turning aside his father's Jewish frown. At times like these, you were thankful to be half-WASP. He sat very still, looking out the window at the lights across the Sound, beyond Middle Ground, the interval of the lighthouse beacon as regular as heartbeat. She said again, "Bill, what's burning?" He smiled an apology. The cigarette was smoldering on the rug. He picked it up with his right hand and stubbed it out, crushing it angrily into the ashtray — and went early to bed, though not to sleep.

In retrospect, all that seemed to carry significance, an irony of some kind, unintended consequence.

Lying in bed that night, he made a list of friends and their recent infirmities: herniated discs, prostate troubles, sciatica, hemorrhoids, and the disagreeable symptoms that announced them. In all these cases he had been consulted, a reliable, sympathetic, worldly friend, no stranger to hard times. Their wives had said to them, Talk to Bill North, he's been through the mill, no-nonsense Bill. He always listened carefully, then gave the obvious advice: See a doctor. And he would give them Brian Fowler's telephone number. But it was the time of life when no one wanted to see a doctor, for fear of what might turn up. It was fear of cancer. He always tried to make a mordant joke, for Christ's *sake,* we all drink too much, smoke too much, work too hard, exercise too little, it's a perfect profile and if we know one thing about our generation we know that nothing's predictable and that perfect profiles don't exist and won't apply. Talk to Fowler.

He'd said to Dick Hartnett, who was nursing a hemorrhoid the size of a golf ball: How many times in your life has the fear of the known been worse than the fear of the unknown?

And Dick had looked at him in amazement. Ah, Bill. You know better than that. *Always.*

Precisely, he'd said.

One by one his friends went to their doctors and one by one they stopped smoking and cut down on the drinking. Hypnotism, acupuncture, Valium, Smokenders, cold turkey. Aperitifs became popular, Lillet, Dubonnet, Campari, vermouth — with Perrier and a twist, and a smile of surrender. Cough syrup, thirty-two proof. Designer cocktails. They hated to do it, the sacrifice of the evening Martini or Scotch on the rocks evidence of mortality no less conspicuous than falling hair, chronic insomnia, or blood in the urine.

Now he could trade stories with them. I've got the damnedest pain in my wrist. And he could grin about that because it was a bagatelle. There was no such thing as cancer of the wrist. Then, clearing his throat: Actually, it was a pain but it isn't a pain anymore. It's a numbness, actually; there's no feeling at all. And the laughter would die away because numbness was a signal, if not of cancer then of something neurological. And these were dangerous, sudden times. Two friends had died of heart attacks while jogging and each man was fifty exactly. Not forty-nine or fifty-one but exactly fifty and both had died immediately, on the spot. One had died in Beirut and the other in Rock Creek Park. And North had imagined them dying at an angle, arms stiffening, eyes glazing, and feet askew, the pavement rising up to meet them — and suddenly the moment freezing, like a film stopped in midframe. The last conscious thought would be an astonishment: a defiance of gravity. Al Murillo, dead on the Corniche in Beirut, had written a light piece for the *Foreign Service Journal* describing the perils of jogging in Lebanon, which sections were safe and which were not, and the signs to watch for. An amusing piece, everyone said so, though the slightest bit — supercilious. In Rock Creek Park near the P Street beach, Joe Deshler had been dead an hour before anyone found him, his body stripped clean as a Mercedes in Anacostia, his watch, wallet, and running shoes gone. He was found by a friend, and immediately identified, otherwise his body would have disappeared into the morgue, tagged John Doe.

These two deaths had happened within a month of each other, part of the same equation, spiritually linked; someone sneezes in Tokyo, and a tornado changes direction in Kansas. They were good, close friends and when they died it was as if part of North's own history had died; his memory was no longer subject to verification. Murillo, Deshler, and North had been members of the same Foreign Service class; all three had served in Africa. They had become specialists in the problems of the Third World or, more accurately, the problems of the United States in the Third World. They had corresponded frequently, long droll letters; nothing had been as expected. Their careers were so different from those of their heroes, Bohlen, Thompson, and Kennan. The Third World, always simmering on the back burner. Adlai had cared, but Adlai was dead. Things changed quickly: the Europeans withdrew, the Russians advanced. Batista fled, the Congo fell apart. Sukarno, Sihanouk, Nkrumah. There were new rules and when Kennedy died and the Vietnamese won their war, newer rules. These were events to which North had been witness — though, amazingly, he had missed Indochina, feeling at the time like a master musician playing Dubuque while the rest of the orchestra was at Carnegie Hall — and his memory, he knew, was no longer trustworthy. It was flabby and unresponsive, like an athlete's body gone to seed. Too much junk food had gone into it, and it was nothing he could rely on in a crisis, or swear to in court. Of course there were the documents, but the documents — memorandums of conversations, action memos, National Security Council directives, CIA estimates, congressional mandates, various minutes of emergency meetings here and there — told only part of the story and often not the most important part, They were like obits. Vital statistics did not describe a life. What was it about Age Fifty, and a career in the government?

How fragile we are, Elinor had said, but he had shaken his head: Not fragile, strong. But soon to be overwhelmed. He had said this under his breath at graveside at the most recent Washington funeral — Joe Deshler's, his wife and daughters seated, stricken, on folding chairs — as the officiating Lutheran spoke of everlasting life, the divinity of Christ, and the pressures of government service.

This was not a cheerful inventory, and it kept North awake. He, Murillo, and Deshler; in the early nineteen sixties, when they were in Africa together, they felt like pioneers. Their ambassadors were political appointees, well-traveled men, but new to diplomacy and ignorant of the Third World. Deshler's ambassador was a man of charm and wit, a midwestern businessman of humane instinct. Son of a gun, he's said after six months in-country, this is worse than Chicago. It was not graft on a colossal scale, because the country was so poor; but everything there to be stolen was stolen. However, the country was free of Communists and that was a problem. Every year a problem with the foreign aid appropriation because there was no Moscow-inspired internal threat. In fact, as the ambassador observed, there were more Communists in Chicago. There were more Communists in one department at the university than there were in B——. But it was a bell curve. Each year, he predicted, there would be more Communists in B——, while in Chicago, of course, there would be fewer. What had Melville said about his whaling ship? My Yale College and my Harvard. That was what North felt about Africa, and wherever he went thereafter, Africa went, too. The continent had not had the same effect on Murillo and Deshler. Poor Joe Deshler — Africa had become an obsession and after 1970, as he freely admitted, he wasn't worth a damn as a Foreign Service officer. He no longer knew where his deepest loyalties lay. When he died in Rock Creek Park, he was on loan to the Agency for International Development.

When Elinor came to bed, he feigned sleep, his left hand tucked awkwardly under his chin. He thought of rolling over, then didn't. He couldn't get his mind on sex and keep it there. His dead hand distracted him. He continued to flex his fingers, feeling her beside him, her heat and the rhythm of her breathing, not quite asleep; she moved and touched his foot with her own. Your move, Jules. Her foot was warm and he backed into her, the underside of his thighs against her knees. Her touch was comfortable and familiar, without reserve. And we haven't needed anyone else, he thought; a two-edged thought. She mumbled something, turning, and he was alone again. He shut his eyes and saw the cigarette, white against the dark shag of the rug and the accusing wisp of smoke.

Then he was dozing, moving back and forth among his dead and troubled friends, his wife, and his absent son. He was trying to ignore his numb hand. By concentrating on his friends he thought he could make a separate peace. But Bill Jr. forced his way inside, an occupying army: Bill Jr. at seven, ten, thirteen, sixteen, nineteen, and twenty-four. He watched the boy grow, taller and broader; listened to the voice deepen; watched the smile disappear.

Sleep would not come so he carefully got out of bed and crept into the kitchen and poured a glass of milk. A low counter separated the kitchen from the living room. On a table at the far end of the living room, dimly seen by moonlight, were family photographs in silver frames, their national archive. Elinor in a bikini on a beach near Mombasa, almost twenty years ago. He and Elinor with Jomo Kenyatta at the race course in Nairobi, the Mzee's fly whisk only inches from her nose, the old bull rank with bed, whiskey, and cigars; Elinor maintained his only equal in pure animal grace was Richard Burton. Elinor with an animated Robert Lowell in a pub in Hampstead, both of them jolly and tight, their moods matching the rosy glow of the pub. He and Elinor in black tie, talking to Lyndon Johnson at a reception in Washington; no, *listening* to Lyndon Johnson at a reception in Bonn, the former President's hands deep in his trouser pockets, jiggling coins and his private parts, telling them about his library, greatest of all the presidential libraries, the most complete, the handsomest, and in *Texas*, magnet for scholars worldwide, he himself overseeing each detail (though North remembered, too, Dunphy, the old man's aide, late

18

at night, with the former President in bed and out of the way, conducting a monologue, he and Elinor listening with the attention you'd give a great cellist playing tragic Mozart in your own living room, the concert for your ears only. They were downstairs in the ambassador's residence, Dunphy suddenly announcing: "We thought he was FDR. And greater than FDR because he was a man of the people, not an aristocrat come down from the Hudson Valley. LBJ knew common Americans at first hand, and was native to the newest region of the country, not the oldest, and had passions — what passions! — and a parliamentary skill that took your breath away. But he could never overcome the manner of his arrival, and then that fucking war. He's brokenhearted now, won't last a year. Hey, hey, LBJ, how many kids did you kill today? He hears it day and night, it won't go away. I thought of the war like this: a storm that had been gathering for a hundred and ninety years, breaking suddenly, a deluge. He had the best minds around him, and he took their advice. The best minds were wonderfully articulate when talking about war. It became their academic specialty. And they were wrong and he was wrong, and there was never a greater error in the history of the presidency. What consequences! If he had come to the presidency on his own, what an eight years he, and we, could have had! That war is going to go on and on, and LBJ will be dead in a year. And I'll go back to Washington and make a lot of money because that's the other change I've seen. It happened just the other day, it seems. Money in Washington. You've never seen so much money, it's a great sea of money, and there for the taking. For the asking. And as for you, you're young yet" — he nodded at them both, his eyes welling — "you and your wife have lived abroad all this time, and you've never served in Indochina. My advice is, Stay away from it. Avoid the war, not because it will hurt your career, because it won't. The Foreign Service is going to need somebody who is not in love with the memory of Indochina. It is not the only memory there is. Indochina is an aberration, an aberration for him, and for the country. Let's go to bed now. I'm going upstairs to check on the old bastard. He's probably reading, not asleep at all. He has insomnia. Many people would say that's a small price for him to pay, and perhaps it is. But, as I say, he'll be dead in a year. And our fellow citizens, or many of them, will be happy. But I like to remember a man on the best day he ever had, so I'll remember him in the well of the House of Representatives, shouting — it was a shout, you'll remember — *And we shall overcome!* And knowing what it meant. Or knowing it as well as any white man can know it, and feel it, too. You should have seen him, after he made the speech. And knew its effect. He spread his arms wide. I think he thought he could fly, that night. He took it all, ears, tail, and hooves. I'm going now, and as you know we leave early in the morning. I don't know what we're doing here, in the Federal Republic of Germany. We go to Paris tomorrow and then somewhere else. And then back to the ranch. I'll be in Washington in a year. When you come back, look me up. I'll be in the book, the yellow pages, under attorney at law. . . .").

Photographs of them together in Cape Town, Madrid, Venice, Berlin (the Wall), and at the summit of Kilimanjaro (Elinor pointing to a pile of bones and insisting that it was the carcass of Hemingway's leopard). And at the rear, partly obscured by Venice and Berlin, Elinor's sketch of Bill Jr. on the deck (in the background, through the windows, the attentive observer could see the table with the photographs in silver frames). Standing in the kitchen, he could not see Elinor's sketch. He could not see any of the pictures clearly, but he remembered them, each detail, and their locations on the table. The sketch was made on the deck late on a sunny Sunday afternoon, Bill Jr. at seventeen, tall and muscular, clad in chinos and a plain white T-shirt, an austere presence. Any stranger would have thought him sullen. His hands were tucked in his rear pockets, his eyes concealed behind dark glasses. He wore no shoes.

The ambassador stepped around the counter and padded across the living room to peer closely at the photograph of him and Elinor with LBJ. Dunphy had gone on to become a private lawyer, exactly as he had promised. He was a lawyer who went in and out of government, often as special counsel to congressional committees, famous for his scowl, his sarcasm, and his contempt for academics and bureaucrats, anyone unfamiliar with elections, and the whims of the voters.

Lawyers, journalists, politicians, diplomats; Washington characters. The ambassador had spent his entire adult life in the milieu of government. On the wall above the table was a drawing of Lincoln, artist unknown, a present from Elinor. In a few decisive strokes the artist had managed to assemble a face broken by remorse. When he looked at the drawing of Lincoln's face, he always thought of the words from the Second Inaugural: . . . *as God gives us to see the right.* And if God was misinterpreted?

It was a face from which all happiness had been erased.

He massaged his hand.

Now he was on the deck. The night was balmy and the Sound restless under a crescent moon, empty of boats. He was startled when the cat suddenly appeared, jumping from the lawn to the railing of the deck and then to his feet, where she rubbed her black body against his ankles. She was still agitated by the memory of the surly southwest wind, the pressure causing her to dart nervously here and there in the house. She spent the nights outside, searching for rodents. He had heard once that a cat's memory was but twenty minutes long, but that could not be true. This cat had an elephant's memory, though she was old, lame, and no longer frisky. He wondered if she remembered Bill Jr. But of course she would. he listened to her purr while he lit a cigarette, looking at the lighthouse, squinting into the darkness, calculating the intervals.

BLINK onethousandandone onethousandandtwo onethousandandthree BLINK

Regular as heartbeat.

That dreadful week in 1975 — Bill Jr. at seventeen, suspended from school. They were on a month's home leave. Bill Jr. had been standing *there,* by the wrought-iron table. Dishes and glasses littered the table; it was a beautiful Sunday in May, and they had taken lunch on the deck. They had been arguing. The argument had begun at lunch and continued into the afternoon, Elinor sitting quietly, sketching, occasionally putting in two cents' worth. He had been trying to explain to his son the consequences of life inside the government, life below decks on the ship of state, the oath of office, your promise to defend the Constitution. How abstract it could seem, yet how grave; it was very abstract and very grave when you were working in countries that had no constitution. Bill Jr. had asked him about the coup, now twelve years old, in the

21

newspapers again that morning. A journalist had been given some documents, and obtained others under the Freedom of Information Act. The documents, and the hack's interpretation of them, were causing a minor scandal. He explained the coup, and how they in the embassy had stopped it. A liberal interpretation of his oath of office, he admitted, since the United States Constitution was not threatened. United States interests were, he admitted; but that was not quite the same thing.

We made various threats and spent some money, he said.

Well then, Bill Jr. said, *they* failed.

With our help, he said.

You had that much power?

Yes. And they didn't want it badly enough.

And you did?

Yes, we did.

How does it look to you now, that decision?

He remembered turning, exasperated. What did he think, that they had never replayed that? Did he think it was forgotten? Did he think they needed some wire-service hack to tell them what they had done, and how they had done it, and the results? One of the results was three weeks in a German missionary's hospital. The newspaper stories were shapely, giving the event the quality of an old film, early Hitchcock or middle Bogart, making visible the creaking machinery of plot, and the hand of the *auteur*, very grainy, the dialogue enchanting.

> *I came to Casablanca for the waters,* Rick said.
> *There are no waters in Casablanca.*
> Rick said, *I was misinformed.*

They stood glaring at each other, father and son, in the unseasonable spring heat. Of course the argument had nothing to do with the Constitution or diplomacy or the coup in the famished African nation. It was a surrogate argument having to do with — citizenship, Bill Jr.'s suspension from school, the headmaster's telephone call preceding the boy's arrival by a day. Bill Jr. was being "sent down" (the headmaster's mid-Atlantic locution) for a week, the week being arbitrary, there being no precedent for the offense in the school's 134-year history. Or at least as far as any faculty member's memory reached. It was very disturbing. An instructor had been badly beaten by a student, a senior, a, ah, troubled youngster, who had been in trouble for most of the year, had in fact been on multiple warning. His name was Mel Crown and he was Bill Jr.'s roommate. Mel Crown had grown up in a difficult environment, an environment entirely at odds with the school's stately brick buildings and lawns, and New England discipline. That was the key. The boy, Mel, was undisciplined and angry, always acting out, and that was understandable, given the family background. There was no father in the home. The mother worked. He's been fired, expelled, needless to say —

Yes, the ambassador had said, exactly what was it that happened?

Mel Crown and Bill Jr. had been out after hours, we don't know where. Probably visiting one of the girls' dorms, though we can't prove that. The faculty member was coming home from a function. It was just after midnight. Apparently there had been a dispute in class that morning. Both Bill and the other boy were in his class, and there had been a contretemps. We still can't sort out the facts. But when the boys saw the instructor, words were exchanged. Mel started shouting, and then attacked him. He gave him a vicious beating, just vicious. The poor fellow's still in the hospital. He's a middle-aged English teacher, very popular. He's not in the best of condition, though he'll be all right, apparently. The headmaster sighed, and was silent.

He said, Where was Bill Jr. in all this?

Bill Jr. didn't do anything, the headmaster said. Then, fearing misinterpretation, he repeated himself: Bill Jr. *didn't* do *anything*. He didn't do anything to stop it. He didn't do anything to encourage it, either. He just watched. He was a spectator. Thank God the campus police happened along, and broke it up.

What was the instructor's name?

Frank Horner, the headmaster said. Of course, everyone calls him Jack.

He'll be all right?

The doctors say he will. He's got a concussion, bruises, cuts, a broken finger. Mel Crown is a big boy, very strong, very, very tough. He's a boy from the streets of New York.

He said, I don't know what to say.

I don't either, Mr. North, the headmaster said. As you know, Bill Jr. has been an excellent student, one of our best. A quiet, withdrawn sort of boy. Not very many friends, and he has that caustic side to his personality. He's got quite a sharp tongue. But he's never been in trouble.

What did he say when you asked him why he didn't do anything? I assume you asked him.

Yes, naturally. It's all a bit vague. He said it wasn't his fight. At the disciplinary hearing, he defended Mel, described the . . . he called it abuse of Mel by the instructor that morning in the classroom. He said there was no power on earth that could have stopped Mel Crown, and that somehow it would have been demeaning to try. I have the feeling that Bill Jr. thought Jack got what he deserved.

And what did Horner say about it?

Of course he's still in the hospital, and understandably reluctant to — go over it again and again. He did say that Bill Jr. did not take part, and was not responsible for what happened.

He said, I'm appalled.

Yes, Mr. North. So are we. It's good that there's only a month left this term, and Bill Jr. will be allowed to graduate. But it's our opinion that he needs help from someone. You or your wife, or a professional. It was a very bad episode.

And his demeanor?

Cold, Mr. North. Cold as ice.

No regrets?

None that we could find. None that he expressed.

It had always been difficult to see Bill Jr. in full light, undressed, in the round. You got the side he wanted you to have, and the rest was always in shadow. His instructors found him an excellent student, conscientious, thorough, subtle — perhaps a bit mechanical in his approach to the liberal arts, particularly literature and politics. He brushed aside compliments, insisting that schoolwork was easy for anyone with an excellent memory. Until the incident with Mel Crown, he had never been in difficulty with the authorities, yet he was quick to say that he found their rules and regulations "unfair" and "stupid," the discipline of the tyrant. Discipline, most underrated of virtues, rose from within. It was an individual response to pressure. That night on the school common, Horner had asked for it; and had gotten it. Mel Crown fought his own battles and did not want or need interference. In any case, he would always have to fight alone and unaided. Everyone did, that was obvious. And what about the victim? North asked. The middle-aged English instructor, unlucky enough to be walking across the campus late at night. Well, the boy said, he too was obliged to fight his own battles. And this time he lost. As you have said so often, he didn't want it badly enough. That must have been the reason. Isn't that why one side loses? That they don't want it badly enough? Isn't that your theory?

As they stood on the deck that afternoon, facing each other, Elinor looking on, he remembered feeling a chill. He thought it was a sudden breeze, but it wasn't that at all. It was the look on his son's face. He was afraid of whatever it was that this boy wanted so badly, he with his mechanical approach and excellent memory, and inner discipline. North understood what Horner felt, the two boys approaching him — the taunts, the shouted words, and Mel Crown's blows, heavy as hammers. And Bill Jr., the silent spectator, the watchman.

He remembered Elinor quickly completing the sketch, and handing it to Bill Jr. He took it without looking at it; he was waiting for an answer to his question. *How does it look to you now, that decision?* The boy's face was frozen, without expression. Its expressionlessness suggested fury, a fathomless anger without object or definition; without face. When Elinor said, "It's a sketch of you," the words seemed as loud as the bang of a door. Bill Jr. put the sketch on the railing of the deck and moved off into the house. Presently they heard the car's engine in the driveway, and the crunch of gravel. Elinor had turned to her husband with a sardonic, inquisitive expression. What did I do? Or fail to do?

It wasn't you, he had said. It was me.

Yes, she said. Politics.

Not politics, he had said. *Me.*

Dummy, she said. It's the same thing to him.

It was all the same thing, one long abrasive conversation: Africa, the coup, Mel Crown, Jack Horner, a single incident played out against that warm first week in May 1975, and when at last the boy left to return to school, Bill and Elinor began to quarrel — about money, modern art, the meaning of Watergate, the price of eggs. It took them days to get back to normal. He wondered if their reckless son united them, in the way that Arabs united Israelis. Was that what he was, a common enemy?

No, not that. He was a stranger in their midst, the mutinous victim of an army of occupation. They were the invaders, conquerors of his territory. He behaved correctly, with circumspection, giving no more than was required to avoid punishment. Yet they knew that when their backs were turned, when he was out of their sight, he was another person. His character eluded them. Even his looks seemed to change from day to day, a fact the boy recognized. Elinor's sketch was a violation of his fierce privacy, his shadowy secret self. Lucky Elinor, she was able somehow to move around him, retreating into her own work, her art. She refused to salute. And the boy did not find her responsible, did not find her guilty, an enemy of the people — or, anyway, his enemy. She was more nuisance than enemy. She was an accessory. All sons were judges, but this one was a hanging judge.

The cat moved against his leg, and he reached down again to gently pull its tail. He leaned against the railing and took a deep breath, forcibly removing himself from the past to the present. He had to concentrate to do it. He flipped the cigarette onto the lawn, then lifted himself off the deck, putting most of his weight on his right hand. Arms stiff, he swung free in the night air, his feet an inch off the deck. The wind was from the west, a sleepy zephyr, so light it barely moved the smoke from the cigarette guttering on the lawn. Still, it caressed and consoled him; it brought a hint of land. It was like a melody, easy to follow, elevating him into the soft darkness.

He let himself down with a thump. He had left his glasses inside and so his eyes glazed, looking at the lights across the Sound, Falmouth and Woods Hole, the lights blurred and erratic around the edges. He smelled the sea, so tart and adventurous, teeming with life under its still skin. It was how he felt about Africa, alive with heartbeats. West, beyond the Elizabeth Islands, was the sullen glow of the lights of New Bedford, the port of embarkation for Melville's obsessed whalers, setting sail into the future, the ocean as life itself, terrible in its torment, angelic in its calm. Beneath the surface, things were always in motion. He smiled in the darkness, looking again at his dead hand, inanimate as Ahab's false leg.

North raised his eyes to the stars, squinting; but he could see no stars, only the fragments of nervous light inside his own astigmatic retina. He guessed that at age fifty a man should be able to navigate by his own lights, with personal charts from a lifetime of experience, a diplomat's intimate knowledge of the world: making choices and then living with the consequences. Of course there was never a single lesson, and nothing discrete. Things flowed into each other, the end of one thing the beginning of another. You tried to look into the future but the future receded, as a shoreline recedes astern, the outline of it always in sight. You could locate yourself only with reference to the shoreline, so it was important to keep it in view; and you were satisfied with anything that lasted from today to tomorrow, durable for a single circuit of the earth around the sun. He tapped a little riff on the wooden railing, leaning forward, peering into the darkness, squinting again.

He had known the last five Presidents, known them as Presidents, not as men; he had no idea what they were like as men. They hadn't known him except as a vague name behind a familiar title, a man with some special knowledge and responsibility, experience in the field. He was known as a field man, uncomfortable in the Department. *Oh, yes, uh, North, good to see you again.* In the meetings in the Oval Office he had spoken only when spoken to; on more than one occasion, he had not spoken at all. The senior men conversed in a kind of code, and it took a moment to decipher. The code differed with the President and the occasion; one President liked the language of sports, another of the battlefield, still another of family life. They usually spoke slowly and softly, and with deft humor; no one raised his voice. This was a way of preparing a line of retreat, postponing a decision, always protecting their political interests without seeming to do so. A transcript would have been misleading. You had to hear the emphasis, where the commas went, where the laughs were; what the faces looked like, and who looked at whom, and when; and in the pauses and the silences there was always ambiguity and nuance, except when the professors were speaking. The professors had a zealot's faith in history and its lessons, and confidence that it — "it," they thought of history as a neutral hard science, like physics before Einstein — repeated itself in predictable ways.

BLINK onethousandandone onethousandandtwo onethousandandthree BLINK

He turned, sensing the telephone before he actually heard the ring, moving quickly back into the house, snatching the receiver from its cradle. Fiercely: "Hello!" A moment's dead air, and a soft click. He held the receiver a moment, then replaced it, hoping that Elinor had not been disturbed. Pleasant to think of it as a misdial; or if he were a jealous husband, his wife's lover, the lover morose at daybreak, needing the sound of her voice. He stood by the phone, looking at it with malevolence, willing it to ring again. But after you were a certain age, a telephone call late at night was never good news. On the other hand, Dick Hartnett once confessed with his bad-boy grin that, infatuated with a young woman who did not return his affection, he regularly practiced telepathy, telephoning her late at night, allowing the phone to ring once, then hanging up. It was his way of saying, *Here I am! I exist! It's me, thinking of you.* He always waited for a call back but it never came; it turned out that she was a heavy sleeper, and never heard the one ring.

This phone call was along that line. *Here I am! I exist! It's me!* And what are you going to do about it?

He returned to the deck, peering into the darkness, squinting again. He hated the early morning, always thick with dampness, his mind still heavy, half asleep, in neutral. He heard a noise and reached down to pat the cat, but she skittered away.

Elinor stood watching him. She watched his body bend and shift position. He stood with his foot hiked up on the railing, his foot beating time. He was muttering to himself, and although the words were not audible she knew he was singing his decline-of-the-West blues, diplomat's ja-da. He wanted people to have the patience and fatalism of the great blues singers. He wanted the secretary of state to have the wisdom of Bessie Smith. Elinor had argued once that his was a plantation mentality, he wanted everyone singing in the fields to the clank-clank of their chains. She watched her husband lift his head, staring at the sky. He said loudly, "God damn it, anyway." He wasn't wearing his glasses so he couldn't see anything. She said, "Bill?"

He turned quickly. Her face was in shadows and her nude body lit by moonlight. The crevices and fall lines of her body were defined by shadows, deep and alluring. His eyes registered all this but his expression was morose. He smiled sadly and made a little gesture with his hand.

"What's wrong? Why aren't you asleep? What are you doing out here? Come to bed." She spoke crisply, fully alert.

He said, "Insomnia." Seeing her, he thought of the boy; he had been just offstage, waving from the wings.

"You were muttering."

"Did I wake you? I'm sorry." He spoke automatically. The boy was at the center of his thoughts, on the edges of the known world.

"You didn't wake me. I woke up and you weren't there. I was having a dream, but it's gone now. So I came out here." She was silent a moment, yawning; it was so still. The breeze was cool on her warm skin. The hair of her forearms rose. "You were shaking the railing with your foot, baby. What's wrong?"

"Nothing's wrong."

She said, "I heard the telephone."

He turned back to face the Sound. "I was thinking about Bill Jr."

She moved to his side, slipping her arm through his. In the east, the sky was lightening, becoming gray. She imagined the sun racing across the Atlantic. Where Bill Jr. was, or was presumed to be, it was almost lunch time. When last they heard, he was in Germany; but he was probably somewhere else now. He could be anywhere. Nearby she heard a bird, the first of the morning. "Listen," she said.

He said, "Whoever it was hung up."

She said, "You know who it was."

"Not necessarily."

"Yes, necessarily," she said firmly. She put her hand around his waist, his skin warming her hand. "It's pretty out here. It's a warm night."

"I was looking at the sketch."

"Not a good likeness," she said.

"A pretty good likeness, El."

"No animation," she said.

He said nothing for a moment. Then, "He was always a good-looking boy."

She said, "I'm surprised. I had the feeling you weren't thinking about him, but about the decline of the West. You had that look. That look you get when you think you've lost your juju. And you were keeping time with your foot."

"No, it was him."

She said nothing.

"I was remembering the time when you made the sketch, the argument we were having."

"That's not productive, Bill."

"Well, it was what I was thinking. Maybe a little of the other, too. Do you think he thinks about us?"

"No," she said.

"I think he does."

"He does not think about us in the way that you think about him. A telephone call in the middle of the night, and when you answer he hangs up. Reach out and touch someone."

"No, El."

"And I don't want to talk about him anymore."

"Just don't — be so rough." He smiled bleakly at her, but he couldn't think of anything more to say, anything that hadn't been said a hundred or a thousand times before, so he shrugged and made a face. She hated it when the mood came upon him but there was nothing he could do about it. He was possessed by him.

"What's wrong with your hand?"

He was absently rotating his left wrist, massaging it. He looked at it, shaking it as if it were wet. "I don't know. It fell asleep. Probably I slept on it the wrong way."

"Well, come to bed." She leaned into him, and kissed his neck. He put his arm around her, squeezing. A second bird answered the first and the eastern sky was now definitely light. Boats were moving on the Sound, fishermen searching for Blues; the lighthouse was dark. New England was waking up, and the morning would be gorgeous. She said, "Come on, it must be almost six."

He looked at his wrist. "It's the damnedest thing."

She took his hand in hers and turned it over, palm up. She peered

30

at it closely, as if reading his palm for a clue to the future. "Does it hurt?"

"No, that's the point."

"Well, you slept on it."

"I haven't slept. I haven't slept at all. I've had insomnia."

She rubbed his hand, playfully pulling his index finger.

"I can't feel a thing. It's numb."

"Bill?"

"The damn thing's been numb since dinner."

"Do you feel all right otherwise?" She was wide awake now.

"I dropped a cigarette and didn't even notice."

"Any pain? Or anything else? Nausea?" She looked hard at him. "What do you think it is?"

He said, "I don't know."

She put her hand on his arm, then her palm on his forehead.

"It's not a heart attack, El."

"We'll call the doctor when it gets light."

"What'll we tell him? That I dropped a cigarette?"

She began to walk toward the door. "We'll start with that."

"El — "

"Are you dizzy?"

"No."

She opened the door to the kitchen and looked back at him. "We'll call the doctor now. I will."

He laughed. He didn't want to be the one to suggest it. He felt a great relief. He said, "We can wait until daylight."

The doctor had no idea what the trouble was, and the ambassador left his office without so much as an aspirin. For a few days, the numbness went away, and the welcome pain returned. Then one morning on Middle Ground the numbness came back, accompanied by another unmistakable symptom. He made the necessary telephone calls and they left the island for Washington. Two weeks to the day after the incident with the cigarette, Ambassador William North, fifty, was in the Washington Hospital Center, a semi-private room, third floor. The Department sent a routine signal to AmEmbassy Bonn that the chargé's leave would be extended at least one month, medical reasons.

2

THE HOSPITAL was crowded and not even the Department's strings could secure North a private room. The boy in the bed next to him was recovering from a motorcycle accident. He had a fractured skull and a broken neck. They wheeled him in early in the morning of North's second day. He was awakened by the creak of the stretcher table and the muttering of the attendants. The boy had been in intensive care for three days, but was now off the critical list and expected to survive, barely; this from the nurse as she tucked in the sheets. That was on Tuesday. He was unconscious for two days, or at any event did not speak or move. He had no visitors. The first words he said were "I'd like it if you'd stop smoking." A sardonic pause. "It just bothers the hell out of me."

He and Elinor looked at each other and put out their cigarettes. Elinor asked the boy if he needed anything and he shook his head. She was conscious of the irony of her words, and grimaced. North introduced himself and the boy nodded, but did not reply. He introduced Elinor and the boy nodded again.

"Do you have a name?"

"Richard," the boy said. His hands were folded primly. He was swathed in bandages, black holes for the nostrils and mouth. It was impossible to know how old he was, except that he was not a child. His voice had timbre. Greasy black hair curled around his neck where the tape had become unstuck.

"Do you know what time it is?"

"Almost seven," Elinor said.

"This is Tuesday?"

"Thursday," she said.

He said, "I was in an accident."

Elinor said, "You're going to be fine."

"Is that what they told you?"

"It's what the nurse said."

He turned his head away from them. His body began to shake, and for the life of them they did not know if he was laughing or crying.

Late that night, unable to sleep, North lit a cigarette in the darkness. It was very still, the only sound the breathing of the boy in the bed next to him. The door was open and he could see the dull fluorescence of the corridor, an unhealthy blue. In this hospital he felt like a laboratory animal, a six-foot one-hundred-and-eighty-pound swaybacked gerbil, "Bill," ill, undiagnosed, ripe for vivisection. And the attendants were so cheerful; they had exciting results from one of the tests. He had looked at them, as if he expected to find the word on their foreheads, like the impression on the shroud of Turin: cancer. And one of them had leaned down and whispered: It's not cancer. We know that much. Whatever it is, it's odd. But it's not that. And you're not going to die from it, whatever it is.

Such an efficient hospital, superbly equipped with the latest medical devices, and only $600 a day plus extras. Still, he was safe enough; he was as safe as if he were in prison. The hospital was built of steel and reinforced concrete, it could survive a direct hit of any weapon short of a nuclear device. The bed was as heavy as a Buick and fully motorized, though not as comfortable. TV on the wall opposite, control panel to the left, steel tray on rollers, plastic thermos, plastic vials, plastic straws for the plastic glass. The place had all the charm of a ship's mess.

He blew a smoke ring. The windows were permanently sealed, the temperature inside always a comfy 76° F. The last time he was in a hospital was twenty-three years before, a hospital run by German missionaries, a bungalow with windows open to the air. The room had a comfortable bed made of wood. There was a thick wooden crucifix over the bed. There were cotton sheets and soft pillows and you could smoke when you liked. Drink, too. Each room came equipped with the familiar triangular ashtray with the Cinzano logo. On the opposite wall, hung where the patient could see it, was an old travel poster, one of Kirchner's neurotic Berlin street scenes, *Potsdamer Platz, 1914,* all vertical lines, the streetwalkers in rayon and ostrich feathers, the buildings sharp-edged and ominous. It could have been the guest room of someone's house. Visitors came and went as they chose. By God, it was hot, though, never less than a hundred degrees during the day, yet there was always a light breeze and the nights were cool and sweet-smelling, filled with the rustling sounds of Africa. The nights were never still.

He blew another smoke ring, his eyes fixed on the closet where his suitcase was stowed. He thought, What the hell, and put his cigarette in the ashtray. Ambassador didn't have cancer, ambassador was owed a reward. He heaved himself out of bed and stood, swaying, lightheaded. He walked slowly to the closet, opened the suitcase, and brought out a silver flask, engraved

To You
From Me
1963

The flask was from that time. He poured two fingers into the water glass and replaced the flask.

He took a sip and smiled. He wished he were back in the African hospital because there was no question then what was wrong with him, and no doubt that he would get well. The nurses were sexy; more sexy than competent. They seemed to have no great faith in German medicine. The doctor was a missionary of an obscure Lutheran order, a field surgeon in the Wehrmacht 1939–1945, and therefore skilled with wounds,. a conservative man. There was a question about whether to open North's stomach to probe for fragments and the doctor decided that was not wise, the risk of infection was too great. Infection was a greater menace than the fragment, if actually there was a fragment; there was no way of knowing for certain. The x-rays were inconclusive and North could tell them nothing, being only intermittently conscious and delirious as well, muttering strange prayers, lying on his stomach in the wide, wooden bed, eyes closed. He remembered all that very well, despite the delirium. His prayers sounded like gibberish to the doctor, whose English was faulty. North remembered the doctor's round face and black beard and what he took to be the sour smell of wine, though it could have been disinfectant. The doctor looked him over (puncture wounds everywhere, legs, back, hips, upper arm, left temple) and decided not to operate, a risky decision but one which he knew that North would approve; doctor and patient, both conservative men. When the patient was compos mentis the doctor would visit after dinner, bringing a bottle of schnapps and a radio. The doctor would look him over, tell him how well he was doing, what a strong heart he had, what a robust constitution. And a robust spirit, Herr North was never pessimistic. Then they would sit quietly, drinking schnapps and listening to accounts of the Profumo crisis on the BBC, laughing uproariously. The German could not restrain himself, he laughed and laughed, saying over and over again, English swine. He did a wonderful imitation of Der Alte, Konrad Adenauer, receiving news of the tarts Keeler and Rice-Davies cavorting in the swimming pool at Cliveden and, later, classified pillow talk with the secretary of state for war and the Soviet naval attaché.

The doctor was glad to have company, it was rare that he had a white man to talk to. And North was glad to have company, too, especially one so droll. Elinor was in the capital with Bill Jr. — it was neither safe nor diplomatic for her to visit daily — and although they talked on the radiophone, it was not the same. He missed her terribly. The doctor had been in Africa for many years; he was distant from Europe, and had no wife. They talked politics a little, but the German was guarded. He had missed everything in the past decade, even Bardot and Romy Schneider, and the Economic Miracle. For an African in Africa, politics was cattle. Sometimes it was a woman. For a German in Africa, politics was — a glass of schnapps and conversation, the perfidious BBC in the background. Time slipped by, a man grew older; a man grew numb; suddenly you were old. In Africa, distinctions were blurred; time had a different rhythm. There was no definite shape to things, other than the land itself.

Sometimes I look at this picture — he pointed to the poster, Kirchner's Berlin in black and white — and think of it as the work of a mental patient describing heaven, a place that exists in the imagination or in dreams. It is impossible for me to believe that Berlin exists, in the way that Stanleyville or Lusaka exists. Nor is it necessary. Do you see?

Yes, he said.

Is it that way for you, too?

No, he said. Honestly, it isn't.

Just wait, the German said.

He stubbed out the cigarette and lit another. The clock on the bedside table read 2:08. He flexed the fingers of his left hand, then nudged the wedding ring over his knuckle. Tight as the bark on a tree, but he thought he felt strength returning to his hand. Or perhaps it was only a vague sense of touch, reawakened by the memories that kept crowding in on him. What else could you expect, at 2:08 in the morning, in a hospital room?

He sipped the whiskey, enjoying himself, moving back and forth in his memory, teasing it, trying to get the facts straight. It was well-traveled terrain, and always easier alone in the darkness, fighting insomnia. Many details had vanished, the specifics of the look of the hospital garden as they drank beer on the verandah. North tried to recollect it all, the process like looking through a file for a misplaced letter, there somewhere, in one folder or another, the paper yellowing, brittle to the touch. Grab at it too eagerly and it would fall apart, lost forever.

He was remembering the coup, from the long-ago time in Africa when he had been so green, his first posting abroad. He and Kleust had gone to see Burkhalter, soldier, missionary, physician. Burkhalter: tall, thick-featured, slow, melancholy, a voice like an organ. He was the same age now as Burkhalter was then. Burkhalter had seemed very old, or anyway very experienced; he knew Africa root and branch. He was the man who knew the answers, everyone agreed. Kleust said he knew where to find him, and Kleust was true to his word. They had driven from the capital in a Land-Rover. The hospital was in the bush, to the back of beyond, in a district officially designated "Disputed." The hospital was off a side road, down a dry watercourse, and over a field. It was backed into a stand of tall, thick trees, invisible unless you knew it was there, knew exactly where to look. In the middle distance the bungalow looked like a native hut, or a piece of sculpture, elegantly proportioned, not a wasted strut or beam, and immaculate. It had a Buddhist intensity and stillness. He and Kleust waited on the verandah for Burkhalter, who had seen them coming and was returning from his garden, a hoe on his shoulder, huge in white shorts and floppy hat. North thought the hospital very well appointed. Back of it, farther into the forest, was a small village, and a landing strip.

Burkhalter greeted them with a shy smile and a *Grüss Gott*. He and Kleust embraced.

The three of them drank beer on the verandah, monkeys somersaulting on the railing, chattering like excited children. The heat was absolute, a physicist's unified field. There was no breeze at all. North had asked the missionary how long he had been in Africa and he had replied, Years and years, here and there, Northern Rhodesia, southern Sudan, the Congo. This hospital, not far from one of Livingstone's encampments. A long and distinguished missionary tradition in this part of the world, he said. English, Dutch, Americans, Germans. A proper place for the teachings of Martin Luther and the natives responded, yes they did; they responded to the idea of the divinity of Christ. They responded a little less well to Heidelberg medicine.

They came at last to the situation. The missionary asked North a few careful questions on the state of affairs in the capital. Who was in charge? Had the government panicked? Was the central market operating, and were prices stable? Was the army loyal? Burkhalter mentioned several names, but North was obliged to shake his head; he did not know who they were. Kleust didn't either. The missionary spoke a peasant's rough German, giving them an appreciation of the situation in the countryside; not good, not good at all. There was a vacuum. There was no authority. The constabulary was no better than the run of common criminals, but of course banditry had been common for years and years; even Henry Stanley had to fight bandits. But now there were automatic weapons. . . . The government was a joke, he said in English; its writ did not run. Then he laughed and gave an eloquent shrug of his shoulders. Nor does Martin Luther's, despite the response to the idea of the divinity of Jesus Christ. He took a swallow of beer and quoted Goethe. North, straining to hear, missed the quote, but Burkhalter's mordant tone told him all he needed to know.

Perhaps, North said, if there was aid.

My God, the missionary said. No. Who would you give it to?

Well, North said, the government. The government has got to prove it is a government. That it can govern. That is has the balls to do what needed to be done.

"The balls?" the missionary said.

I beg your pardon, North said. He had forgotten that Burkhalter was a missionary. In his shorts and floppy hat, he could have been anything; a doctor, for example, or a soldier.

I don't understand the expression, the missionary said in English.

North repeated it in German.

Burkhalter sighed, and said nothing for a moment. Then he began to reminisce about the village where he was born and raised. He was from the island of Sylt, in the North Frisians. In German legend, people from Sylt were idiots, *Dummkopfen*. Sylt, barely more than a sand dune in the North Sea, now a resort for Hamburg businessmen, their robust wives, and noisy children. Frisians were always considered inferior, unserious, without imagination. The terrain was too bleak for seriousness. It lacked Wagnerian grandeur. As was well known, Germans were passionate about their physical surroundings. Yet Sylt had never been conquered. Among the German tribes, Frisians had the reputation of — and he swept his hand in a bold arc before him, including the bungalow's vicinity, every tree, bush, animal, and human being, although there were no human beings in sight other than Kleust's driver, sitting motionless in the shade of a giant baobab — "these people," he said.

"Or Americans," Kleust said.

"Herr Kleust," the missionary complained, clucking with disapproval.

North ignored Kleust. He did not understand the missionary's anecdote and was not certain how he could explain the American position, in this atmosphere. The heat, the driver dozing under the baobab, the monkeys. "The struggling democracies of the underdeveloped world deserve our support. They cannot do without it." There was nothing damp or sentimental about the policy. It was pragmatic. Given time, it would send a signal to the old men in the Kremlin.

The missionary nodded. It was a admirable policy, certainly. The missionary complimented the American administration on its perspicacity. *Weisheit*. Then, inevitably: "How long have you been in Africa, Herr North?"

"Fifteen months." Long enough, he thought but did not say. "I was in Washington for three years." There was a silence and North looked up. Two vultures circled lazily. He said, "Things are different, with our new administration, younger men with different ideas. Our President has the means to defend democracy here and everywhere. The Communists — "

"Yes," Burkhalter said sadly.

"— don't neglect these areas. Weapons, advice."

"The Americans are not considering an intervention." It was half statement, half question.

"No," North said.

"Not directly," Kleust said.

The missionary smiled and chattered, tickticktick, in imitation of his monkeys. The monkeys fell silent, and the missionary laughed. "This part of the world seems so far from your capital." He opened his mouth as if to say more, then didn't. He sat quietly a moment, sipping beer. He said, "Of course, the world has shrunk. I suppose that nothing is mysterious anymore." He looked at the American. "This, right here, is important to your government?" He stared out across the tawny veldt, where the heat was rising in waves. Nothing moved. The land was profoundly still, simmering in the heat. The baobab had the look of an ancient icon. "Well," he said at last, "I know what you want. You want names. Who they are, their background, what they believe in. What they want. How they intend to get it." Burkhalter thought a moment. "I can give you the names, but the names don't matter. This is not 1848, or 1917. This is not Berlin or Saint Petersburg. It is true they call themselves Marxists. But in office they will behave like model capitalists. They will steal." That is what powerful people did in this part of Africa, stole. Everyone stole. The importers, the exporters, the moneychangers, the mining concerns, the merchants, the army officers, the civil servants, the missionaries. "These boys will be no different," he said. Identities were irrelevant. They are somewhere out there, he said, his voice rising. *"They are somewhere out there. The land is theirs. They have no single leader. No one man to send to parley, even if they were interested in parley, which they aren't. Don't search for Russians or Chinese, they aren't there. Some of their weapons are, but they aren't. What do those out there want? They want to run things. And before long, they will. I have lived here a very long time, Herr North. And that is what I have learned. That, and the simple truth that God is present here."

North looked at him. He guessed that Burkhalter was about fifty. But it was difficult to tell. He could be sixty, even seventy. He was fit, powerfully built with iron-gray hair as stiff as wire, and a military bearing to go with an often wistful expression. He said, "What's your guess? What will happen next?" It was what Washington wanted to know.

"Killings, perhaps hostages. Whites, if they can get to them."

"And if they can't?"

"They will," Burkhalter said.

North suddenly had a thought. "You?"

The missionary laughed. "No, I think not." He looked again at his monkeys, tickticktick. "I am just an old missionary doctor, and besides I have the baobab juju." He gestured at the tree with its great branches.

"You could come back with us, Kleust and me."

"But this is my home," Burkhalter said. "If I am not safe here, I am not safe anywhere." He took a long swallow of beer. "Things are insecure everywhere, would you not agree? Even in the capital."

Their driver had disappeared, but now he was back, pointing at the sun. There was just enough daylight to reach the government zone. The missionary offered the driver tea, but he shook his head. It was time to leave.

North said, "Can they be bought?"

"Oh, yes," Burkhalter said, "I expect so."

North stood up, Kleust following; no more questions. Burkhalter thanked them for coming, he did not often have visitors from the outside. They were all sweating, saying good-bye. The missionary walked with them to the Land-Rover, its skin hot to the touch. Kleust sat in the front seat with the driver, North alone in the rear. The German stood scuffing his foot in the dirt. He seemed to have something further to say.

"Do you intend to buy them, Herr North?"

"Not my decision," he said promptly, and watched the German frown. "Thanks for your help."

"I do not know if it would be a good thing."

"You have been very helpful." North said.

The German nodded. It was nothing. Anything he could do in the future —

North said, "If you hear anything —"

Yes, he said. Then, "My sympathies are with the people here." He looked at North, and then shyly away; he leaned close to him and said suddenly, "Did you say you worked in Washington?" Without waiting for an answer, he went on. "When you were in Washington, did you know the President?"

North said that he didn't.

"Such an attractive man. And his wife, also."

North agreed.

"And their children."

Yes.

"Such a large family!" He laughed and slapped the side of the Land-Rover. "Do they mean to populate the world? Is it true that the father is a Croesus?"

"He is very rich," North said.

"I would like to meet your President. Do you think he will come to Africa?"

Sometime, North said. Certainly he would.

"He is very popular and respected, even out there" — he waved his hand — "they know who he is. Such a young man, it is very good for your country. Once I had planned to study in the United States, but then I came here. Do you think, if he visits —"

"Absolutely," North said.

The driver said something to Kleust, who nodded. He turned to the missionary and said that his ambassador, Herr Zimmerman, sent his fondest regards; then he handed him a bundle of German newspapers and magazines. The missionary's eyes lit up. *Danke, danke.* The only news he had had for months was via wireless, the BBC, and the English were not always trustworthy. He grinned and held up one of the magazines, a German picture magazine. The President and his wife and children were on the cover, a formal pose in one of the reception rooms of the White House. They looked like sovereigns of a lucky country, the colors royal blue and a fierce red, the family so poised. The missionary chuckled as if this were a coincidence too bizarre to credit. He backed away and told them to drive carefully, and have a safe journey. God bless, God bless. He waved them off, then retreated into the hospital with his cargo of magazines and newspapers.

The driver grumbled, they were late; they had stayed too long. Driving down the dry watercourse, back to the dirt road, North had asked Kleust to translate the Goethe quotation. Kleust shrugged, he couldn't remember. Perhaps they were the poet's last words, "More light!" Come on, North said; they were a dozen words in idiomatic German, spoken so rapidly he could not understand them.

Kleust smiled wanly. Very well, he said. "In English, it is this. 'The Germans make everything difficult, both for themselves and for everyone else.'" North smiled and reminded Kleust that he himself was of German extraction. German, and Jewish also. But of course Kleust knew that.

Kleust said, "I think the point he was trying to make about Sylt was that no one ever conquered it because no one ever wanted it." An excellent point; but one North neglected to make a month later, when he was back in the United States, summoned to explain to the assistant secretary what he was doing riding in an embassy Land-Rover outside the government zone, in an area specifically forbidden to foreign diplomats; he had exceeded instructions. And the fact that he had been almost killed; *that* was an embarrassment. No use explaining that he was traveling with a letter of safe conduct, the letter festooned with seals and signed by the colonel in charge of the district. The men who suddenly appeared at the roadblock had not been told, or did not care, or did not read; probably all three. The driver had been killed right away, and it was due to the

42

skill and nerve of his friend Kleust that they had survived — had, in fact, *won*. That was the truth, but the truth was too simple to be plausible. In any case, it was not a "mature" sequence of events. The assistant secretary prepared a memo for North's file, the salient sentence being "This officer displayed questionable judgment." The assistant secretary was a humorless diplomat of the old school, his caution a legend on the seventh floor.

But in 1963 caution was not everywhere admired. When North was debriefed at Langley the DDCI had smiled warmly, shaken his hand, and said, "Well done!" In the roundabout way such exchanges were made, the DDCI indicated there was a place for him at Langley should he ever become disenchanted with the Department or, smile, vice versa. North was flattered but declined the offer. He had a weekend of celebrity, and in due course received a note from the attorney general. The attorney general definitely admired daring and implied, without quite saying so, that the President had been informed. Everyone knew the President admired daring. Of course within a few months the President was dead. The attorney general went to the Senate and a few years after that he was dead, and there was a new crowd on the seventh floor; and the assistant secretary's memo was still in North's Department file, an official file five inches thick (though now perhaps on an acorn of microfilm, the Department being fully computerized and interfaced). Preserved in a vault underground, it would endure as long as the government itself, surviving plague or holocaust or scandal, as the paintings on the wall at Altamira outlasted the civilization that produced them. Dossiers were never destroyed: they were part of the permanent record, the institutional memory. "This officer displayed questionable judgment." Read that: You fucked up, and we knew you fucked up. At Altamira there was a drawing of a bull escaping a lance. The lance was poorly thrown. A sixteen-thousand-year-old fuck-up; a fuck-up from the Ice Age.

The assistant secretary was now retired, though occasionally one saw him walking the halls, a consultant to the Secretariat, always in a hurry, impeccably tailored. He was an influential Old Boy, having retired with the rank of ambassador; everyone knew he had a photographic memory, and never forgot a friend.

"Shit."

On the other hand, he had survived, too; a career minister now, soon to go to Bonn as chargé, running the place while a Sun Belt entrepreneur entertained industrialists and made speeches about the American Way —

"SHIT!"

He turned, irritated, his reverie broken. Kleust and Burkhalter, the Land-Rover, the dark green forest, the attorney general, and his own twenty-seven-year-old self feathered away into the darkness, out of reach. He was back in the present moment, in the moody fluorescence of a Washington facility, surly nurses and steel furniture. He looked at the clock: 2:30. He had gotten it all back in twenty-two minutes, his memory on fast forward. Well, not all; it would take another few minutes to get it all. The boy was moving his hand in front of his face, dispelling the disgusting odor. North shifted position to extinguish the cigarette, then changed his mind. The boy irritated him; he did not want company. He wished he were alone in a wooden bed, with the ashtray with the Cinzano logo, talking to the doctor who smelled sourly of wine. He had a hard time believing in the African hospital, in the same way that the missionary doctor had a hard time believing in Kirchner's Berlin; but that was where he wanted to be. And thinking about that, and about Africa, he shivered. He realized suddenly that he was slick with sweat, and trembling; his hands were trembling. He stared at the ceiling, composing himself. He was a fifty-year-old man, he told himself; and Africa was long in the past. Perhaps Elinor could find a Cinzano ashtray, and a poster of a violent African dusk. He said, "What did you say?"

"The smoke. It stinks."

"Sorry. I thought you were asleep." He put the cigarette out. He looked at the ashtray and saw three cigarette ends; he had been chain smoking.

"It woke me up."

"Sorry about that."

"You don't know what it's like."

"No, I don't." He closed his eyes.

"It's a son of a bitch," the boy said. "And you were talking to yourself. I couldn't make out what it was," the boy complained.

"Just as well," North said.

"My neck itches."

"Shall I call the nurse?"

"No."

The boy fell silent and North turned over, fluffing the pillow. The cotton was cool on its underside. Elinor had brought the good linen. He closed his eyes, listening for sounds in the corridor. He was half in, half out, of Africa. That Kleust, what a Fritzie piece of work. They had been friends for more than twenty years, following each other around the world, one posting to another, always of equivalent rank, usually embassies in the Third World, until Kleust got a Class A embassy five years ago. Kleust was more popular in his Foreign Ministry than North was in his. North had sent him a congratulatory cable in German, Goethe's quotation. Kleust had been in Ottawa, and now was back in Bonn, a director at the Foreign Ministry. He had been hoping for Washington, perhaps as minister. Bonn was hypnotized by Washington, the American connection so fraught, Bonn always nervously deferential, worried that in its frenzied obsession with the Evil Empire the U.S.A. would forget the ally on the Evil Empire's western doorstep, the first cat to be kicked. And the neurotics who conducted the nation's business in Washington! Playboys, megalomaniacs, felons, Baptist preachers, film stars. To be a minister in such a capital! And Kleust loved the embasssy building on MacArthur Boulevard, a great hulk of glass and hardwood; its Wagnerian superstructure bore a resemblance to the Gneisenau.

"I really hate it here," the boy said.

So he wanted to talk. Bye-bye, Kurt. North said, "They said you're lucky to be alive, and that you'll be all right, good as new. No spinal damage, and your head's all right." One of the pleasures of the Foreign Service was staying in touch with friends, and he and Kurt could have quite a run in Bonn, until the administration selected a Sun Belt banker or entertainment lawyer to show the flag. North's was an interim appointment, and when the new man arrived he would drop a rank. It did not make a great difference, though; he would run the embassy, more than likely. As Kurt would run the Foreign Ministry.

He said, "No, it isn't."

North came back again. "What happened on the motorcycle?"

"Gravel. I spun out."

"Christ," North said, turning away. He had given Bill Jr. a trail bike when he was fifteen and on the second day he owned it he had run into a ravine and broken two fingers, and given himself a concussion. Elinor was furious and refused to speak to him for a week. Had refused, in fact, to speak to both of them.

"My girlfriend was killed."

"Christ, I'm sorry."

"She was a savage all right." The boy didn't say anything more for a moment. North closed his eyes again. He said, "I took the curve too fast. I'd never been on that road before. She was holding on. It didn't seem fast at the time, but it was."

"I'm very sorry," North said. He was listening now.

"Thank you," the boy said, "But it's all shit. Shit as far as the eye can see."

"How old are you?"

"Nineteen," he said. "I'm not even from here. I'm from Worcester, Mass. I don't know what the hell I'm doing here anyway. It was her idea, she wanted to go to the concert. So we climbed on the bike and rode down here, ten hours."

He slipped away again, thinking about Kleust. He hadn't heard from Kleust for a while.

"I'd rather be home, to tell you the truth."

"Worcester's a nice town," he lied.

"You're from Mass," the boy said. "I'd guess Boston. I can tell by the accent, though there's a lot around that accent. Like, it's a band with too much acoustic guitar. The bass line gets lost and you don't know where you are, jazz or R and B or rock or what. It's true what they say about people who can't see, their hearing improves. I've got dynamite hearing. You must've lived a lot of places, though Boston's still there somewhere."

North smiled, "Back Bay."

"I figured," the boy said. "All you guys sound alike."

"I haven't lived there for over twenty-five years."

"Your wife has a nice voice, quiet."

"Yes," he said.

"But she's not from Mass."

"No, Chicago. From around Chicago."

"No kidding," he said. "My sister lives in Chicago. But she still talks like Mass."

"You never lose it completely," North said.

"You got any kids?"

"One," he said.

"He hasn't been around," the boy said.

"He's out of the country," North said. He fingered a cigarette out of the package on the night table, then put it down. "He's a — student."

"What's he studying?"

North thought a moment, then said, "Law. He's studying law."

The boy grunted. "My dad's a lawyer." He didn't say anything for a moment; the atmosphere was suddenly charged. "They all talk the same. They all talk as if there's some secret room somewhere and they're the only ones who have a key, and you've got to pay them to get it. Then they talk at you, talk talk talk. And then they let you watch while they open the door and say some mumbo-jumbo."

North laughed.

"And it only costs a hundred dollars an hour."

Maybe in Worcester, North thought.

"If you're lucky," the boy said.

"Go back to sleep," North said.

"I'm wide awake now."

"You need your sleep."

"No shit, Sherlock."

"We can talk tomorrow."

"What's wrong with now? You woke me up."

"Well, I'm tired."

"They're all shit," the boy said.

North said nothing.

"So your kid's going to be a lawyer."

"That's what he says," North said. That's what happened when you told an innocent lie, a story meant less to deceive then to deflect. You got Watergate. It made him uncomfortable, and he wished now that he'd said he wasn't sure, which, while not precisely truthful, was not a complete lie, either.

"They're great, the lawyers. They're terrific with people, their relatives especially. They've got a real human touch. That's why my old man hasn't come down to see me, or telephoned either. Probably afraid I'd die of a heart attack if I heard his voice."

North said nothing to that.

"His secretary checks with the doctor every morning, though."

"Well," North said.

"But maybe your kid'll be different. Maybe he's a great guy and'll make a great lawyer."

"I'm not counting on it." North said.

"Maybe it'll be cool," the boy said.

"Maybe," North said.

"I suppose he's telephoned."

"No," North said.

"Well, he's in the great tradition, then."

"Look," North said, then paused.

"Sorry," the boy said, "I didn't mean to piss you off."

"He's not studying to be a lawyer. He's in Europe, that's all."

"Sounds like fun," the boy said.

North closed his eyes, feeling drowsy. He knew that sleep was near. "I suppose so," he said.

"I've never been to Europe."

"Well, you're young."

"You're sure he isn't a lawyer?"

"I'm sure," North said.

"He sure sounds like one," the boy said.

3

T HEY WERE PUNCTUAL, Hartnett and Carruthers, arriving
within minutes of each other, cool and tidy from their air-
conditioned cars. And they were cordial, shaking hands and
talking about Sunday's game. Carruthers and Hartnett were great
football fans; it was only the exhibition season and they were already full of opinions. North introduced them to Richard, Hartnett his personal lawyer, Carruthers a lawyer for the Department
of State; Richard nodded his head but did not speak. He was certain to be smiling, though. The most desirable of all of Washington's locked rooms was RFK Stadium on a Sunday, and the mumbo-
jumbo was superb.

North put on a white terry-cloth robe and slippers and they
walked down the hall to the solarium. Two women were leaving as
they walked in, and he made way to let them pass; they moved
painfully, shuffling, and did not return his smile. There were three
empty chairs in the corner and a small table with a child's checkerboard. Carruthers put the checkerboard to one side and took
out a sheaf of papers and began sorting, wetting his thumb to separate the sheets. North and Hartnett said nothing, waiting for Carruthers to begin. It was his meeting, arranged at his request. The

call had come that morning, a bit too casual it seemed to North. He had known Carruthers for years, and heard something odd in his tone. Carruthers concluded the conversation by suggesting that Dick Hartnett might join them. Carruthers knew that Hartnett was North's lawyer and, as it happened, an occasional consultant to the Department of State. This will save time, Carruthers had said.

"So," Carruthers said at last. Then, looking around, as if surprised to see where he was, and suddenly remembering. "How're you feeling, anyway?"

"Paul," North said.

"Just asking."

"I'm feeling fine, let's get on with it."

"Hate hospitals," Carruthers said.

North looked at him and smiled, not unkindly. "No shit, Sherlock."

"I hear you're going to Bonn. Congratulations. Isn't that what you've always wanted? The Jerries. Not me. When I get my reward it'll be the sunny south, a nice consulate, Oporto or Marseilles. Though as I understand it you'll be interim, until the new man arrives. President wants a *friend* in Bonn, you understand. A good, close friend he can shmooze with. The friend can tell him all about the pinko assholes in the Foreign Service. Then they can trade anecdotes about the Jerries then and now. An anecdotal history of the Holocaust. I wish you luck in Bonn, Bill." Carruthers sighed, and cleared his throat. "I'm here at the suggestion of the under secretary, and I'll be reporting to him. We're all on the same side here. This meeting so far's I'm concerned is informal, no written record." He bent down to squint at the top sheet of the pile of papers in his lap and gave a little exhausted laugh. "We're just getting a ton of paper from the committee. Senator Winston is working overtime, one piece of paper after another, and he's not giving up. No, sir. He has a good, young staff, zealous and confident. And he has Dunphy. And they've turned up some information, it's such a nuisance. What I'm saying is that some of the paper is *our* paper, that they're dealing back to us, and asking questions. The Department of State is a god damned sieve. They have a lot of stuff, is what I'm saying. Hired one investigator from the UPI. Couldn't make a name there, I guess he figured to make a name on the Hill, ha-ha. He's quite a gumshoe, this lad." Carruthers paused, his thumb on his tongue. "He's a god damned good man with a document, I can tell you that. He has a law degree, too. And a litigious turn of mind. Christ. Another lawyer, comfortable with documents. Know how to get them, knows how to *read* them. And that's the big thing, isn't it? Knowing how to read them." Carruthers sighed. "Damnedest thing, they used to go from the committee to the UPI or the *Post* or the *Times*. Now it's the other way around because it looks like Senator Winston and that son of a bitch Dunphy have reinvented the wheel. They've discovered that they've got subpoena power, and that's just set the gumshoe atingle. The UPI and the *Post* and the *Times* don't have that. Sometimes they act like they do, but they don't. Goodness, but they're zealous." Carruthers laughed pleasantly as though he had made a joke.

North lit a cigarette, his third of the day, flexing the fingers of his left hand. This was going to take a minute, Carruthers being cute, composing his overture. He looked out the windows at the gray shape of the building two, three blocks away. It was an old government building, one of the anonymous departments or agencies, an annex of Commerce or Labor or the FCC or ICC. When North first came to Washington they were important, their secretaries or directors men with influence. Twenty-five years later it was hard to remember the names of the current Cabinet, and no one did except the army of lawyers and lobbyists hired to manipulate them. Today a department or agency didn't count unless it was involved with national security. Everyone wanted a piece of national security because that was where the money was.

"So," Carruthers was saying, "the main thing is that Warren Winston wants to make a name for himself this session at least as big as he did last session, when he won the hearts and minds of all America. He has all those friends in the news business. And now with Dunphy and that young staff and the gumshoe he's got a whiff of something. Maybe more than a whiff, because he knows more than I'd expect him to know. It's likely there's a leak somewhere, there usually is, though with all those young people working eighteen-hour days they can look through wastebaskets. They don't give a damn about home life or a Dubonnet at the end of the day." Carruthers paused again and North felt that the drumroll was coming to an end at last. "They're meeting in closed session and they're taking depositions and the gumshoe has got some of his friends waving the Freedom of Information Act. That's according to *our* sources, *our* leak. This leak, *our* leak, is an older fella, he goes way back to Senator Joe, doesn't care much for zealots. And I think there are three or four personality conflicts. It's probably sexual jealousy, these young women on the staff are particularly aggressive. So" — Carruthers took a deep breath, evidently preparing to strike a clear note — "our man thinks Winston's got something. Winston thinks he's got an example of a red-hot security leak. And of course that's only the tip of the iceberg that he thinks he has. What he's really got on his mind is terrorists, and he's trying to link the two. Do you see what I'm saying? Our man thinks Winston sniffs a cover-up." He smiled sardonically, a man ill at ease with cliché. "A cover-up," he repeated. "So there's some interest in you, Bill." He smiled again, having jumped three hurdles at once.

"That won't get them very far," he said.

"Bill," Carruthers said, disappointed, "Bill Bill Bill." He had a round face, without definition, like the face painted on a balloon. It was not a soft face, nor an especially cheerful one, and if at forty everyone has the face he's earned — well then, Paul Carruthers had led a life of perfect self-absorption. Like Buddha's, his was not a face to register emotion of any kind. He had extinguished the pain and care of the external world by the simple method of ignoring it. He was a fierce competitor and often underrated because of his bland looks and droll preludes. Those who knew him well listened carefully to his voice, a tenor. His emotions were communicated not by any expression in his face but by the tone of his voice. His face was as neutral as the dial of a radio.

"They're interested in your son, and the approach that was made to you in Africa. I'm talking of course about the last tour, the 'eighty-two–'eighty-three tour, the winter of those years, the year the 'Skins went to the Super Bowl, just knocked hell out of Miami. You remember the strike, the short season, the anxiety, we were so disappointed. Sundays were out of synch, we didn't know what to do with ourselves. That's the year they're concerned with, Winston and Dunphy and the gumshoe." Another short pause while Carruthers consulted a paper. "Bill, where's your son?"

"I don't know," North said. "And Elinor doesn't know, either."

"Where was he, last time you heard?"

North paused fractionally. "Hamburg."

Carruthers sighed. "You want to add 'to my knowledge'?"

"No," North said.

Carruthers lowered his voice, not quite an apology, more an explanation. "These are questions I have to ask, Bill. It's my brief. They're being asked at the other end of the avenue, and I have to ask them here. It's not personal."

Hartnett intervened. "And he's answering them freely, of his own free will, without consultation. The record can show that."

"There is no record, counselor," Carruthers said, disappointed again. "I'm not even making notes. This is informal, as I've said. This is a conversation among the three of us, simply trying to get to the bottom of this matter. Us three."

"Who are on the same side," Hartnett said.

"Well, of course," Carruthers said.

"I don't know where Bill Jr. is," North said. "I wish to Christ that I did, but I don't."

"Uh-huh," Carruthers said. "And he would now be —"

"Twenty-eight," North said. Born in 1958, a vintage year. Elinor regularly had his horoscope cast. And the astrologer invariably predicted a sunny and productive future in some creative field, conceivably films.

"Unmarried?"

"So far as I know."

"Dunphy has a report —"

North smiled. He was trying to gauge the degree of sarcasm in Carruthers's voice. He said, "I don't think Bill Jr. is into marriage licenses, or ceremonies. I think, in the circumstances, that this is a detail. Wouldn't you agree? He is still with the German girl. Woman. Last I heard."

"In the late autumn of 'eighty-two?"

"Yes."

"And you have not seen him since then. Nor have you heard from him. Nor has your wife seen or heard from him. And there have been no communications, to and fro."

"No."

"Dunphy thinks otherwise."

North said, "Dunphy can think anything he likes."

"At this last meeting, the 'eighty-two meeting. He was in good health?"

"Very good health."

"But the meeting was not a success."

North leaned forward and stared into the balloon face, so seamless and inflated. "One does not have a *meeting* with one's own son, Paul. We had a visit, he and I and Elinor. The three of us, in Hamburg, I did not want Elinor to come but she insisted. And she was right to come. The visit was not, as you say, a success. He did not convince me and I did not convince him and, as a matter of fact, if you had seen us that afternoon you would not have guessed that we were father and son. You would have said I was conducting a hostile interview, the kind that comes along occasionally when you are a Foreign Service officer. Except of course we were not interviewing him; he was interviewing us. We were his prisoners. He called me 'Ambassador' and I called him 'Bill Jr.' That is not the name he uses now, but it is the name I know him by. He was abusive to my wife. So you could say that the visit was not a success."

North took a breath, then looked away out the window; the drab government building was in shadows. He did not like talking about his son to Paul Carruthers, who did not have a family and would not understand about fathers and son; perhaps he understood about sons, being one himself. But not about fathers. Strangely, North's most vivid memory of the afternoon in Hamburg was not of his son but of his wife. They were seated side by side on a low divan, Bill Jr. on a ladder-back chair. They looked up at him, he down at them. Elinor looked at their son as he had seen her look at pictures at an exhibition, a hard concentrated stare — as if she were trying to see the bones under the skin. She had not seen Bill Jr. in three years, neither of them had. The tears seemed to slip effortlessly from her eyes. He did not notice right away and when he moved to take her hand, Bill Jr. grinned wolfishly and poured a glass of water from the carafe on the table between them. Then with two fingers he pushed the glass toward his mother. She took it, whispering thank you as if he were a stranger performing an unexpected courtesy. Furious, North half rose, preparing to leave, having no more to say; he and his son looked at each other across a great chasm. But the boy had not finished. He had a lecture prepared, and proceeded to deliver it. North thought he had never seen a more resolute face, humorless, fierce, his blue eyes — Elinor's eyes — flashing, cruel as a hangman's, talking rot — literally that. But North listened, thinking that somewhere among the polysyllabic German constructions he might find something to hold on to, and assimilate. In his lifetime he had listened to all sorts, and had assimilated so much. Why was he unable to assimilate this? He listened particularly for family words and phrases, the private language of parents and children, the *no* that meant *maybe*, the *maybe* that meant *yes*, the special idioms. Members of a family were different provinces of the same country. But he heard nothing familiar. It was as if his son had no childhood memory, was in fact an exile with no recollection of the old country. At last, when Bill Jr. had finished, he'd said, with conscious inelegance, "Oh, come off it." And the boy had smiled coldly, his eyes narrowing — and that expression, too, was unfamiliar, nothing of him or of Elinor or of the little boy with the skinned knee or perfect report card, or the adolescent caught in a lie. That boy had been voluble, never at a loss for words; for that boy, silence was an admission of guilt. Injustice enraged him. His favorite word, injustice, he had learned it at five and it had been a family word, applied equally to underdone hamburgers, a Red Sox loss in extra innings, a quarrel with the houseboy, a missed airplane connection, or a death. Bill Jr. took everything personally. But this hard, silent look, it was not recognizable. And it was manufactured in the way that a newspaper or magazine "profile" of a close friend is manufactured, and renders the close friend unrecognizable. Life on the page was different from life in the flesh, and a career was never what it seemed. But then North remembered that when he was profiled in *The New York Times*, Bill Jr. read the piece and remarked, "I feel as if I know you for the first time." How odd, he had thought; the profile was standard stuff, our-man-in-Africa-doing-a-hard-job-well, vital and not so vital statistics, "the diplomat is married to the painter Elinor North. They are the parents of a son, William Jr., a student at Columbia University." That was the last paragraph. The rest of it was data, reinforced by a quote here and an anecdote there, all of it unexceptional. What was there to discover in a Man in the News?

Paul Carruthers would understand none of that, however.

Carruthers said, "I suppose it's hard to know where it all began."

You suppose right. Maybe it was when the kid down the street gave him a bloody nose, and North was not sympathetic enough. Or sympathetic in the wrong way. Or not around, "not there for him." North shrugged and cleared his throat. Yes, it was hard to know.

"And I gather his views . . ." Carruthers's voice changed key, and he sighed. *Views* was not the correct word, and he knew it. "Ideals. Objectives. Have not changed?"

North laughed harshly. Right again, Paulie. In Hamburg he came on as a nasty Marxist thug, hard as nails, pitiless, a mean piece of work, waving his bloody shirt, probably a killer, though that had yet to be definitely established. Yet the boy did say, in caustic German: *We will hunt you down like game. We will stalk you. We will make mistakes, but you must be constantly alert. You will know no peace. And we have to be lucky only once.*

"You have the report," North said. "I made a full report to the Department and filed it, along with my resignation. The report was accepted. The resignation wasn't." And how he had hesitated before signing the letter, signing his career away, more than twenty years in the Foreign Service, his entire working life. He was certain they would accept it, it would give them one more ambassadorship to offer an amateur; though central Africa was not Switzerland or Scandinavia, or Bonn. He thought they would accept it, regarding it as damage control when the news leaked. However, the news hadn't leaked; and it still hadn't, amazingly enough, though it would not be long now with Winston and Dunphy and the gumshoe on the scene. He'd sat at his desk in the embassy, pen poised above the paper, and wondered, What will I do now? There would be various opportunities. He could become a consultant to an oil company or investment banking house or multinational corporation, or an exporter — or an importer! He knew people, heads of state, foreign ministers, ministers of the interior, police chiefs, and their sons and sons-in-law and brothers and dear friends and wives, and *their* friends and family. It was lucrative work. He had signed the paper and sent it up through channels, but they did not accept it. Word came back from the under secretary. Stay at your post. They kept his letter, however. And his report, which was immediately classified Top Secret. It had never occurred to him to withhold the report. He wrote it as he would write any confidential memorandum of conversation, supplying the salient facts, and using direct quotations, and including an "appreciation" of the tone of the exchange. Editing the cable, he cut his appreciation to the bare bones; a few sentences. It was the report of a professional diplomat, an experienced man with an excellent memory. Looking at the completed cable, he recalled that the root of the word *diplomacy* was the Greek *diploma,* meaning a folded letter; a letter folded so that its contents were concealed. He typed his resignation, two sentences to the President of the United States, as required. Then he wrote in longhand a covering note, personal to the under secretary, and sent both to the under secretary at the Department. He was a security risk.

He felt very tired suddenly. Two patients shuffled into the room and, seeing the three men in the corner, shuffled out again. Carruthers and Hartnett in their blue shirts and drawn indoor faces looked like doctors. North thought of Richard, so silent and alone in the bed down the hall. Shit, all of it was shit. Lawyers and their secret rooms, and the mumbo-jumbo inside.

"As the report stated, we talked to him for an hour." He was about to add "and then they let us go," but didn't. Carruthers could figure that out for himself. He said instead, "We left, Elinor and I, after the harangue. I suppose that's what it was, a harangue. The usual stuff, nothing original. It's all in the report. A few fancy German phrases from Marx and, I think, Spengler. His German is excellent, he speaks it like a native. He sounds like a Hamburg businessman."

"Explain that," Carruthers said.

He explained about Bill Jr. speaking German and then English. His English had a slight German accent. The intention, successful, was to put more distance between them. As if more distance were needed. He explained at length, remembering how, afterward, he and Elinor had gone to a café, ordering coffee and Cognac, and Elinor looking at him and saying, He looks so thin. And different. His appearance is altered, she said. She'd said, His hair grows in a different way. He did not understand what she meant, and said so. She touched her own hair, pulling at it and making a face. It isn't the haircut, she said. It's something else.

He remembered her drinking her Cognac, and leaning across

the table. Her eyes were so bright. She said, Maybe he dyed his hair. The color wasn't right, it wasn't his color. What I mean is: His hair *had been* dyed. I think he had been dyed blond. Do you think that's possible?

It's very possible, he said.

She said, Oh, God, Bill.

He ordered more Cognac and they sat in silence a moment.

She said, What I wonder about all the time is whether I'm responsible.

He said, You aren't. I'm not, either.

She looked at him and said, Oh?

I'm not responsible for him any more than my father was responsible for me.

Bill, she said.

He said, I'll give him the successes but not the mistakes.

She said, He's so different.

Damnedest thing, he said. My mother always said we were alike, two peas in a pod. Same pod, same peas.

She looked at him wanly. I mean Bill Jr. *Bill Jr.'s* so different.

Yes, he said stupidly.

And if we aren't responsible, who is? God?

He's like a ghost you meet on the staircase.

Yes, she said. But who made him?

It was so painful, He wanted to deflect her. He did not want to consider responsibility. He said, Even Charles Manson had a mommy and a daddy.

He is not Charles Manson, she said fiercely.

No, he wasn't Charles Manson. He remembered Manson's eyes, and the young women who surrounded him. He said, I don't believe in theoretical responsibility. Those who are guilty are guilty. Those who are innocent are not guilty.

They were silent a moment, and then she began to talk, aimlessly at first, circling. She felt part of him, she couldn't help it. She knew he was hers, a part of her in a way that even her husband wasn't and she thought that they, she and Bill, were as close as it was possible for two adults to be. And she didn't mean only that he was of her flesh; it was more than that. She said, I feel there is this — wonderful boy there somewhere behind the mask. Masks:

he seemed to have at least two. I try to look behind the surface, but I can't. It's like a secret place you loved as a child, a place entirely natural, a beach or a field, ruined now with hot dog stands and a gas station, leaking sewage, a place with the sign of the skull and crossbones. It's like America, you can barely remember what it was like back then, before the atmosphere was poisoned, before the selfishness and megalomania, cant, rant, and thirty-second updates. . . . Listening to him is like listening to a commercial. What offends me is the slovenly logic, and the slogans, and the absence of anything *human*. And the absence of doubt. And the absence of motive. How can he be ours? How can he be mine? I don't understand what it is. What is it all for? Or is it just theater?

She·had taken a sip of coffee and another long swallow of Cognac and excused herself to go to the *Damen* to be sick. He had watched her go, her words still in his head. He did not want to think about responsibility. But if he did not take responsibility, who would? They had gotten good and drunk in Hamburg, the end of the evening a blur, a bad boiled dinner somewhere, wine, more Cognac, and then a long meandering walk back to the hotel. He thought they were being followed but every time he wheeled around the street was empty. He could imagine the little superior smile of the man or woman watching their Spenglerian progress to the hotel, whose architecture was reminiscent of one of Ludwig's castles. How had it survived the war? He went to the window and looked into the street, drawing the curtain to one side, like a man on the run in a spy movie. There was nothing suspicious. They were drunk, but not so drunk that they couldn't make love. Elinor had said, Let's go to bed. And do it with a minimum of inelegance.

Falling asleep, the ambassador had a vision of his father in the Brahms-brown study on Marlborough Street, examining his texts. The nature of sin, the nature of righteousness, the nature of justice. Man and God, God and man. Or, as he wrote it, G-d. The essence of the faith: scholarship, inquiry, contradiction, and a long memory. What a strange trio they were, his father, himself, his son. What linked them, other than nationality? His father and his son were parentheses, enclosing him as surely as the oceans. His father was of the Old World as surely as his son was of the New,

59

the past and the future enclosing the present, pressing in on it, mocking it. North had always thought of himself as an outsider banging on the gates, to the Gentiles he was a Jew and to the Jews a Gentile; to his son he was a puppet, evil as Pahlevi. To his colleagues, a man who knew the score. Perhaps, he thought, perhaps I assimilated — too much? Too soon? Too readily? Too eagerly? He had wanted to join the club. The truth was that he was not Jew nor Gentile nor shah. He was a diplomat, with a diplomatic immunity. A black passport, thick as a paperback book; government paycheck, government pension. And his duty to have a say in matters of the greatest consequence. His right to be heard. His obligation to speak, to quarrel with the government as he had quarreled with his father, and as his father quarreled with God. He was very different now, he doubted that he would recognize himself, a man who had spent a lifetime inside the government. From time to time, he had defended the indefensible. No doubt some of his uncertainty, his belligerence, his hostility, his refusal to withdraw, his indulgence, his cynicism, his frequent despair, his good intentions, his *work*, had crippled his boy. Perhaps it had left Bill Jr. with nothing to hold on to, nothing that would last from today to tomorrow, a humane faith. Instead, there were unredeemed promises. . . . The house on Marlborough Street, so still, thick curtains drawn against the sun or the cold, had been his Valley Forge. He remembered its heavy silence, and its library. Then he fell asleep in his wife's arms.

"Just you, your wife, and son at this visit," Carruthers said.

North looked up. "In the room, yes. He had friends in the building because once there was a knock on the door and a conversation. I didn't see who it was outside. I assume one of his colleagues. Or confederates, whatever you want to call them. And we didn't hear the conversation, except I believe they were speaking in German."

"And you haven't heard from him since, or seen him."

"No, for Christ's sake."

"Bill." Disappointed again.

North said evenly, "He has no reason to get in touch with us. and he hasn't. And won't."

"He did before."

"That's right."

"He's smart," Carruthers said.

"Right again."

"And tough."

"Plenty tough."

"No known loyalties."

"I guess that's right."

"He's determined, he won't give up."

"He's very determined."

"He takes after you, then."

"I wouldn't say so," North said.

"He doesn't resemble you. I mean physically."

"No."

"We've done quite a lot of checking," Carruthers said. North nodded, waiting. "We've run him in and out of every computer in town. And that's what everyone says, that he's tough, determined, resourceful. And subtle." North nodded again, weary; his attention was beginning to wander. "Do you love your son?" Carruthers asked softly.

Hartnett said, "Jesus Christ, Paul."

The gray had turned to drizzle and the drizzle to rain. Outside the light was failing. North sat expressionless, looking out the window at the rain. From somewhere he heard music, a popular tune, adolescent voices. Could you love the idea of a thing, and not the thing itself? Or a thing as it was, and not as it had become? Could you love a memory, the substance of it, not the soft silhouette —or was it the reverse? Did he love his son? Or was he only nostalgic for a childhood shadow, a supple sentimentality as airy as a daydream? But of course that was not Paul Carruthers's real question. That was not what he was asking. What he required was an affirmation of loyalty — to the state, no less. He wanted to know whose side the ambassador was on, push came to shove. Love was where you began. It was none of Carruthers's business by which process North arrived at his answer, if he chose to give one. He was not interested, anyhow. He wanted a loyalty oath. Carruthers would like to see him in the position of Colonel Moscardo, defender of the Alcazar in Toledo in 1936. The commander of the people's militia, laying siege to the city, put the colonel's son on the telephone and told him that unless he surrendered, the boy would die. Moscardo told his son, "Put your trust in God, my boy, and die like a man." "A big hug, Daddy." "A very big hug, my son." The boy was twenty-three and so not technically a boy but a week later he was put to death, as promised. Later, the Alcazar fell, and later still Moscardo became a general in Franco's army, and the story part of the passionate fabric of the Spanish Civil War. Everyone knew the Spanish had a fondness for the dramatic act, and a strict sense of honor. Perhaps the key words were "Put your faith in God." It was not good enough to say that no man should have to make such a choice, because there it was. Was it courageous to betray your country in order to save your child, or your friend? Betray your country in order to save yourself? No, definitely not. That would be an act of cowardice, though perhaps unavoidable if your enemy was determined. Cowardice seemed too harsh a word, too laden. It would not be one's finest hour, however, It would not be a very fine hour either way, but he thought that of the two men he admired the colonel more than the commander. Was life, *living*, the most precious thing of all? Perhaps it was, but North did not think he could betray his country, which also, in its way, was a living thing; and he had taken an oath. He said to Carruthers, "Of course." course." Not entirely responsive, and he watched Carruthers for a reaction.

Carruthers said softly, "That was a question prepared by the under secretary."

"Is that right?" North said. "I would have thought Dunphy. It's Dunphy's kind of question."

"But not Dunphy's kind of answer, Bill. Actually, it was the under secretary who wanted to know." He glanced at the little pile of papers in front of him. "Dunphy doesn't have anything to do with this conversation. He's on the other team, he's offense; we're defense. It's something to keep in mind, Bill."

"I'm glad you set me straight," North said. "The under secretary has always been great at defense. And isn't that the essence of football?"

Carruthers said, "I just wanted you to know whose question it was." He shifted in his chair, irritated. "The under secretary likes things tidy, shipshape. No surprises. In case the matter should ever get to a hearing room, all those lights and cameras. Everybody sweating."

North said, "As the Spanish say, 'Authority that does not abuse loses its prestige.' "

Carruthers said, "That's a hell of a thing to say, Bill."

He was very tired. He said, "So where are we, Paul? What do you want?"

"It isn't what we want. It's what they want, the committee and Dunphy. It's our best guess that they want an embarrassment. Terrorism's quite the thing, now. Reasonable that a committee of the Congress would want to look into it. Is there an American connection? That's on the surface. It's the hidden agenda that's the difficulty. That's Dunphy's property."

Hartnett turned to North. "Will you please tell me. Who the hell is Dunphy? Name's familiar, just barely. Kind of name you find in paragraph six, or mentioned on the Sunday morning programs. But who is he? I mean, what does he do when he's not advancing Warren Winston?"

North said, "He was a spear carrier for Lyndon Johnson. He was back in the woodwork in the West Wing and then when LBJ bowed out, he went to Johnson City to help him with his papers. When LBJ died, he came back here, set up a law practice. He's a casualty of the 'sixties, that's the truth of it. He loved Johnson. I met him once in Bonn, years ago when I was in the political section. I drove them around, did a little interpreting, fetched him a Scotch and soda when he wanted it. I mean LBJ. Dunphy fetched his own Scotch, beginning about ten each morning."

Hartnett smiled. "Well, that's something. Drunks're easy."

"He's not a drunk," North said. "He was drinking because there was nothing for him to do, except look after LBJ. The old man wasn't well, you could see it. He was drinking because he hated to see what was happening to the old man. He was devoted to him. He said that LBJ would be dead in a year, and he was. Pat Dunphy is an awfully angry man. He's a son of a bitch."

"What's he doing with Winston's committee?"

"He goes in and out," North said. "Public, private, public, private. Loves trouble. Loves stirring it up. Loves watching it happen. He loves to get even."

Hartnett was thoughtful a moment. "Why?"

Carruthers cleared his throat. "He's got an idea that it was the government that failed LBJ. Made him withdraw in 'sixty-eight. Killed him."

"So he doesn't care much for the Department of State."

North smiled, "I think that's fair to say, Dick."

"There's something else," Carruthers said. "LBJ wanted to make him an ambassador. Nothing big, he wanted to do his boy a favor. He sent out the word just shortly after he withdrew from the race. We dragged our feet at the Department, and one or two gents spoke out of turn. Passed the word quietly to the Foreign Relations Committee that LBJ was trying to pull a fast one, place one of his hacks as chief of mission to a *very important country*. Pat Dunphy: not qualified. Before you knew it, it was summer. The Democratic Convention, poor Hubert, all the trouble, LBJ despised and pitied. The Foreign Relations Committee never got around to holding hearings, and the nomination was dropped. But Pat Dunphy didn't forget."

"Well, well," Hartnett said. "So it's personal."

Carruthers screwed up a tight smile. "It usually is," he said. He consulted a document, then laid it face up on the table. It had the seal of the Department of State at the top of the page, and was stamped

SECRET — SENSITIVE
EYES ONLY

An internal memorandum, something for the under secretary. North couldn't see the date. Carruthers covered it with another piece of paper. He said, "Everybody's got a history. Entangling alliances, old enmities. Enmities," he repeated. "So that's what we're up against, Pat Dunphy wanting to get even. Warren Winston wanting to make a name for himself. And others on the committee simply *curious*." He looked up. "I know this is hard."

"Yes," North said. "It is." Then, "But I've been through it before, and you have my report."

Hartnett looked at his watch. "It's eight o'clock."

Carruthers said, "We'd like to talk to Elinor."

"You know where to find her," North said.

"It would be . . . very helpful if she'd cooperate."

64

"You'll have to ask her. But she doesn't know any more than I do."

"Yes, of course," Carruthers said.

"She doesn't know anything."

Hartnett said, "When do you think we can wind this up?"

"Our problem is, we have to know everything they know. When they come snooping around with their pieces of paper. Dunphy and the gumshoe. We have to be able to say, Oh, yes, well, there's a simple explanation for that. So if we might." Carruthers looked at Hartnett, raising his eyebrows. The look said, A little while longer. His soft voice caused the two men to lean forward, the better to hear him; each word was carefully enunciated. "So if we might, just so I have it clear in my own mind, to smooth some of the rough edges. Can we go back to the embassy, the week before Thanksgiving 1982." He looked at the ceiling, as if trying to assemble his thoughts. "You see, the other thing that's interested them, that they can't pin down, and that worries them, is the German connection. So. You're in your embassy, your office, and the Germans come to call. They have made a request to see Ambassador North —"

"Paul, this wasn't the Court of Saint James's. Kleust rang me up and said he wanted to chat and I said fine, when, and he gave me a time and I said, fine, any time you want. I didn't know what was on his mind. Maybe he wanted a tennis game."

"— and you granted it. What happened next? I mean the names of those present, our side and their side, what you said and what they said and so forth and so on."

"You have all that."

"Yes, and so does the committee."

"And it wasn't our side and their side. It was not a confrontation, or démarche. It was a chat, them and me."

"Whatever," Carruthers said.

"Not 'whatever,' " North said. "Let's get it straight. It's important. I didn't know what it was about. It turned out, as you know, to concern my boy. They wanted to give me some information. Kleust's initiative."

"Kleust?"

"Kurt Kleust, an old friend."

Hartnett said, "You have Bill's report. He has nothing to add to that. There *is* nothing to add to it."

"We want to make certain that nothing was inadvertently omitted. That sometimes happens, no? And now there's a little bit of urgency. And any time the Germans are involved —" He raised his hands and let them fall. "That committee, there's so much mischief to be made."

Hartnett switched on the lamp at his elbow. They had been sitting in near darkness. "This isn't the best time for Bill," he said.

"I know," Carruthers said. "Alas. But it's the time we have. Winston and Dunphy aren't going to wait on Bill's health, and we can't either."

North said, "Tell me again what Winston wants."

"Winston?" Carruthers paused, steepling his fingers. He reached into his shirt pocket for a cigarette, found one, and lit it. The smoke hung in the damp air. "He wants a conspiracy. I don't think he can get one, but that's what he wants. The ambassador, the ambassador's son, the Department of State."

"Christ," Hartnett said, laughing.

"A conspiracy to suppress."

"What?" North said. "Suppress what?"

"The *connection*," Carruthers said. "They have an idea that your boy is a dangerous character. And they're not the only ones who have that idea. Young Bill has an unpleasant record, and has had access to classified information. The way our embassies are secured. Or not secured. The procedures, the encryption system. I don't have to spell it out. And you and Elinor are the last people to've seen him and we didn't know about it before, we knew about it *after*. Do you see?" he smiled encouragingly.

"You mean, our loyalties."

"That's correct."

North said pleasantly, "Are you taping this conversation, Paul?" His smile faded. "No."

"Good," North said.

"And I don't take it kindly that you'd suggest such a thing. It's against the regulations. I wouldn't do it. And the under secretary wouldn't allow it."

"Of course he wouldn't, Paul. Apologies."

Carruthers was silent a moment, then nodded at Hartnett. "Is he wired?"

"You wired, counselor?"

Hartnett opened his coat, as if he were about to be frisked. "Not me," he said.

"I guess no one's wired," North said.

"It's a hell of a thing to accuse someone of, a colleague," Carruthers said. "It's important that we have mutual trust here. We are on the same side. We are in the same boat, and it's important that we have our ducks in a row. You don't want to be surprised, I don't want to be surprised. We want no embarrassments, not you, not the Department, not the under secretary. And when we're up there in front of the television lights, Winston and Dunphy on the high dais, if that's what it comes to, we've not only got to be clean. We've got to be seen to be clean, doesn't that make sense? Don't you think, Bill? Isn't that wise? Because otherwise we get our clocks cleaned, and there's just a hell of a lot of embarrassment all the way around. So let's have no more talk about wires. Let's concentrate on the main thing. And the main thing's the committee, what it has and what it doesn't have."

North listened, nodding, distracted. As Hartnett said, everything was personal; to think, after all these years, Warren Winston, back in his life. The last time he had seen him, almost ten years ago, they had reminisced about being young in Washington. A favorite pastime of the middle-aged in the capital. The nature of things in '61–'62, and how the town had changed, how contemporary it had become. Winston seemed not to have aged, proving once again that appearances are not always deceptive. He was turned out in a fawn-colored suit, his hair blow-dried, his eyes clear as window glass, his skin as tight and rugged as a mountain climber's. Jogging and Nautilus. He drank soda water and spoke frequently of "cognition." North remembered feeling disappointed, Winston seemed a parody of a modern politician. He had the smile and manner of a talk-show host, as slippery and cold as ice. In the old days he'd imitated the President, altogether a more attractive model. What are you doing now? Winston had asked, and North replied that he was political counselor in Bonn, but was shortly to leave to become ambassador in central Africa. That right? Winston had said with a show of interest; but he had not asked which country, and his eyes continued to roam. Presently he excused himself, took a colleague by the arm, and went off into a corner; the senator was not interested in reprising the old days. Watching Winston, North was aware of a paradox: as the city had become more cosmopolitan, it had also become more self-centered. It was like Paris, except there was no École Polytechnique; instead, there was television.

North looked at Carruthers. "Didn't you work in the Justice Department in the old days?"

"For about a minute and a half."

"Civil rights?"

"Antitrust," Carruthers said. "But I wasn't much of a trustbuster, and I always wanted to be at State. I wanted to be a diplomat, like you. An ambassador, or an assistant secretary. But I didn't want to do the Foreign Service drill, counsel in Ciudad Juarez or wherever. So I went to the Pentagon for a year, and then back to the White House. And then, two years after Dallas, back to my old firm." He laughed. "Except it wasn't mine anymore. When I got back there were fifty partners, the kids'd taken over. My name was on the door, but that was it. So I stayed a couple of years to find my feet, and then took the three best young ones and the two really good old ones, and formed another firm. Amazing, how many contacts you keep; in Washington, there are only a hundred people and they all know each other. But I got bored so I came back inside. I had more money than I could ever spend. That was five years ago. I like the government, so I came back to it. I like it on the inside."

"I knew Winston, back then."

"Everyone knew Warren Winston. That house he shared with whatshisname. The one in Georgetown. Bachelors together. There was plenty of action in that house."

"He used to drink. Now it's sermons and soda water."

"Yep." Carruthers nodded. "And jogging."

North said, "In the old days, they all wanted to be President, but knew they couldn't. It was a harmless fantasy. Now they know they can. Anybody can, given money enough and hard work, and some luck."

Carruthers looked at Hartnett. "I wouldn't depend on luck, Bill.

I wouldn't depend on that at all." He put out his cigarette. "See, he's got something, doesn't he? And now with your interim appointment, the suspicions're piling up. It's bad luck and bad timing. We know this has been in the works for some time, and I guess you'd have to say things kind of fell between the cracks at the Department. But Winston looks at it. It just bothers the hell out of him. See, he's not like us. You and I, we haven't believed in coincidence for so long that when there's a real coincidence, we can see it. Only a cynic can identify a saint."

Hartnett laughed. "Do that again, Paul?"

Carruthers sighed. "He wants something the worst way."

"You want me to tell you about Africa," North said.

"Yes. I want you to tell me about Africa, the day the Germans came to call."

Hartnett groaned, looking at his watch.

North thought a moment. "Come by tomorrow morning, and I'll tell you about Africa."

4

NOTHING MOVED, but he sensed restlessness in the hospital, a kind of fever. Restlessness everywhere in the city, the sound of whispering, marching feet, pressure. His own feet were motionless, sticking up at the end of the bed like two exclamation points.

! !

Insomnia, memory's snake eyes, the reward for an uneasy conscience. *That which I should have done I did not do.* Insomnia, and a numb left hand, medical tests, and now they wanted to know all about Africa. On the bureau opposite, Elinor had placed a self-portrait, what the Germans call a *Selbstbildnis.* It had been painted more than three years before, when they arrived in Africa the second time, his first ambassadorship. He had been worried about the reception, his role in the coup almost twenty years before; perhaps there would be a snub when he presented his credentials to the president. But there had been four changes of government since then, and the coup was referred to only as "the events." Many of the participants were dead. The president had been cordial, and had held his lecture to two hours flat. His government had an urgent need for money, there were so many schemes begun: electrification, the railroad, an installation for the air force and its fleet of MiGs. The president was eloquent with a poet's command of image and metaphor. North listened politely, with his ambassador's grave expression, and tried to remember himself as he had been twenty years earlier, a callow second secretary, so eager to get into the game. His instructions as ambassador were different. The aid budget was down; and there would be no military hardware, period. Make friends, the under secretary had told him; enjoy the country, there's wonderful hunting and fishing. Watch the Russians. Be nice to the Chinese. Meet the leaders of the opposition if it's possible. Don't make any promises you can't keep, which meant: Don't make any promises. This country, the under secretary had said, is not on our leader board.

He had found himself lulled by the president's musical baritone and at the end had shaken hands and said how pleased he was to be there. You were here before, the president said. Yes, he had replied, as a very young man. At the time of the events, the president said. Yes, he said. Only yesterday, the president said. Nearly twenty years ago, he said. And so much has changed, he added. And the president had smiled, showing an enormous gold tooth. Welcome back.

Africa had a sexual effect on him. Elinor had never seemed more desirable. The *Selbstbildnis* showed her as she was then, thinner, less gray in her hair, her skin soft and tan. She had painted herself on the lawn, the little bouquet of a garden behind her, the white African sky overhead. She was leaning forward, her hands primly clasped in front of her, her expression one of the most open desire. He had titled it *A Woman Waiting for Her Lover*. She had dismissed it as kitsch, a sentimental view of their mornings together. It was a powerful mnemonic, for he had always regarded his tour as ambassador as an extended holiday, AWOL from the world; what fun they had had.

They were always up early, making love. Most mornings, the power was off, the house silent as a desert. He thought of them as Bedouin, austere before the world, loyal only to each other. They were a tribe of two. It was warm in the big bedroom, the sun already climbing, the glare fierce. Lying back stretching, he watched

71

her do her hair. She refused to cut it short, despite the heat; it takes more than that, she said. Her hair was thick. She brushed it a hundred strokes each morning, concentrating, her tongue between her teeth. The whish-whish of the brush and the creak of the bed were the only sounds in the room. Her shoulders and back glistened with sweat; he was languid, loose as rubber, filled with energy. When he tried to help her with her hair, she said, softly, no. They sat cross-legged at the end of the bed, amid the tangled sheets, and always she turned to him and laughed, a womanly, throaty chuckle, tossing her head, her hair bouncing on her shoulders. He was randy as a teenager. *So proud of yourself,* she said.

In the dense heat of Africa they would remember things from their American childhoods, episodes that had lain buried, hidden all these years, now miraculously available. The stories enchanted them, one story leading to another, serving to remind them that they were people with individual histories, each with a life that predated the other's. The stories were presented with high good humor, so surprising; they were precious as antiques. Why, you never told me *that!*

"I went with a boy, brief time, a year or so before we met," she said, pausing tilting her head, smiling privately, listening to the whish-whish of the hairbrush. "He was a boy from Connecticut. He had the strangest family. No one worked. One night after dinner his mother and I were alone in the study. We began to talk and she asked me how her son was *in bed.*" Elinor looked up, grinning; she hadn't thought of the boy or his family in years. "What kind of lover he was," she said. "Was he — was he *ardent?*"

Bill began to laugh.

"Well, you know, those days. We weren't sleeping together. We were making out a little, you know, in cars. We were kids, teenagers."

"I remember," he said.

"Remember the Chevrolet?"

"Of course I remember the Chevrolet."

"You'd better," she said.

"What did you say to her?"

"I —"And Elinor faltered, turning away, her hair covering her face, the brush motionless. She reached for his hand in the silence and heat, turning toward him, her eyes bright; she took his hand, squeezing it, her eyes beginning now to patrol the big bedroom, the family pictures on the bureau and on the walls, as if by sheer force of eyesight she could summon the teenager, not the long-forgotten boyfriend but her own son. Did he have a girl? Did they neck in the back set of a car? Well, he was no longer a teenager but that was how she remembered him, a boy, not yet formed, not prepared for the world. Was he *ardent*? She had no idea. Probably he was. He burned in other ways; why not that way. She looked down at the bed closing her eyes.

He said gently, "El."

"I don't remember what I said to her, she was such a fool." Elinor tried to nudge her memory back to that place, a large house on the Connecticut shore, the two of them alone in the study, the boy's mother anxiously leaning over the coffee table, her own stunned surprise — and then it was gone, vanished in the silence of the present moment. "I think I was too shocked to say anything. Let's forget it."

He said, "All right."

She gritted her teeth and looked at him helplessly. "Damn it." Then, "Now you tell me about some episode. And make it funny, Bill."

But memory did not work in that way, so those mornings when their son would arrive unbidden they would wait quietly together until he disappeared, as he always did; they knew he would disappear, as they knew he would return. They just didn't know when.

In the mornings when he lifted the window, they heard the sound of birds and the occasional cough of a motorcycle. For a while it would be cooler outside than in. The power always failed around midnight, and toward dawn the refrigerated air would grow stale and humid. They lay in bed, feeling the warm breeze. He rolled over on his stomach and turned on the radio, the BBC World Service. Ba Owen tapped at their door and withdrew, leaving coffee and fresh fruit, and a flower in a fingerbowl, and *The Boston Herald*. The *Herald* arrived in bunches and was kept in the kitchen. Each morning, Ba Owen would select one and place it on their breakfast tray. The newspaper was damp in his hands and the ink stained his fingers. It did not matter that the news was weeks old;

in Africa, a month was the blink of an eyelid. And the *Herald* did not contain news. It was colorful Boston propaganda, a long whine of complaint directed at Cambridge academics, welfare cheats, the proprietors of local sports franchises, phony docs, killer dogs, gay nuns. And it was as easy to read as a comic. Later, Elinor took it to the pool, where she read it as she floated on a red rubber mattress as the vultures circled overhead.

That was the morning. Some days, he couldn't wait to get home from the office. A couple of times he faked headaches, it being unseemly for the ambassador to leave the office at three in the afternoon, setting a bad example for the junior officers. But he could not keep his mind on his work. He saw her sitting cross-legged on the bed, brushing her hair, watching him. He saw her delighted look, the half smile, the curve of her thigh. So he made an excuse, a headache, and went home at once, telling his driver to hurry it up, he was late for an appointment. He'd yell, *I have a headache,* and they'd tumble into bed. Then he realized that this embassy was not Moscow or Peking, or even Pretoria or Ottawa. This was a country at the nether end of Washington's list of serious missions. Any business that needed doing could be done before noon.

In the morning, and again in the evening, they would swim in the pool. After thirty minutes in the water he would go to work at the embassy and she would move upstairs to her studio, if the power had been restored and the air conditioning was working; otherwise she would stay outside, setting up her easel in the shade of the big tree, unless it was so hot that her oils melted. There was always a reception or dinner at night. Once or twice a month they would have house guests, visitors from Washington, or a traveling foreign correspondent, occasionally a colleague from a neighboring country. The visitors brought gossip from the outside world.

That morning — the morning in question, the morning the Germans were due at the office — they swam together as usual. Then on impulse he went back into the house for a second pot of coffee. It was very hot on the terrace. When Bill brought the coffee tray to poolside, Elinor was out of the water, drying her hair with a towel. They sat on the edge of the pool, watching Ba Owen move in the shade of the large tree near the guest wing of the house, the wing that sheltered their visitors. Odd-looking tree, he could never remember its name; it resembled a linden, and that reminded him of Berlin. He started thinking about the Germans.

At the sound of a car in the street, they both looked up. The guard moved his head out of the sentry box at the end of the driveway. It was a British embassy Land-Rover, the minister on his way to the office. Through the shrubbery they recognized the color and the long whip aerial on the rear bumper. The guard left the sentry box and suddenly began waving his arms.

She said, "What's he doing?"

He said, "I don't know. Get inside." He was already helping her out of the water, keeping himself between her and the guard twenty yards away. A woman appeared in the street, and they heard a high keening, a kind of wail. She was one of the lepers. The guard moved to cut her off, and force her back the way she had come, out of sight. The guard shouted at her but she did not move. Her face was shrouded with a red bandanna. She commenced to yaw, rocking from side to side, her face to the sky. The guard had his carbine at port arms, moving her away from the driveway. Ba Owen had slipped out from under the tree and had joined the guard, standing a little behind him. They were both shouting at the woman, Go back! She came from out there, the district away from embassy ghetto, across the golf course and railway tracks. She did not appear to hear them, but continued wailing. Bill and Elinor put on shirts and walked down the lawn. Elinor told the guard to stop, but he and Ba Owen had advanced into the street, moving the woman back. She stumbled backward, her fists moving from side to side. Her face was concealed, but one enormous bangle hung from an ear. Her face seemed to be misshapen. Bill called to her and she gathered her skirts and in a moment was gone, as quickly as she had come. The guard and Ba Owen stood watching her go. They were talking in low tones and shaking their heads. Then, to the white people, the guard said it was all right. She was gone now, back to her place, back *there*.

"What did she want?" Bill asked.

Ba Owen shook his head. He didn't know.

"Did she want money?"

Ba Owen said no, he didn't think so.

"Then what did she want?"

"She sometimes comes here. She evades the security." He meant the police vans that patrolled embassy ghetto.

"Do you know her name?"

"She likes the flowers," Ba Owen said. "She wanted to pick the flowers from the garden." He solemnly pinched his nose between thumb and forefinger. The woman had been fetid, and surrounded with flies, huge bluebottles.

"Let her, then," Elinor said.

Ba Owen shook his head firmly. "No, Mrs." Then, to Bill, he spoke in rapid dialect, gesturing. He avoided looking at Elinor. He said finally, "The woman is a leper." He and the guard turned and strolled up the street to assure themselves that the woman was gone. The odor of her was still around them, clinging to the street and the shrubbery. Bill and Elinor walked back to the pool.

Elinor said, "What did he say to you?"

"Ba Owen says she has bad juju."

She said, "I can't get used to her wail. It's unearthly. I've heard it before, but this is the first time I've seen her."

Bill said, "She shouldn't be here, in embassy ghetto."

She looked at him archly. "Too exotic for our delicate sensibilities?"

He said, "No. This area is off-limits. Embassy ghetto is supposed to be secure."

Elinor said, "The poor thing."

"Ba Owen says she's a witch. Powerful witchcraft. He advises us to be careful. She has bad juju." He smiled. "She scares Ba Owen."

Elinor snorted. She dipped her hands in the water and splashed some on her belly and thighs. She lowered herself into the water, pushed off, and floated on her back to the middle of the pool. The heat was rising, and the dense smell of Africa with it, overwhelming the chlorine in the water and the fume of the flowers. She floated on her back without moving her head. Bill watched her a moment, then said, "Kurt's coming by today."

She lifted her head, paddling slowly. "Here?"

"The office. But maybe I'll bring him home for lunch, after. Would you like to lunch with Herr Kleust?"

"Of course."

"Maybe I'll bring him home with me, then."

"All right."

"He and some of his people are coming by this morning." She moved her arms, sending little ripples over the surface of the water, looking at him steadily. He looked very tall, standing by the edge of the pool. "They didn't say what it was about. But I think it's Bill Jr. Something about Kurt's manner."

She scissored to where he was sitting and lifted herself out of the water, standing dripping at his side. "Call me when you leave the office, will you do that? I'll plan lunch for three on the terrace. Do you really think so?"

"Yes."

"Is that what Kurt said?"

"It's just a feeling."

"Bill —"

"That's all I know."

"But why in your office? Why doesn't he just come here?"

"He has some people with him. Who knows? Maybe he wants to make it official."

"Oh, God," Elinor said.

He remembered leaving Elinor at the pool, dressing quickly, and driving to the embassy to read the overnight cable traffic: bulletins from the West. His DCM, Harry Erickson, had brought him the folder and now sat in the leather chair in the corner of the room, silent while the ambassador read. There was nothing new and he read swiftly, initialing each page. The last document was a transcript of the President's latest press conference; loose questions, casual answers. It was the performance of a nimble public relations man. The ambassador scanned the cable for references to Africa; there were none. No surprises, Africa was low on everyone's list, and the President had no interest in the continent; he had never been to Africa. His generals had never been to Africa either, so the region was the State Department's problem. Of course it was no different in the Soviet Union. In his forty years as a foreign policy specialist, Andrei Gromyko had never been south of the Sahara. They knew nothing firsthand so naturally they saw the continent as an abstraction. The people in it were not real. This

President and every President since Teddy Roosevelt saw Africa in the faces of her *mzees,* in their English suits or tribal robes; or in the fiction of Hemingway or Waugh; or from the films, America's memory.

When he was done he rang for coffee and handed the folder across the desk to Harry.

Harry said, "God, he is a yo-yo."

North looked at him. "Is that what you think?" Harry Erickson smiled and shrugged. "Well, he isn't. He is a lot of things, but he isn't that."

"I'm entitled to my opinion. He's the *baas,* I'll go along with you there." Harry looked at him, a suggestion of belligerence. "I thought, if you don't mind, I'll go upcountry today. There's a ceremony in the north, I'd like to see it —"

"Go ahead," North said.

"— tribal ceremonies." He smiled. "Centuries-old customs. Weird rites. Fertility dances."

"Go ahead, Harry."

"Interior minister's invited me. I thought I'd take Josh along, that's right up his alley." Josh Pafko was the station chief. Harry stood looking at him. "Alice is taking a trip. She and Jan are going to Salisbury. For the shopping."

"Nairobi would be better."

"Alice hates it here. She just hates it and feels she has to get away, to take a trip somewhere. Africa's not her cup of tea. The atmosphere, she doesn't like it. Of course she's excited about this trip. They've been planning it for a while."

"How long are they going to be away?" He was thinking about Kleust, due any minute.

"A week, she says," Harry said. He stood tapping the file folder into his open palm. "Jan Francis is a cunt."

North smiled, nodding. He wondered how many people Kleust would bring with him. Kleust liked to travel in groups, the more spear carriers the better.

"There's nothing to be done about it," Harry said. "Alice doesn't travel well. She said she did, before we were married. She said that was what she liked about the Foreign Service, the travel. But she doesn't like Africa."

"I can try to hurry up your transfer."

"The hell with it," Harry said.

North rose and went to the window, and looked down into the embassy courtyard. He watched the guard rise slowly from his chair, his hands on his knees. He stood a moment, swaying in the heat, then walked slowly to the barrier, where a car waited, its engine idling. Waves of heat rose from the skin of the car. The barrier was a simple red-and-white-striped pole, comical to look at; it resembled an elongated barber's pole. The guard, Benson, stepped over it, inspecting the flag that hung limply from the car's left fender. He bent his head down as the driver's window descended. He tipped his hat, then checked the clipboard, his finger moving ponderously down a list of names. And with a great smile, saluted and turned to raise the bar. It lifted easily. The Germans.

North said, "We have visitors."

"It won't do any good," Harry said.

"I can talk to the under secretary."

Harry shook his head.

"Alice —" North began.

"Alice can go to hell," Harry said.

North watched the car float into the courtyard, a mirage. Benson slowly lowered the barrier and returned to his chair in the shade. He was smiling and fanning his face. Air conditioning in cars was a great thing.

North said, "Have you read the new security orders?"

"Sure. It's all crap. Nothing ever happens here. But we have to do it."

North turned from the window. The security division's orders: an iron gate and ashcans filled with sand so that a car or truck would have to approach in a tight S-curve. No one could get into the curve until an embassy civilian checked papers. There were four marines, one at the entrance to the S-curve, two flanking the gate, a third out of sight in the guardhouse. Mines left and right, everyone armed. The ambassador's office would be relocated at the rear of the building, next to the code room. Bulletproof glass, reinforced doors, a safe that would explode at the twist of a key. This was an order that confirmed the task force report, two years in the writing. Or was it three? In that time, two ambassadors had been kidnaped, and three killed. Threats were routine. How quaint it was now to read Kennan's memoirs, his descriptions of wandering alone late at night through European cities, listening to café chatter, getting a feel of things in the streets. "It's not crap," he said.

Harry said, "All right, it's not crap. But why don't they give us combat pay?" He signed, and shifted direction. "She doesn't know what she's getting into. She doesn't understand anything. She's just a small-town girl."

"Jan's been out here a long time."

Harry said, "She's native. She's slept with every man, woman, and child. And animal. I've heard she sleeps with animals. That's the rumor."

North watched the car doors open and three men hastily exit, hurrying across the asphalt to the embassy entrance. White men in white suits. It was only twenty yards but he knew they would be sweating by the time the Marine corporal opened the door to admit them. The flag of the BRD hung damp as a dishrag. Almost as damp as Harry Erickson, he thought.

He said to Harry, "I can arrange some leave, you and Alice, get away together —"

"There isn't anything to be done about it."

He saw the younger man's reflection in the window glass, a slender, thin-lipped, thirtyish man, white short-sleeved shirt, blue cotton trousers, a shock of sandy hair; he had a tattoo on his forearm, an anchor. He did not look like a man who would have a tattoo. It was as incongruous on him as love beads would be on Averell Harriman. He and Alice, midwestern stoics; except she had begun to lose it. They were from a small town in Minnesota, the upper Midwest, the winters so cold steel would snap. For three years they had been trying to have a baby. They had been two years in Washington, two years in Morocco, a tour on a desk in the African bureau, and now here. Harry's record was excellent. On paper, he was formidable.

"It's easy for you to be cool about it, Bill. You've got Elinor. And I know you think I'm not fitting in and that's why you want my transfer speeded up. But how is that going to look, wife trouble in Africa? They know how to read between the lines. The Department hates instability, and you can't deny it."

80

"I wouldn't," North said.

He tucked the file folder under his left arm and took a step to the door. "It's Alice who needs the transfer, not me. She's the one who's fucked up." He opened the door. "I want to do a good job, Bill. She's never left Minnesota, that's the problem. I don't know what to do about Jan Francis. You know what Alice does all day?" He looked away, hesitating. He said, "Never mind. I'll see you tomorrow."

North watched him go, then sat down heavily in his chair. Neither one of them had left Minnesota. What the hell were they doing in Africa? Africa was a bad place to create another self, though people often tried. Africa could add another layer to a personality, but you had to keep it away from the center of your being. You had to build a wall around yourself. Africa was too extreme, and the Ericksons were too ordinary. Ordinary people in an extreme situation. The culture of North America was not thick enough to absorb Africa. It could colonize, but it could not subdue; it could destroy, but it could not defeat. It was wise not to fight Africa. The ambassador knew there would be trouble from the first time he met Alice Erickson, with her prairie zeal and her passion to *understand*. With understanding would come sympathy, Q.E.D. Short, blue-eyed, plump, understanding Alice; tall, blue-eyed, slender, condescending Harry. She wore Moroccan bangles and brightly colored slippers, like a character out of Ali Baba. She confided to Elinor that in Morocco she had tried kif, though Harry would have none of it, straight-laced Norwegian that he was. Emotionally, he was still in Eagle Bend. "My Harry," she said grimly, seeking a reference that Elinor would appreciate, "belongs to the school of Edvard Munch."

Bill North smiled in spite of himself, thinking of all this.

But the performance this morning was something else. Personnel problems seemed to vary in inverse proportion to the importance of the assignment. Nevertheless, he made a mental note to speak to the assistant secretary, or send him a message, back channel. It was not important enough for the under secretary. Geography was destiny, and Harry and Alice belonged in a chilly northern climate.

His secretary put her head in. "Ambassador Kleust is here."

He rose to greet them. Kurt Kleust, and two others whom he

didn't know. He and Kurt shook hands and Kurt introduced his companions: Major Bruch and Herr Duer. North had seen Bruch at a distance, but Duer was unfamiliar to him. Major Bruch was the military attaché; Herr Duer was tactfully unidentified. They were all sweating. North buzzed Cynthia for iced tea, and indicated the couch and the two chairs flanking it. He offered cigarettes while the Germans removed their jackets.

Kleust said, "Bill, you look tired."

He had brought a fat art book for Elinor, a collection of the German Expressionists, mainly the school known as Die Brücke, the Bridge. Kleust believed that she was devoted to twentieth-century German art; in fact, Bill was the enthusiast. He and Kleust looked at the plates while Major Bruch and Herr Duer sat politely silent.

"Squalid German politics, marvelous German art." They were looking at a Käthe Kollwitz woodcut.

"They go together, night and day," Kleust said.

"Is it not true everywhere?" Major Bruch inquired. "Even America?"

"No," Kleust said.

They talked German politics for fifteen minutes, Herr Duer silent on the sidelines. The talk turned to polo. Kleust and Major Bruch were great horsemen. Last week they had played the annual match with the British, and won, as they had the year before. North had thrown out the ball, feeling overweight and out of place on a huge stallion; he hated horses. He had invited the Chinese ambassador to watch the match, and spent an hour and a half explaining polo through an interpreter. It had been an interminable three chukkers, and not a black face in the spectators' enclosure; they might as well have been at the Myopia Hunt, except for the heat and the flies. Major Bruch told an elaborate anecdote about his opposite number, the British military attaché, an overage captain who broke his mallet and was unhorsed. The British were fine sportsmen and played with dash, but —

The preliminaries continued. The essence of the diplomatic life: haste makes waste. Fresh cigarettes were lit. North was watching Duer while listening to Major Bruch. Bruch reminded him of an illusionist distracting the audience with his easy mouth while his hands were cooking the deck, stuffing aces up his sleeve. He judged Duer to be in his middle thirties. His face and arms were white, and his forehead beaded with sweat. He was evidently unused to the tropics. Coming inside from the heat, it was always wise to sit quietly and wind down. Duer was leaning forward in his chair, coiled, waiting. He was clean-shaven but for some reason North suspected that he normally wore a beard. Herr Duer was not with the embassy, he knew that much; he wore the distracted air of someone committing a thought to memory. He had the manner of a detective, and the unkempt appearance of a Fassbinder fugitive, the sort of man who would automatically be singled out at the airport security barrier.

At last the major came to the end of his story. He cleared his throat and passed the attaché case to Herr Duer. North wondered if they were wired, Bruch and Duer.

Kleust said, "This is informal."

North smiled.

"Bill, let me show you some pictures." He nodded to Duer, who opened the attaché case and handed a manila envelope to North. It was not sealed. There were three eight-by-ten glossy prints, taken with a long lens; three middle-aged men at a café table, all of it foreshortened.

Duer said, "Hamburg, last month. The fifteenth of last month, at four in the afternoon."

North's expression did not change. His hands were trembling slightly. He walked to his desk and took a magnifying glass from the center drawer. He had to push the Smith & Wesson to one side to get to it. He returned to the chair studying the photograph, noticing as he did so a sigh and a rustle in front of him; impatience. He looked at only the top photograph. He did not recognize any of the three at the table, they were ordinary middle-aged men in dark suits and open collars, apparently Germans. But his eyes were elsewhere now, at a table in the rear of the café. He needed a moment, so he looked at Kleust and shrugged.

Duer said softly, "Look again, please, Ambassador. The upper right of the photograph."

He looked through the glass again. A smudge of a face, but unmistakable, a positive sighting. His stomach turned as he looked through the glass. He said, "Last month?" He was concentrating on the photograph, all the details. The face was in profile, bearded under a black beret. The right hand held a cigarette, the angle of the hand was unmistakable. Bill Jr. was talking to someone across the café table but his companion, whoever it was, was concealed by the waiter's body.

North said, "It's him. Who are the three in the foreground?"

"Our people have an interest in them," Major Bruch said.

"Are they connected?"

"We don't think so. We have no reason to think so and it would be unlikely. The three in the foreground are not political. At least they are not political in that way. In the way of your son."

North nodded, looking at each of them in turn. For a brief moment, he had an urge to thank them but he didn't. Whatever Kleust said, this was an official visit. It was not personal, so appreciation didn't come into it. "Who is he with?"

"A female, according to the waiter. He remembers her because of her good looks. And she wore a short leather skirt. She was a good-looking young female."

"German?"

"The waiter thinks she was foreign, but is not sure. Your son spoke excellent German, very fluent. But the young woman did not speak at all, according to the waiter."

North looked from Bruch to Duer and back again.

"That is all we know about that," Herr Duer said.

"Hamburg," he said.

"Hamburg," Colonel Bruch said.

"And nothing since then?"

"Nothing positive," Duer said.

He looked at the other two photos. They were essentially the same scene, taken from different angles. The clearest of them showed Bill Jr. in corduroy trousers and a dark sweater at the café table, raising a cup of coffee to his mouth, a characteristic gesture, his elbows out, holding the cup in both hands. His expression was pouty, like an infant's. Smoke curled around the cup, from the cigarette in his left hand. He was frowning, annoyed at something. The photograph was not clear enough for North to see his eyes. A waiter was bending over the table, the waiter in white shirt and black tie, his body concealing the young woman. North recognized the expression on his son's face. He and the young woman were having an argument. He was talking and she was listening; or, anyway, she was silent. She was probably not listening. Talking was one of his long suits. His thoughts would be on his own arguments, what he would say next, and how, particularly *how;* when he was hot, his speech became almost Edwardian, elaborate, rich with sarcasm, a literary monologue in complete sentences, subject, verb, predicate. The moral life of the young.

"We are trying to find out about the young woman," Kleust said.

North looked again at the picture and wondered what the argument was about. The waiter was present, so it would not be anything personal or political. Probably the coffee was foul. The sugar dish was empty. He had complained and the young woman had objected, perhaps to his tone of voice. One could be wonderfully rude in German. He said, "The three in the foreground —"

"We photographed your son by the sheerest chance. It was Herr Duer who noticed him in the background of the picture. Herr Duer has an — interest in your son. And his associates. And their plans for the future, insofar as they effect the BRD. Herr Duer's eye was drawn to the beret, it is not usual to see berets in Hamburg. Something about the angle of the face, and the hands holding the cup of coffee . . . Herr Duer has an excellent memory."

Duer said, "By the attitude of the waiter we are guessing that this is a familiar café to your son, though the waiter denies that he has ever seen him or the young female before. Look at the waiter's feet. They are crossed, and he has one hand on the table. This is the attitude of one who is conversing, not merely taking an order."

German thoroughness. "Seems so," he said.

"We thought, looking at your son, that perhaps there was an argument of some kind. His face is dark. But the waiter could remember no argument."

North nodded but did not reply.

"Then, looking at some of the other photographs we have collected, we thought that perhaps his face was always dark."

North said, "The waiter is lying."

Kleust leaned forward. "That was what we thought, Bill. We have the café under surveillance, but there is no sign of them, your son or the young female. And the waiter behaves normally. And of course until now we were not certain that it was your son. We had no positive identification until today. It was only a guess on Herr Duer's part. Give thanks to the beret."

He said, "Where is the café?"

"Around the corner from the Hotel Prem. An expensive neighborhood, fashionable. A neighborhood where tourists often go. Of course there are not many tourists in Hamburg. Hamburg is not Munich. And this was in October, so there are even fewer tourists."

Duer said, "Does your son normally wear a beret?"

"No," he said.

"Nor a beard."

"Nor a beard."

"Do you know the Hotel Prem?"

He nodded. "Stayed there once, years ago." Subtle of Kleust, remaining silent. Three years earlier they had had dinner at one of Kleust's haunts on the harbor, a fish house. He and Elinor and Bill Jr. and Kleust, the American consul general, and the resident spook. Bill Jr., bored and sullen, did not speak so they ignored him. It was an excellent dinner, very jolly; the consul paid. Bill Jr. left them in front of the restaurant, walking away through the gauntlet of wharf whores. And that was the last time he had seen his son. He disappeared into Germany. He remembered that Kleust had returned them to the Hotel Prem and they had a nightcap in the bar, a half bottle of Fürst von Metternich. He and Elinor did not miss Bill Jr. until the next morning, when the receptionist reported that his bed had not been slept in. Will your son be returning? Bill thought a moment and said, No, he won't be, knowing he was gone, knowing they would not see him again for a very long time.

"Your whole family?"

"Bill Jr. was with us."

"Well," Kleust said.

"What do you intend to do now?"

"We have the café under surveillance, as the ambassador said," Herr Duer said. "And the authorities in Hamburg have been alerted. We have the waiter under surveillance also, but we do not expect anything to come of this. There is nothing in. The waiter's background. To suggest any connection with your son or your son's associates. Of course that, in itself, is perhaps suspicious." Herr Duer smiled.

North smiled back. Quite a piece of work was Herr Duer, squaring the circle. Heads I win, tails you lose. He handed the photographs back to the German, who put them in his attaché case and closed it. For a moment no one said anything.

North said, "The other three, in the foreground —"

Duer made a little gesture of dismissal, but his eyes were bright.

North said, "Could be a coincidence."

Kleust sighed. "I am afraid Herr Duer does not believe in coincidence."

Herr Duer leaned forward. Half moons of sweat showed under his armpits. He gave off an odor of cologne mixed with sweat as he shook a damp cigarette out of the pack on the table and lit it. He smiled fractionally, displaying yellow teeth. "With your permission," he said politely. "This is a formidable lead, the best one we have had. In fact the only one we have had, that is verifiable. They are very careful, these people, very professional, very meticulous." He paused again, glancing at Kleust. "We thought you might be able to help us. We thought you might be persuaded to come to Hamburg, Mr. Ambassador."

"To help you find my son."

"Yes," Duer said.

"How would I do that?" he asked softly.

Herr Duer cracked his knuckles. He was trying not to show his excitement, but his voice rose and he spoke rapidly. "It is well known, people return to that which is familiar to them. The Hotel Prem, for example. You have been in Hamburg with the boy, you might remember places you visited with him. And you could recognize him, in a café or across the street, with a beret or without a beret or a beard, or however he chose to present himself. I don't have to say to you. It is in everyone's interest to find your son, before."

"Before what?"

"He is a violent boy," Duer said sharply.

North looked at Duer, then turned to Kleust. There was a moment of silence, and then Kleust nodded at Duer, almost apologetically. Duer immediately rose. "You and the major," Kleust said. "Please to wait outside for a moment. I wish to speak to the ambassador privately." He turned to North for confirmation. It was North's office and North's embassy and Kleust did not wish to seem — Teutonic.

"Sorry about all this," Kleust said when they were alone.

"It's hard as hell, Kurt."

"I know it is."

"I don't care much for your Herr Duer."

"Nor do I. He is interested only in his work. But he's good, he's the best we have, though he has the personality of a . . ." Kleust sought the word and North said, "Bowling ball." Kleust thought a moment, then smiled. "I would have said polo mallet."

North stepped to the window and stood looking down into the courtyard. Harry Erickson was walking to his car, talking animatedly to the station chief. They looked like boys without a care in the world, playing hooky from school. He said, "I suppose Duer's efficient."

"Very," Kleust said.

"Unorthodox or by the book?"

"Both," Kleust said. "That's why he's so good."

"You've got quite a file on my boy, haven't you?"

"Yes," Kleust said.

Harry Erickson looked up and saw the ambassador in the window, and quickly looked away. He and the station chief got into the big Land-Rover. "One of my officers," North said from the window, "young fellow, good record, except that he's younger than springtime. Wife's having an affair with another woman. Or that's the story. That ever happen with your people?"

"I know all about that."

Of course he would. There were no secrets in embassy ghetto.

"Jan Francis is a friend of mine."

"I'd forgotten," North said.

Kleust laughed. "You remember my commercial attaché. Fell in love with Bruch's deputy, a darling captain. Fine horseman. They were discreet about it and it didn't matter except it drove Bruch crazy. He had the captain transferred to South Africa, which ruined the polo team last year. But I understand the move produced benefits for the security services. The commercial attaché cried for a month and tried to follow his boyfriend, though he didn't try very hard. Not much for a commercial attaché to do in South Africa and this lad was very much the careerist. So he's in Athens now. You have too many people in this embassy, Bill."

"I know that. It's called bureaucratic creep."

"Well, you're the ambassador —"

"They keep sending me people. And they are usually people who can't stand the climate or the Africans. They think it's exotic until they get here, and then they want to be somewhere else. Oslo or Geneva or Rome."

"Jan Francis likes to make trouble. She likes to make trouble for the Americans, particularly."

"She has a husband," North said.

"He does not count," Kleust said.

North watched Harry Erickson and the CIA man get into the Land-Rover and drive away. Benson raised the candy-colored barrier and saluted smartly. Harry returned the salute casually, a weary general on friendly terms with the ranks. He tried to imagine Alice Erickson and Jan Francis in bed together, doing whatever women did. Well, he knew what they did; but it was hard imagining them doing it. He wondered if it was fun for Jan, making trouble for Americans. Whether or not it was fun, it was certainly easy. "She ought to pick on someone her own size," he said.

Kleust said, "That's difficult, in this country."

"So you still see her?"

"Not often," Kleust said.

"I wish she'd lay off," North said.

"Your people have to learn," Kleust said.

North nodded, that was true enough. He said softly, "Can I see the file?"

Kleust said, "I don't have it. Duer has it."

"Will he let me see it?"

"He hasn't let me see it," Kleust said. "They guard things closely, you know."

"Have you asked to see it?"

Kleust said, "No."

"All right," he said. "Tell me about Herr Duer."

"Trained with your people, and the British. He's not a fool and so far as anyone knows he's actually on our side." Kleust smiled. There had been another spy scandal in the security services of the BRD. "And he's too young to've been a Nazi, so he's clean there, too."

"And he wants me to go to Hamburg."

"Perhaps the boy made an error. Uncharacteristic. He is a careful lad. The truth is" — Kleust joined North at the window — "Bill Jr. does have a connection with the three men who were there. They have had financial dealings, and it was not exactly a state secret that these three had attracted the attention of Duer's people. It was very foolish for Bill Jr. to be at that particular café. Duer thinks perhaps it was significant."

"Significant," North said. "Significant of what?"

"Maybe he's trying to send a signal. He's clever enough to know that these three would be under surveillance, that there would be photographs."

"It's a hell of a roundabout way of going about it."

"It's the way they are."

"And who is the signal meant for?"

"Maybe you," Kleust said.

"Is that what you think?"

"It's what Duer thinks. And this is Duer's business."

"Duer-who-doesn't-believe-in-coincidence."

"Yes."

"He wants me to go to Hamburg to finger my son."

"There's something else," Kleust said. "Duer has been picking up little bits and pieces of information. Sometimes I think" — he smiled and beat a little tattoo on the window glass, S.O.S. — "that they have the entire country wired for sound. But he has 'indications' — and don't ask him what they are, because he won't tell you, or if he does tell you what he says won't be the truth — that Bill Jr. and his *gruppen* have an operation going. We are certain that he and three others robbed a bank in Bremen, so they have funds. The operation is something serious. His word, not mine. Duer thinks they have. That they are planning an assassination, probably an American."

"I don't believe it."

"Duer's serious. He didn't fly six thousand miles for nothing."

"I still don't believe it."

"Duer knows his business."

"What do you think?"

"I think that Duer knows his business, and that he is not a fool."

After a moment, North said, "You never knew him as a little kid."

"But I did, you know. Back in the early days, remember —"

North nodded, they had a photograph of Kleust holding Bill Jr., age five, Victoria Falls in the background. "We do go back a long way, don't we?" Slumped against the window, he looked out into the heat. In a country wired for sound, they had picked up the boy's voice and deduced that he was preparing to kill someone, probably an American. He was studying his own reactions, and was not surprised to find himself neither astonished nor insulted. He had not ordered them out of his office, had not challenged Herr Duer to prove it.

"Remember, the pictures, at night?"

North shook his head. He didn't remember.

"He was very little, maybe four years old. And when you took him up to his bed at night, he'd refuse to go to sleep until one of the pictures on the wall was removed. It was a different picture each night. He'd select one that had to go, and you'd put it outside the door, and replace it the next morning. It was very funny. Very cute. He wanted a different — vista. Each night."

North smiled, remembering. Outside, Benson yawned, rising, pulling his chair farther into the shade.

"Did you ever figure it out?"

"No, never did. All kids have quirks. This was Bill Jr.'s."

"And it was harmless," Kleust said. "But he was so insistent."

North looked at the German. "Did that reminiscence go into the file?"

Kleust shrugged.

"It must be quite a biography."

"He's dangerous, Bill."

North looked at his watch, almost noon. He said, "I'll have to talk to my people." When Kleust said nothing, he inquired softly, "Have *you* talked to my people?"

"No," Kleust said. "I meant what I said. All this is off the record. We came here to get a positive identification. There was no need to clear that with your people."

"I wondered," North said.

"This is not an interrogation. We have no right to interrogate you. We came to you for help and you gave it. Isn't that right?"

"Right, Kurt."

"The other thing is, Bill. We don't know exactly where the boy fits in. No doubt that he does fit in, but we don't know whether he's leader or follower or free lancer or what. We don't know if he's giving orders or taking them. He's a puzzle, your boy. And from our bits and pieces we aren't sure about his motives, either."

"What are you sure about, Kurt? Tell me one thing."

"He's a dangerous boy." Then, putting his hand hesitantly on North's shoulder: "You have a right to be angry, Bill. Throw us out of here. Challenge Duer. Accuse me of disloyalty. I'm surprised that you're not angry."

The ambassador continued staring out the window, a ghost of a smile on his face. There was a German word, *Grübelei,* meaning a grubbing among subtleties. It often resulted in *Katergefühl,* a state of self-reproachful irritation that cannot be rendered by any English word. It was no anger he felt, but fear. He was not angry at this any more than he would be angry at hearing a doctor's diagnosis that he or Elinor was dying. In the circumstances, anger was cheap. He was not special, nor was Elinor, nor Bill Jr. except in their connection to one another; they were not special in the eyes of God. He had always thought the most fatuous three lines of modern poetry Dylan Thomas's

> Do not go gentle into that good night,
> Old age should burn and rave at close of day;
> Rage, rage, against the dying of the light.

A Welshman's autistic image of an old geezer — doing what? Cursing nurses, tearing out the IV, overturning the bedpan, sobbing, railing at God — for what? Dealing bad cards. Poor me, boo-hoo. He said, "Who should I be mad at, Kurt? The twentieth century? Columbia University? That they didn't give him better instruction in the humanities? The American culture? Me? Elinor? This is a terrible sickness, and I don't see what anger has to do with it. I'm scared to death." He held out his hand for Kleust to inspect the tremor. "Look at that." As he spoke he could feel his anger and indignation rising. He hated explaining himself, nor had he any taste for proposing rules of behavior. Every time he did he sounded like a relic of the nineteenth century, *Grübelei* among varieties of religious experience. Dour, discredited stoicism, without the pinprick of contemporary irony. A relic, a throwback, an antique; but without self-pity. He could claim that much for himself, and for Elinor. Enough of that. He said, "Is Duer wired?"

Kleust smiled. "Duer is always wired."

"Have you ever worn a wire?"

"No," Kleust said.

"Damnedest things, they work like a charm. No bigger than a wristwatch."

"Are you wired, Bill?"

"No, for Christ's sake," he said.

They were silent a moment. Then Kleust said in German, "I will tell you everything that we find out. Please tell Elinor that, for me."

"What about the file?"

"I'll see about the file."

"Duer can find a way to do it informally."

"Perhaps," Kleust said.

"He can do it orally, if he wants. Though I'd rather *see* it."

"I'll talk to Duer."

North watched old Benson drag his chair into the deep shade. He said, "Remember the missionary, what was his name, Burkhalter?"

Kleust smiled. "How could I forget?"

"Is he still alive?"

"He's back in Germany. He's a very old man."

"In Sylt, I suppose."

"No, he's in the DDR. The East."

North considered that. Conceivably he wanted to be closer to Wittenberg, the soil of Martin Luther. He said, "I owe you one for that afternoon."

"No, you don't." He shook his head. "It was an escapade."

"We were a couple of Georgie Pattons, weren't we? Elinor found another hunk of shrapnel the other day, size of a pinhead. Emerged south of my liver. A billet-doux, she called it. Souvenir of the early days."

"I'm sorry about all this, Bill."

"Remember what Burkhalter said, the quotation from Goethe? I didn't catch it, and I had to ask you to translate. And you didn't want to, but you did. 'The Germans make everything difficult, both for themselves and for everyone else.' " North smiled, but Kleust did not. "As you say, Duer is a good man, the best you have. God damn him. I'll talk to my people. I wish to Christ you'd stayed out of this, Kurt."

Kleust said in German, "It is important for us, Bill."

North was looking out the window again. He thought he would not invite Kleust to lunch. They could save the Riesling for another day. He noticed a commotion at the candy-striped barrier, Benson rising from his chair. One of the Marine guards stepped out from under the portico, then halted. The woman in the red bandanna was approaching, her arms in motion. He could hear nothing. The Marine took another step forward, then turned. Benson went to the barrier and stood there, talking with the woman. She moved from foot to foot, her gold bangle glittering in the sun. Benson took something out of his pocket and gave it to her and she bowed, stepping back. Benson waved his arms, and for a moment the ambassador thought he was rudely dismissing her; but he was only shooing away the flies. She moved off, looking slyly back at him. Her face was concealed by the bandanna. The Marine stood quietly, stunned. Benson watched her go, then shuffled back to his chair in the shade. North shook his head.

Kleust was at the door. "Shall I call the others?"

"Go ahead," North said.

"You're a good man, Bill."

"I feel like the last Jew in Berlin," North said.

5

ORE OR LESS, that was the story the ambassador told them the next morning. And in the sudden silence that followed — North uncomfortable, restless, truly exhausted though it was not yet noon — Carruthers clucked mournfully. "They really shouldn't have spoken to you without speaking to us first, really they shouldn't've. And you shouldn't've *gone*, without clearance. You said you were going to clear it, but you didn't."

Hartnett leaned forward, ever the professional, watching, worried but trying to remain nonchalant, the customary protocol of the healthy in the presence of the sick; an unbalanced transaction.

"I considered it a private trip. Still do."

Carruthers shook his head. "Not good enough, Bill."

"But it'll have to do, won't it?" He said, "I went to Hamburg. We were let strictly alone, and in due course Bill Jr. made contact. The usual jargon. Very skillfully done and if Duer and his people were following us, we lost them. We had the visit with Bill Jr. that I described, and then we went back to Africa."

"Irregular," Carruthers huffed.

"Did you make any report to the Germans?" Hartnett asked.

"No formal report," North said. "But of course I talked to them.

Why not? I told Kleust roughly what had happened. A couple of weeks later we went upcountry, Kleust and I. We went to hell and gone to shoot crocodiles. And I told him roughly what had happened."

"Endangered species, tut-tut," Carruthers said with a small smile.

North looked at him blankly. There were twelve thousand crocodiles on the lake upcountry. Crocodiles were common as flies.

"They have all this, you know, the committee, Winston and Dunphy. The approach from the Germans, your trip to Hamburg, your meeting with your son." Carruthers consulted one of the ever-present documents. "They call it a rendezvous."

North looked at his watch. "They can call it anything they like. Look, I'm tired. I'm due upstairs for tests. So if you don't mind."

Carruthers cleared his throat, not neglecting to shoot an alarmed sidelong glance at Hartnett. North looked terrible, gray-faced and weary; he said he had slept poorly, insomnia. Well, it was an incredible story, Carruthers said, fascinating. But there were still one or two points that he wanted to clear up, one or two loose ends —

Hartnett concentrated, listening. That was what he was supposed to be so good at, listening. Listening for the life behind the words, the unspoken thought, the undertow. In the lawyer's world, as in the diplomat's, context was everything. The atmosphere, the history, the *stakes:* the state of mind now, as a function of the state of mind then. And not only what you remembered, but what you knew. Really, it was the reordering of the past in order to secure the future. He would have to listen to each of North's many voices, and they were not always easy to distinguish. Bill North was a subtle character. He was a government man trying to live in obedience to his good conscience, mindful of his oath of office, a worldly man, not easily surprised. A little bit of a cynic. Who wouldn't be, given the circumstances, twenty-five years of work for the American government?

And when did such a man surrender, throw up his hands and declare that the struggle was no longer worth waging? It would be when putting a good face on things no longer counted, had no purpose; when the weight of events was too great. A client would say, *The hell with it, you work it out, do the best you can, but settle it quickly.* Meaning: I am not innocent, and time is short. Listen carefully to those instructions, counselor, and decide at once not to put your client on the witness stand, or in the negotiating room, or anywhere near the enemy. The stakes were too high.

Yet such a man would not want to turn his face to the wall, either, and if his life contained disloyalties, if there were the usual misunderstandings and contradictions, he would want to explain himself, not to justify or to atone — that was the trouble! — but simply to get the facts straight and in sequence, knowing that a life was not a narrative written by a single author but a miscellany. Such a man would think that at the end, all there was was memory and blind faith.

Carruthers was still talking but North's eyes were closed. Hartnett tapped him on the knee and he looked up, blinking. Then he closed his eyes again. Hartnett said, "Paul," and they both stood. This session was at an end. Hartnett thought of the son, looking at the father. To Bill North, his son must seem an undiscovered part of himself, an unmapped, uncharted territory of his own continent. My God, he thought, something had gone terribly wrong. North was motionless, eyes closed, sitting in his chair, waiting for the doctor, waiting for them to leave. And waiting for his son, too; that was foregone. Such a man would abandon his fortified self, and move far afield. Such a man would make an excellent and large-minded amanuensis, but a terrible witness. He would not hesitate to testify against himself.

"Look, Bill," Carruthers said. "They have something else, something new. I don't know where they got it, maybe from the West Germans. Maybe from your friend Kleust. Nobody's heard anything about him for two years, but now they're hearing things again, and they think he's coming up from underground."

He heard the door close softly, and he opened his eyes. He was alone in the solarium, except their words were in the atmosphere. The light hurt his eyes, so he closed them; it was less painful in the dark. But he could hear the humming of the fluorescence. What did parents say to children? I have eyes in the back of my head, and I can see you wherever you are, and know what you are doing. You did, too, as a young father; a particular noise or, more usually, a particular silence and you'd put down the paper and cock your head.

Bill Jr., what are you *doing*?

97

I'm not doing anything.

Yes, you are.

It was good enough propaganda while it lasted; not as durable as Santa Claus or the Tooth Fairy, but good for four or five years, a fragile cease-fire, administered by the eyes-in-the-back-of-the-head peace-keeping force.

Yes, and you could shut your eyes but the humming of the electricity remained. The trouble was, he felt that *he* was the one who was being watched. Everyone had a hidden pair of eyes, as each word seemed to have a hidden meaning. He had spent too long listening to Hartnett and Carruthers, and himself, too. He was tired ot the sound of his own voice, blah blah blah. There was too much pressure behind his words, too much left unsaid, too much that couldn't be said; and so much that wasn't known. Too much of the past in the present. He wished Kleust were there, with his bred-in-the-bone naturalness. His fatalism and his fables, and his paradoxical faith in the future; no future could be worse than the past, probably. Kleust reminded him of the African continent in its variety and density, and endurance, and restraint.

Africa had thickened them both. And coming so close to death there, at such a young age. For a time it gave them the feeling that they were invincible, capable of deeds beyond their wildest imaginings; the truth was, it made them romantic in their own eyes. They never spoke of it, for the truth was too ludicrous. Kleust no doubt saw himself as Lohengrin, the Knight of the Swan, Wagner's Shane, who arrives out of the forest as if by magic. It was not a comparison to be pressed too far, but it was irresistible. North did see himself as a Western gunfighter, Bat Masterson cleaning up the town; a pacific man, no stranger to irony, but a good man with a gun and brave as an eagle. *That Bill North, he's quiet, but a hard man when aroused.*

The predictable union of Western movies, the Hardy Boys, and Ernest Hemingway's publicity. And it was also true that of those who died, they gave no thought at all: who they were, or the lives they had led, or what they believed in. They were just extras littering the landscape, earning a day's pay for a day's work with no billing whatsoever. It was all physical, the look of the land and the weather, the Land-Rover's terrible racket, the odor of the vegetation. They drove out of the watercourse and onto the road, scarcely more than a path. Huge anthills flanked them. In the distance was a herd of antelope, scampering in the opposite direction, away from the car's noise. Only a few hours more to the capital, through the savannah, purple now at dusk. The driver was muttering under his breath, Kleust nervous, looking left and right. From the rear seat he watched Kleust; there was too much noise to talk comfortably. It was hot and he began to doze, thinking of the report he would make, to the ambassador, and then, if the ambassador agreed, to Washington. In Washington they were anxious to do something, anything, to retrieve the situation. They were weary of negative publicity, do-nothing liberals. They wanted a recommendation but it had to be effective, something decisive, no more halfway measures, nothing amateurish; it had to succeed, the assistant secretary was most insistent on that point. He made the point again and again in his late-night conference calls to the ambassador. In Washington, they wanted guarantees. He would advise the ambassador that it was time to place bets, the wheel on its last circuit. *Rien ne va plus.* No doubt Kleust would make a report as well, though the Germans had no assets in the region and would not act. And perhaps Washington would not act either, though he doubted it; the administration wanted to play.

He opened his eyes when the car abruptly slowed, then accelerated when Kleust yelled. They were surrounded by armed men, and suddenly explosions were all around them. He had never heard gunfire, nor the sound of grenades, and for a moment he did not understand what was happening. He had the absurd feeling that he had wandered onto a skeet field. Then he was pushed forward, stunned, the air out of him; it was as if a great hot hand had cuffed him. The windshield splintered and the car careened to one side. The driver was there and then he wasn't; his vacant seat was wet with blood. The car came to rest.

An acrid, sour smell filled his nostrils. He was upended, his head in the front seat, his body in the rear; he could not move. Things flew around him but he heard nothing. Kleust wrestled him out of the car and into the ditch. He was on his back. The sky was violent, a brilliant African violent at twilight. Kleust was beside him, firing a pistol. He methodically pulled back the hammer, aimed, and fired.

The driver's rifle was on the ground beside Kleust. It took him a moment to identify it, its use. He picked it up, balancing the barrel on the car's fender. The barrel chattered on the metal. It took him a moment to pull the trigger; he did not want to hurt anyone. But he fired once, and again, after a hesitation. It was likely that this was all a terrible mistake. He and Kleust were diplomats, with diplomatic immunity. Kleust seemed to think it was for real, though. He pulled the trigger again and seemed to find a rhythm to it, pulling the trigger, and feeling the kick against his shoulder. It seemed so very slow and silent, almost languid. He heard nothing except music, unfamiliar modern music. Someone had a transistor radio. The music was monotonous.

When at last the scene in front of him organized, he noticed the driver on his back in the middle of the road. A flash behind him, a grenade. The stench was awful. Someone was bending over the driver. He aimed and fired and the man twitched and fell. This was simple enough to do, point the rifle and fire and the man you fired at was dead. His mind was working so slowly, all his movements in slow motion against the violent dusk, mares' tails across the enormous sky. He was humming to the music now, believing himself most clear-headed. These were not live human beings, though the moment itself was real enough. The blood on his hands and arms was real, and the music inside his head was real. The two men in the road were not real.

He saw another rise from behind a bush: khaki shorts, no shirt, and a lean black face. He thought this khaki-shorted man had the face of a musician, a bass player perhaps; he was heavy-bellied and thick-legged. His back was to the man lying in the road, and he looked to be running away. Wonderful, if true, but there was no amnesty for musicians. He fired, aimed, and missed. He had got things turned around. Aim, then fire. That was what he did, but he missed again. He said, Damn. His hearing was returning. He heard Kleust's pistol, the click of the hammer, and the report. Kleust was talking to himself. He aimed again and fired as the target was nearly out of reach. That was what he was, this musician; he was a target.

He lay back on the ground, exhausted. The ground was soft. He'd gotten that one. One dead bass player. He saw the musician's head come apart, a fragment of bone flying off into the bush. The musician's hand flew up, as if he were trying to catch the bone fragment. He had a big hand, long fingers, graceful as a musician's should be. Kleust was saying something to him. He was speaking German and grinning. He felt as if he were under water. He could not breathe, owing to the strangling weight on his chest. His hands were filthy and sticky with blood. The sudden silence was terrifying. Kleust was yelling at him in German.

His legs wouldn't work, though he struggled to rise. Overhead the sky was darkening, little pinpricks of light high up; perhaps they were stars, but he thought not. Things went in and out of focus, and he could not trust his eyes. He saw the thorny tops of trees. He was rising, Kleust's arms around his shoulders, dragging him out of the ditch.

Kleust repeated, You're all right.

He said, I'm not.

He did not know what in his life had led up to this. There had been no preparation, no way to forecast the awful sudden violence. He never saw it coming. He was unprepared, and mystified. What was he doing here, he and the German diplomat? Yet he had killed a man, perhaps more than one man; it had been nothing like what he had expected. That was the trouble, all of it was unexpected. In the slowness of things he had felt a great anticipation, the sense of momentous occasion. History twitched, his life would never be the same. This would be a memory against which all other memories would be measured. He had no doubt that he would live and Kleust, too. He felt a great exhilaration. The others were not real to him. He lay again on the hot brown earth, the grains scratching his cheek, each grain before his eyes. A thin line of ants communicated between black pools of blood.

They were in the dark. Kleust held his hand, as if they were teenagers on a date. "Bill," he said. *"Kamerad, Kamerad."*

He said, "Are you hurt, Kurt?"

"No," Kleust lied.

He began to laugh. Kurt's hurt. Hurt Kurt.

Kleust's face was fixed in a dark German anger. Presently the silence returned, thick and painful. Kleust continued to speak but he did not listen. Dusk was nearly complete. It was cold in the car.

When he opened his eyes, everything moved in slow motion, helter-skelter. Kleust had given him something from the first aid kit, so the pain was not so bad now. It was located way inside, where he could feel it but not locate it. He was dizzy. So he kept his eyes closed, shutting out the lights. He saw the President and his family, all of them in blue. The President stretched out his hand, in a kind of salute. Accepting the good wishes of the President, he flashed a cocky smile, listening to the monotonous music that replayed itself in his head, a dirge. Then he saw Elinor's face, and heard her voice.

This was a moment fixed in his memory, the car speeding and lurching, and the President, and the music. He remembered not another thing until he woke up in the hospital, the doctor and Elinor standing by his bed, Kleust sitting in the chair near the window. He remembered her great smile as she bent down to kiss him, then brought him their son. The boy was so grave, for a moment he did not recognize him as his own. In any case, he did not have the strength to embrace him; and he was marvelously elated, and did not need sympathy. So she quickly took him back.

PART TWO

I

T HERE WERE TIMES when she thought her father a specter, part of the air, everywhere and nowhere. He came and went without warning. There was no pattern to his movements. He was not predictable. She would be sitting quietly by the window, deep into her memory, and she would hear a noise and there he'd be, massive in the doorway, filling it, blocking the light. Often he would approach her, to say something or to touch her hair or shoulder. She would hold herself motionless, waiting for him to leave. Her mind would commence to race, and the noise began. Her mind was like a rushing stream, tumbling downhill over rocks and boulders, eddying, bouncing, shifting direction. When next she looked up he would be gone and the words he had spoken vanished also, though if she listened hard she could discover them somewhere in the room. His words were as spectral as he was. And yet when she looked at him, always out of the corner of her eye, when he was preoccupied, she could see the resemblance. Their eyes were similar, being large, dark, and luminous. They were alike in no other way. Her father was large, barrel-chested and heavy-armed, dark hair thick on his arms and hands. That she was terrified of him went without saying.

Gert and her father did not have very much to do with each other. She missed her mother, who was dead; and he was gone so often. They met occasionally at breakfast and at the dinner table, rarely speaking. They exchanged no information, and she understood that she must never ask about his work; and should anyone ask her, she should ignore the question. He usually went out after dinner, offering no explanation; and she did not expect one. She spent her own evenings in her room, sketching and listening to music: Wagner, Bartók, the Rolling Stones. She sketched scenes from her early life, as she remembered her early life. She had no social life, because of the fear she carried with her always.

Once, late at night, she saw her father on television, sitting at a round table with other men, talking about public affairs. His performance surprised her, the other men listened to him with respect, almost deference. Dressed in a sober dark suit, he had affected a little black mustache and horn-rimmed glasses. He looked like a raffish professor, though she knew he called himself a journalist. For a moment, she was not certain it was he. She had to look closely at the screen. He seemed to have changed his personality along with the clothes and facial decoration. He was apparently very witty, for the other men laughed appreciatively at things he said. And he, too, would chuckle, a man entirely aboveboard and at ease, a man comfortable on French television discussing public affairs, his dark side concealed. She watched him carefully, wondering how he did it. The sound of his laughter was unfamiliar to her, however. She had rarely heard her father laugh. He never laughed at home.

There was much she tried to forget, and much she could not remember. Gert had left the school at eighteen; her real life seemed to begin at that time. She was skilled with her hands and a willing worker, and through the school found employment with a dressmaker in the Sixth Arrondissement. She enjoyed the back room of the dressmaker's shop, with its bolts of expensive, brightly colored cloth, old Singer sewing machine, and silent mannequins. She listened to music while she worked. Her wages were not high, but she was content; she was as content and untroubled as she had ever been, working with needle and thread, and the machine.

One afternoon Gert was pressed into service as a model. An important customer was in the shop and the regular model had called in sick and so the dressmaker, with an air of resignation, asked her to fill in. She proposed this not without misgivings, for she thought Gert a strange young woman — of course, naturally, coming from the school. But in the event the dressmaker was astonished. With her slender figure and air of complete self-absorption, Gert was an immediate success, a natural in the salon. She could model anything, from sportswear and lingerie to the most formal ballroom gown. With the right make-up, she looked almost Asian, with her high cheekbones and Slavic eyes; with no make-up at all, she could pass for a troubled American teenager, an innocent abroad. The dressmaker thought her sympathetic and advised her to sign up with one of the large agencies, her look was very much the mode; put you in combat fatigues, the dressmaker said cynically, and I guarantee the cover of *Elle*. Gert did not understand the reference to combat fatigues, nor to *Elle*. But she said no. She was happy in the shop, sewing and modeling. She did not mind when the customers looked at her, for she was not expected to say anything. She was not expected to have personal contact with them. They could look at her and she did not have to return the look. When they spoke to her, she was not obliged to reply (and she was thought enchanting, a grave gamine). She could remain within herself, an inhabitant of her own world, or worlds. She said none of this to the dressmaker, contenting herself with a simple *Non, merci, Madame*. And of course the dressmaker did not press the point, recognizing a bargain when she saw one.

Gert saved her salary, cashing the checks and putting the money in a hatbox she kept under her bed. Of course she said nothing to her father, who in any case did not inquire about her work. She remained at the shop for three years, until one afternoon, having coffee in a café, she met a young American. He spoke German to her, anticipating somehow that German was her nationality. She was charmed by the young American's voice, so soft and sure. He seemed to glide over the gutturals of the German language. She thought his voice as soft and sweet and full of promise as Mick Jagger's.

When he first spoke to her, she did not reply. She had not listened to what he said, only the rhythm and timbre of the words.

Often when she had coffee in a café, men tried to speak to her.

He asked her if she wanted to go walking along the quai.

She looked at him boldly, but did not reply.

He turned back to his newspaper, the American paper in Paris. They were seated side by side at small tables. It was May and the sun was warm. She was drinking coffee and he a beer.

Why did he think she was German?

After a moment, he said, It's a nice day for a walk. We could walk on the quai, and then walk over to St. Germain, look in the bookstalls. See what's happening, he said in English. He did not smile but his voice was warm. Check out the Frogs, he said. Do you speak English? No matter, I would rather speak German.

She looked away in confusion. She did not speak English. Her eyes flew upward. She saw pigeons floating and diving, and in the distance the square sullen façade of Notre Dame. Her eyes made a transit of the rooftops of Paris, so familiar to her now, and then she looked at him again, sideways. He was absorbed in the American newspaper. He was dressed in blue jeans and a gray sweater and sneakers, unmistakably an American except for his saturnine face, well formed with full lips and large ears, and a cleft chin. A northern European face, she thought, distinctive, well groomed. She could not see his eyes but believed them to be blue. A distinctive blue-eyed young American then, but subdued; there was a kind of hush about him, so different from the forward Americans who came into the shop.

He turned to glance at her as he turned a page of the newspaper. The sun turned the hair on his arms golden. She quickly looked away, fiddling with her coffee cup.

He said, Would you like another?

She stared at her empty cup, feeling her face go hot.

I'm having another beer, he said. Or we could go to St. Germain.

Instinctively she shook her head.

He had said, in the softest German, Who are you afraid of?

And she had answered, My father.

Well then, he had said — rising, carefully folding the newspaper, putting a few coins in the saucers, hers and his, taking her hand and helping her to her feet and finding no resistance — well then, we are comrades. My father is afraid of me.

They walked only a little way that afternoon, along the quai in the direction of St. Germain. They stood for a minute, watching the barges on the Seine. Her shop was around the corner and although she had the afternoon off, she needed an excuse. She could feel herself being pulled into his orbit, like a moon to a planet. She was trying to make sense of his remark, spoken so casually yet with a kind of dramatic flair. His voice was soft as cotton. She wondered what there was about him that his father was afraid of; he did not seem menacing. Then she wondered vaguely what his father looked like, and what kind of person he was. Probably he was an agreeable person, without brutality or guile, even though he was an American; she reflected that Americans were frequently afraid. To an American the world was a dangerous place, though this young American seemed fearless enough. He said something and moved a little away from her. She liked to look at him, so tall and robust, loose-limbed and well mannered. He was looking into a bookstall now, thumbing through volumes, as if he had forgotten about her. She turned and walked across the street. He called after her to wait and she stopped and looked at him. The sun was in her eyes, reflecting off the river, blinding in its brilliance. He had put on dark glasses and she could not see his eyes. She explained that her hour was up, she had to go to work; she couldn't take a walk to St. Germain or anywhere. He cocked his head, having failed to hear what she said. Her voice was barely above a whisper. He asked when he could see her again. She indicated the café up the street. She was often at the café, at noon and again after work. He asked her where she lived, an address or a telephone number. Do you live alone? Are you in the book? He was standing with his hands in his pockets. They were talking across parked cars. He smiled and spoke his name. She didn't hear, and shook her head. Then he asked for her name so that he could look her up in the telephone book. Where did she work? He made a little pantomime of writing her name and number. They could meet again for coffee, and take a walk to St. Germain. He did not make a move in her direction, and that gave her confidence. She lifted her head high, as she did when she modeled the most expensive gowns.

Guten Tag, she said.

They met the next day, and the next. He did not ask her any

more questions. They talked of neutral things, or rather he did. He explained that he was a student, in Europe to study. He was studying politics and social change at the Sorbonne, he said. But his studies were not demanding and he had free time, except most evenings he went to lectures, at the university and elsewhere. He did not have many friends in Paris so he went to the lectures *faute de mieux*. The lecturers were stupid but he went anyway: French logicians, he said, jacking off. He had used the American expression and when she looked at him, wrinkling her nose, obviously puzzled, he had explained in street German. She blushed, then laughed, imagining French logicians masturbating on a well-lit stage in a drafty lecture hall at the Sorbonne. Her laugh delighted him, and he elaborated. Sometimes they masturbated each other, but mostly it was just themselves, each to his own, one on one. A complicated masturbation, he said, the lecturers looked like circus contortionists, and of course they continued long after orgasm. It was a measure of their ingenuity and endurance, and mastery of the theoretical material. That was the point of it, to wring every last drop of semen from their exhausted testicles, beating themselves up in the process and, it went without saying, seducing the audience.

She laughed and laughed.

He went on: The audience. A hundred students, mostly French with some English and Germans, and little bands of publicized nationalities with grievances. Vietnamese and Chinese at the rear of the hall, separated by a wide aisle, declining to recognize each other. Dutch, South Africans, Egyptians, Cubans, Palestinians, Portuguese, Basques. Half a dozen Americans, four black, two white. Five women, one man. The Portuguese were interesting, always making careful notes, rarely speaking. They were a dark, wet people, superbly sullen. He had attempted to strike up conversations with the Portuguese, but it was impossible. CIA. They thought I was CIA, he said. It was also difficult to speak to the Dutch and to the Palestinians, and to the American women; they all thought he was CIA. He got on well with the lecturers, however. The lecturers spoke of "objective conditions." So many stations of the cross, or points on the compass. They had a childlike faith in "objective conditions," social, economic, political, sexual.

They know nothing, he said.

Then: Do you want to know how little they know? I'll show you.

He disappeared into a wine shop and emerged with a parcel. They continued to walk, near the Louvre now. The great formal garden spread out before them. He put his arm around her, nuzzling her neck as if they were lovers. She did not object, understanding that this was part of his demonstration of how little people knew. Still, she liked his arm around her, and the way he smelled, and his soft talk. She knew he would protect her, though the garden was peaceful. It was dusk and strollers were about. Lights winked on. They fell into step behind a middle-aged American couple. The woman's voice was high and hectoring; it was a complaint about money, he said. He translated for her, muttering into her ear as a lover would. They had been cheated in a restaurant, the god damned French, thieves. The man walked slowly, using a cane. They were well-dressed Americans, obviously prosperous; no doubt on their way to the Crillon or the Ritz for a cocktail. Walking very slowly now, the man indicated a bench; he wanted to rest. He guided her to the same bench. The prosperous Americans sat at one end of the bench, they at the other. He kissed her, lightly on the mouth, and spoke a few words of German. The American woman nudged her husband. He said, You are very beautiful.

After a moment, he rose and took her by the hand and they walked back the way they had come, to the Louvre. He did not pause to nuzzle or kiss her. He was walking quickly and when they had gone a few hundred feet he stopped, and they turned around. The American couple were still sitting. While they watched, the man struggled to his feet and they moved off together, in the direction of the Place de la Concorde. The woman was still complaining.

He said, See how easy it is.

They walked back to the bench, where he retrieved his parcel, a bottle of Beaujolais.

If it had been a bomb, he said, "Boom."

Oh, she said.

Objective conditions, he said.

Boom, she said.

He said, They are representatives of the American race. The objective conditions of the American race, though premature. He said they reminded him of his grandparents, the grandfather who drank too much and the grandmother who was never silent. She was a handsome athletic woman who never shut up. She believed she was being cheated always; the proles were out to get her. An ignorant woman married to a drunk, both of them with money to burn. But they didn't burn it, they drank it up, or bought furs, or a swimming pool for the back yard, and club memberships, and congressmen. But they could not buy security, the house in Lake Forest was double- and triple-locked; it had dogs, a costly security system, and live-in servants, and still they were frightened. For good reason. They talked of the way things used to be, and would never be again.

She said nothing, looking at him with curiosity. He had spoken rapidly in German and although she had listened carefully, she had not understood it all. Yet it thrilled her, hearing about his grandparents; she thought she knew him better now. She looked at him and saw not just him but others, forebears; an American world, people with money to burn, a grandmother who never shut up and a grandfather who drank. She wondered whether these were his mother's or his father's parents. Now she took his arm, leaning into him. The American couple were almost out of sight.

He said, My father's father, my other grandfather, one tough *mensch*. He's dead now, cancer. He knew when to fight and when not to fight. A worthy adversary, not like the other one. He lived in America but his heart was in central Europe. He never really left central Europe. He liked listening more than talking, knew that things were different, and wanted to know how, and what. He already knew why.

She nodded.

He said, We shall see.

She said, What?

He said, Would you like to go to a party? Meet some friends. Exciting people. No French or English. No Americans. No lecturers.

She did not understand. She thought he had no friends.

They are not from the university, he said. These are other friends.

She said, I have to be home.

He said, All right. I'll walk you home.

She nodded, surprising herself; but things were different now. He had told her about his grandparents, and their life in America. It gave her a feeling of security; there was a background to things. She took his hand. He did not know where she lived, and had never seen her apartment. It was not a long walk and along the way they stopped at half a dozen places — fountains, statues, a bench, a trash barrel — to plant the bottle of Beaujolais, loitering nearby for a minute or two. And always, when they returned, it was there in its inconspicuous brown wrapper. No one paid any attention to them or to it. It was just litter.

She said, "Boom," and laughed.

They walked slowly hand in hand. She lived in a shallow cul-de-sac off the rue de Sevres. He expressed delight, so near St. Germain. He opened the front door and she checked the mailbox in the courtyard, rooting around amongst the letters and magazines. And that was how he came to discover that she was the journalist Max Mueller's daughter — or mistress, or ward. He had not known that Mueller was married, and it would be unlike him to have a young mistress. Max Mueller was puritanical, conventional in his personal habits, no man to draw attention to himself. At any event, that was his reputation, and now there was his name on the doorbell, and on one of the letters that she held in her hand.

He said, You are going to have to tell me your name.

Gert, she said.

He said, I am Wolfgang. Wolf.

She looked at him in an odd way, unable to express what was in her mind. She was unable to form the words, but as so often happened, he guessed her question, the hope being father to the thought.

He said, I meant what I said. You are very beautiful.

She smiled shyly, pleased.

He said, I am going away tomorrow, but I will be back in a week. It is nothing much, just a little business. Perhaps we can meet again when I return, and go to a film. She nodded agreement. And have a bit to eat after the film? Yes, she said.

He asked, Do you like me?

She replied, Yes.

He said, Why are you afraid of your father?

And standing in the courtyard, night coming on, she did not know what to say, how to reply. She looked up at him, so tall, his face solemn in the darkness, waiting. She felt as if she had known him all her life. Her thoughts seemed to crash into one another, like bumper cars at the amusement park, wheeling and butting and random. But she could neither sort out these thoughts, nor arrange them in sequence. Her own history, she knew, was a stubborn violent muddle, never continuous; she was always at the edge. But while she knew it, she could not say it. She could not give voice to her deepest self.

He smiled at her.

Dead men on furlough.

What did he say?

But she knew very well. It was Lenin's phrase. Where had he heard it? Lenin's words echoed without warning from another region of her mind, suddenly loose like animals in a cage. She willed herself to stay still, and say nothing more. It was an expression of her mother's; Lenin's description of old Bolsheviks, exhausted by overwork, and the years of violence, poverty, conspiracy, and fear. Nothing could surprise them, and their emotions were wrung dry; yet they labored on in cold devotion, believing neither in God nor in man but in fate. That was now her mother saw her father, in her fear and hatred. The first time she said it, he slapped her. The second time, he beat her. She was forced to watch the beating, her father's arm swinging steadily as a metronome. She remembered he used only one hand, hold her, Gert, close to him with the other. She could smell the heat of his body, and feel his muscles move. He held her head so that she had to watch. He was hitting her mother with his closed fist. Terrified, her mother never moved from the chair.

2

T HEY WAITED, mother and daughter, for the times when he would leave. "On business," he said, as if he were a bour-geois on a commercial journey to Leipzig or Prague. They stayed apart from the others in the house; at night her mother wept. Then one day she left the house earlier than usual and did not return that evening; there was no explanation. Her father was away also, but was due back soon. She remembered the others whispering, a dense sibilance in the little house; she thought of it as the hissing of snakes. Later — a week, a month, perhaps longer — she was taken by one of the men to the nearest city. En route, they stopped so that the man could relieve himself. It was an autumn day, when mist covered the hillside. She ran, but he caught her. Her dress was torn and she was bloody. She knew he was close behind her, in pursuit. She saw his shadow. She stumbled and crashed down the hillside, rolling over and over; she fell a long way. She remembered her fists bouncing against the earth, and the mist overhead, and her own strangled cries as she came to rest in a shallow gully, his arms around her. But to her dismay that was all she remembered, her eyes squeezed shut, deafened by the fall, hurting everywhere.

In the city they lived in a small apartment. She never knew its name, it was a drab apartment in a gray industrial city somewhere in the east. The man never left the apartment except to buy food and newspapers; and then he locked her in. He did not touch her again, but looked at her as if he wanted to, or to explain something; but he never did, and she always turned away, stunned and silent. She did not speak, pretending that she heard nothing, understood nothing, felt nothing, knew nothing. When one morning she discovered that she had begun to menstruate, she said nothing about that, either; she recalled a conversation with her mother, about an episode each month. It was normal, a natural, physical thing. Blood was evidence of life. She knew she must remain absolutely silent about her episodes, because while they were normal they were also private; they were hers, not his. She forced all sensations, all knowledge, inside. After a while, she did not have to pretend. There seemed to be several worlds that she could enter at will. Part of the time she was in one world, part of the time in another. When she was asleep there was a third, the most vivid and consoling, a world of primary colors in violent combat, and her resolute mother nearby — an exhilarating and vivifying solidarity between them. She replaced the mother she remembered, conjuring up this: a muscular, strong-minded, determined woman, very like the heroic stone figure in the little square outside her window. She looked at it every day.

One afternoon she heard the man talking. He had a visitor. She put her ear to the keyhole, being careful to make no sound. It was Max this and Max that. They spoke in an undertone, a mixture of German and another language. The visitor was a haughty figure who never removed his hat. He did most of the talking. She understood him to say that her father was arriving soon, perhaps tomorrow. She did not know how long he had been gone, but it seemed a very long time. He had gone away suddenly, destination unknown, and now he was returning. So he had not forgotten her after all. She listened patiently to the two men talk, smiling when the haughty visitor raised his voice, silencing the other one. She heard her own name, but could not discern the context. She did not like it, hearing her own name. Then, after a final whispered instruction, the visitor went away. There was something strange in

116

his voice, a sinister undertone, something unsaid. She turned quickly to her bed.

She did not sleep that night, terrified of what might befall her. She knew her father would punish her for what she had done, and what had been done to her. He would beat her as he had beaten her mother. She would have to sit quietly in the chair as her mother had done, accepting blow after blow to her face. She lay in bed thinking and when the idea came into her mind, she was not surprised; it had been there all along, an idea as obvious as left and right or north and south. She slipped out of bed and walked into the living room. She could hear the man snoring on the couch. It was a warm night and he was nude, his back to her. She stepped quickly to the closet and reached into his leather jacket, where she knew he kept his revolver. She had seen him cleaning it. She believed that if she killed the man who had taken her from her home, she would be absolved from her father's anger. What he had done to her would die with him; killing him, she would kill the deed as well. She would take revenge herself; no one else would have to. So she took the revolver from the man's jacket and walked to the couch and shot him in the right temple, just above his ear. She was surprised, the gun made no sound. He groaned once and turned his head. He looked at her, his eyes wide with surprise. There was just the smallest hole above his right ear, and almost no blood at all. She watched his eyes glaze and his eyelids flutter. He moved his hands over his chest as if he were an orchestra conductor; then they fell down, covering his sex. At the last moment, perhaps he had been embarrassed. He groaned again and collapsed, settling into the couch. All the tension went out of him. She stood looking at him, smiling; then she began to laugh. There was something comical about him now, modestly covering himself in the presence of a young woman; a dead man absurdly concerned with his sex. She leaned forward, staring at him in the steely moonlight; his face was a ghastly slate gray, scarcely recognizable. In some ways this one had seemed puritanical, he had a peasant's rough morals; but he had been corrupted, and his last conscious thought was shame. Or mortification. Or perhaps it was only a dying man's reflex.

She moved back a step, into the shadows, wrinkling her nose at the smell of gunpowder, and shit. From the shadows his silhouette was indistinct, a smudge in the darkness. She still had the weapon in her hand, the thing heavy, hard to hold, but lethal; it was slick with oil. How quickly life left him, no time to say good-bye, or anything at all. No time to make peace. No time to protest. He'd looked at her with the most open surprise: one minute alive, the next dead. He knew it, too. He'd looked down the gun barrel, and had not moved. It was so easy, it was the easiest thing she had ever done. And she was the only witness, her word would be potent. She had to think now of her explanation, for surely the authorities would be notified. The explanation could not be personal, and it must be true. All her life she had lived in a political world, even if she knew little of theory or practice or dialectic; she knew that some acts were correct and some not. She could not tell a lie, and did not want to; that was for others. She was moving back and forth among her various worlds, stepping out of the shadows, staring at the dead man's silhouette. The truth was, the fact of it was, that he had killed himself. His morbid world killed him, he had reaped what he had sown. He was a suicide from the moment by the side of the road when he had reached for her, his fingernails tearing her skin, his decadent laughter filling the air. And she had been obliged to run. There were many millions of people in the world, and he was but one; he had had the bad luck to want to interfere with her. It could have been anyone else, but it was him; he was nothing special, or different. He was not disciplined, though. He had made his own appointment with death, had arranged for it as surely as any of the savage martyrs. And when the time came, his life was taken from him; it was not important who pulled the trigger. That was a detail, one word in a long-running sentence. Truly, he had set the events in motion himself, by his behavior; as had her father when he went away and did not return; as had her mother when she went away without explanation. When things went out of control, when there was no discipline, when there was no reliable history, *there was no reliable future.* It was left to her to guarantee the future. Someone had to act, and all acts had consequences. History was indifferent, but it must be served. History had no scruples.

She bent over the dead man, hesitating while she thought. Her thoughts were not coherent, nor consecutive. She knew she had authored a unique event, something particular, and now she had to shroud it in mystery to conform to history's laws. History was anonymous, and inscrutable; though not to her. She knew she could read the time. She had the capacity to intervene; she had the will. She turned the dead man's right hand palm up and fitted the revolver into it. His fingers were supple, as if made of putty. She lifted the heavy hand and let it fall, and it dropped on his stomach, the revolver barrel making a little red mark, a scratch. She stepped back, smiling, scrutinizing what she had done. He did not look peaceful, this dead man. His lips were drawn back from his teeth, and the look of surprise had been replaced by a look of profound malevolence. With her forefinger she pushed his upper lip over his teeth, but the moment she released her pressure the lip crawled up again. But his expression had changed. Now it was almost benign; it was a kind of benign contempt. Fine, she thought, appropriate to the circumstances. She craned her neck to look out the window into the moonlit square, and the female carved in stone, a muscular woman holding a banner. Then she walked into the kitchen and washed her hands. She drank a glass of milk, and then she went to bed.

It was eight in the morning when she heard the door open and someone enter. She held her breath. She listened carefully for — something, a gasp, a cry of surprise, a shout. She heard a grunt, heavy footsteps, and silence. Then she heard an exclamation in German. Her father opened the door and looked in. He was so big, he filled the door. He did not greet her in any way, only looked at her incuriously, as an official might. She sat up in bed, rubbing her eyes. She had been in a deep dreamless sleep. She said, "Papa." He did not reply, but closed the door firmly. She heard him moving around, muttering to himself in German. Five minutes later he opened the door again and told her to collect her things, what things she had, that they would leave immediately. When she emerged from the room with her bag, a sheet covered the man on the couch. Her father was standing by the door, looking at his watch. He said that Jerzy was dead. He had killed himself.

And you heard nothing, he said.

She did not know if it was a question or a statement. She shook her head. No, Papa.

Nothing in the night.

I was asleep, Papa.

Remember that you were, darling.

What?

Asleep, all night long. That you heard nothing. Saw nothing.

Yes, of course, Papa.

Did you like Jerzy, darling?

No, Papa.

Yes, I understand. Did you quarrel?

No, Papa.

The door to the apartment was always locked?

Yes, Papa.

And there were no visitors?

She looked at him closely, wondering what it was that he wanted her to say. She tried to read his face as she read the time. But he frightened her so. She began to tremble, looking at his eyes, and his tremendously dark brows. Her mind was racing, her worlds colliding. She said at last, Yes, Papa. One visitor.

He smiled broadly. And when was that, darling? Was that yesterday, in the afternoon?

Yes, Papa.

Did you see his face?

She shook her head vehemently. No, Papa.

He had a car in the street outside. They drove to another apartment in the city. The remainder of the day was a blur to her. Officials came and went. There seemed to be a great consternation. Her father had told her to sit in the kitchen, away from the commotion, and be very quiet. Do not speak unless you are spoken to, he said. Tell them what you told me, he said sternly. Two men had interrogated her, but as their questions were confused her answers were also confused. When she did not understand the question, she said nothing. They did not appear to have the straight of it. At the end of the day, she and her father were driven to the railroad station in an official car. She sat in the back seat, her father in the front with the driver, an older man whom he seemed to know. They chatted all the way to the railroad station. After a short trip by train they were transferred to another car, and driven to an airport, through a gate at the far end of the field, and directly to the plane. Once inside, she fell asleep and when she woke up and asked where they were, her father said, "Paris."

In Paris they had a large apartment and a housekeeper, who accompanied her every day to the school. The streets were colorful and animated, not at all like the streets of the other city. Her father said that she would attend a special school and that if she was attentive she would do well. She took him at his word, listening carefully and rarely speaking. Every few months there would be an examination. Sometimes she did well, sometimes badly; it depended on her frame of mind, and the nature of the examination. She knew that it was not wise to disclose everything, so she withheld knowledge as a matter of course. She believed all the students did; they all knew more than they said. She had a few friends at the school, girls she'd play cards with, and talk to when no one was watching. The school was run by nuns, large women for the most part, austere and peculiar in their black and white costumes. Each morning and each evening there would be a prayer. Promptly at five P.M. they would be released; she would be met at the gate by the housekeeper, and they would walk home to dinner. Her father was often gone on business, sometimes for a month or more. He seemed very prosperous and sure of himself, and she never lost her fear of him. She remembered him beating her mother. She would never forget the thick hand pressing her temple, forcing her to watch, and her mother's terrified, stoic acceptance.

There was all that to account for.

Dead men on furlough, he said again.

She looked at him.

A phrase of Lenin's, he said. When young revolutionaries become old revolutionaries.

She smiled, nodding. Suddenly she stood on tiptoe and kissed him, a lingering kiss. They stood a moment in the shadows, kissing. He did not seem passionate, his thoughts were elsewhere. Gert knew this, she could taste it, taste his distance; she felt him recede. She was now absolutely certain that he would never hurt her. She knew also that she was protecting him, drawing him closer to her, drawing him inside. That was where they would both be safe, where the darkness was absolute. His words — but what did they mean, beyond that they said? She spoke his name. But he was still waiting, so solemn, a motionless American. She could not even feel his breathing. She looked at him helplessly.

He held her at arm's length.

She said, Do you want to see the apartment?

He said, This is where you live with your father?

Yes, she said.

He said, I have to go away for a while. Not long. When I return, I'll tell you why my father is afraid of me. And then, perhaps you can confess, too.

She said again, Do you want to see the apartment?

It was the most she had ever said in one breath. She moved away, across the cobblestones of the courtyard. She looked up; the apartment was dark. She waited a moment, and when she turned back — in one motion, her arms at her sides, a model's slow pivot — he was gone, as she knew absolutely he would be. As she knew absolutely that when he returned to Paris, he would come to see her, as he had promised, and explain about his American father.

Two weeks later they were alone in her bedroom, the windows thrown open to the drowsy summer. Gray light: it was raining, a welcome sprinkle, muffling the morning sounds from the rue de Sevres. Someone was baking bread, the sweet smell of bread in the room, too, along with the rain. She watched him sleep, dozing a little herself, warm and content in the big familiar bedroom with its single poster: one of Picasso's blue women. He lay on his back, his hands folded on his chest like a pharaoh, his mouth slightly parted as if he were preparing to speak. She lay beside him, her eyes half closed. She noticed stubble on his chin where it rested against the sheet. She touched his skin with her fingernail. He did not stir. They had talked through the night: talked, made love, talked, made love again, more talk, more love, fierce talk, fierce love. He was a fierce lover, though never rough or egotistical as she imagined men to be. She knew there was brutality in him, and recklessness; sooner or later it would show itself. She did not see him clearly yet. His soft humorous voice mesmerized her, his voice soft even when describing with ferocity. Now she was trying to find room for the information he had given her. She was trying to surmise the look of things behind his words; words alone were never enough and always deceptive, a smoke screen of sound. She believed her eyes. She wanted above all to *see,* to go beneath the surface as Picasso had done. So she tried to imagine America, his America, its shape and the life it accommodated. America was as vast as the Soviet Union, and as exotic to her as Japan or South Africa or Argentina. She wanted to know what it was that inspired such passion. She was a European, and had never heard America described at first hand by a member of the family, an intimate familiar with its rules and geography, its legends, its civilization — not a destination after all, but a journey. A civilization was never finished, or stable, or defined finally; it was always growing and in flux. America had forever been a mysterious country, widely feared and hated, but also a riddle, unpredictable, fathomless, yet magnetic. And ludicrous; people laughed at America, its oafishness and low taste, and its pretension.

In the night when she had cried out, her emotions loose and volcanic, he had embraced her, his arms like great muscled wings; he had crushed her to him in the Paris darkness. They were alone in the world. Breathless in his embrace, she had expected torment. He had lifted her off the bed and she was free of gravity at last, floating with him, emancipated from the earth. They were free, beyond restraint or reach of any authority. She was ecstatic, knowing she would never leave him. Then when he began to speak again, his mouth close against her ear, his breath hot, she imagined an hourglass turned upside down, grains tumbling from the bell to collect at the bottom of the glass to be read, each grain, like tea leaves; she saw the future racing toward her. She had listened, rapturous, dreamy, seldom interrupting, attentive in her fashion — seeing a tale, a narrative, Wolf's song.

Oh, a narrow, careless, unhappy country. Unhappy with itself, unhappy with what it had wrought. Unhappy with its civilization: broken promises, contracts not honored, a drawer full of bad debts. Negative vibrations, a pervasive melancholy among the glitter. In America, unhappiness was not a virtue, it sapped the strength of the people. Like prairie topsoil, optimism was a national resource. Heartbreak and nightmare. America talks in its sleep, he said, a feverish voice from the back country, no longer a frontier. No longer potent. No longer young. No longer new. From the chorus, a growl of complaint and helpless outrage. In the nightmares were ayatollahs, redheaded strangers, love gone wrong, unfaithful women, erratic men, and terror everywhere, a breakdown not of law but of order. America's sleep-talk, obsessed with legend and myth; but the grammar was elusive. Americans were not reluctant to tamper with their own history, trying to make things nice, and that was why living in America was an adventure — a world of science fiction, a lake one day was a forest the next and a desert the day after. And no one was in charge. America reinvented itself each day, why couldn't the world do likewise?

That was why the present situation was so laughable. The people were distressed with the holy men in Iran. There was an atmosphere approaching war fever. Americans did not understand that acts had consequences; ignoring that rule had allowed them to sleep easily in the twentieth century. Bad news? Keep it out of the paper. Forget it! Americans did not believe in atonement, an hour of reflection. So there was outrage and astonishment over the capture and internment of the diplomats and spies (there was no difference between them in any case) employed by the embassy in Teheran. Uncivilized barbaric behavior, Khomeini a sixteenth-century mystic, an Islamic Cotton Mather, an evil, evil man — an *antique*. However, there was no astonishment from anyone who had read the Koran and took it seriously, not as poetry but as history and prediction: as an article of faith, like the Bill of Rights. To anyone who knew the history of Iran under the puppet shah the taking of prisoners of war was logical and necessary, inevitable, symmetrical, fulfilling the requirements of history, meaning revenge. That was the reality "on the ground," as the ambassador was fond of saying; that there could be more than one reality in the world always came as a surprise to Americans, and an insult that the local reality was always the controlling reality.

His own father was obsessed with the captivity, being a — commissar in the American diplomatic service, an ambassador. It was his life. It was his entire life, and anyone who knew him knew that; he believed in diplomatic immunity, diplomats as a separate class of citizen, like priests or army officers. So the seizure of the embassy was an unspeakable breach of courtesy, an appalling turn of the screw, and could not be permitted to go unpunished. But he was impotent, they all were; they did not even have the intelligence to acknowledge a guilty conscience, meaning: responsibility for the fate of the Iranian people. Now they did not know what to do. They organized a rescue mission, and that failed; they organized a boycott, and that failed. The world they made was coming apart, piece by piece. Hard for a European to understand, beyond the understandable, even laudable *Schadenfreude*. But the distress of Americans was palpable, architects watching the house collapse of its own weight, and this was a house that was supposed to last a century! This house, made with the finest American materials, constructed by America's most adroit and subtle craftsmen, turning to dust. Cuba came apart, Indochina came apart, and now Iran and the Gulf. What would be next in the Northern Hemisphere? Germany? Wasn't it only a matter of time before the Germans began to think again, and the nation slowly move its shoulders, uncomfortable in the American jacket. Ostpolitik, Deutschpolitik. Germany had a right to control its own affairs. Germany had a right — no, a duty — to sit at the head table, as the strongest power in Europe. Germany had done its penance, had reconciled its past, and the new generation insisted on charting its own future, having suffered long enough for the sins of the fathers. *Ja?*

He had looked at her and smiled. "Boom," he said.

"Boom," she replied.

The Koran was not far removed from the Old Testament, in its definition of law and order. An eye for an eye. Quite specific, and no provision for an appeal. Perhaps Americans could be brought to understand the principle, Americans who enjoyed the exercise of power, who so loved their ostentatious killing machines, weapons of war utilizing the latest technologies, each new advance in the state of the art further removing the killer from the victim. Was it that Americans did not like to look their enemy in the eye? But — he smiled again, and she could see his words looping and floating, hesitating, finally homing in — concealed weapons were effective also, a bomb that could fit into your overcoat pocket, a handgun scarcely larger than a deck of cards. All that remained was to select the target, and there were so many, human beings, installations. Random targets. That is, targets selected at random.

Not the obvious targets, not men of notoriety, but men who were cogs in the machine. Men without whom the machine would founder, the kind of men who would routinely look over their shoulder, knowing that there was always a possibility, because naturally they were part of it. They were the sort of men who were routinely imprisoned in the client states, Iran, Korea, the Philippines, Israel.

It would set them back, he said.

He had kissed her tenderly in the darkness, and disclosed that his father had killed a man, an African, while on diplomatic service in Africa. He did not know the name of the African, whether the African had a family, what the African believed in, or if he believed in anything; but he had shot him dead. They gave him a medal for it. He was commended by the attorney general. When I asked him about it — What really happened, Ambassador? Was it necessary to kill him? — he refused to talk. Refused to explain or justify. My impression was that he shot him as easily as he lied for his government, his employer for a quarter of a century. Or as he lied to me. Silence, also, is a lie.

She said, Yes.

He said, The ambassador was without remorse.

She had nodded in the darkness, imagining the dead African; the African with no name and no history, no grave and no headstone, murdered by an American in Africa. She wanted to know if his father had ever dared to hurt *him*, if he had ever raised his fist or pointed a weapon at him. But she did not know how to ask. She assumed the answer was yes. She was thinking of the future now, the two of them together in Europe. They would be happy in Europe, with its many national boundaries; it was a natural hiding place. In Europe, they could disappear; millions of people had disappeared in Europe. And there were many targets, human beings, installations of an official nature; they could search for the targets together as they had the afternoon they had walked near the Louvre. Of course she would have to think up an excuse for her father, in order to leave the apartment. He would want some explanation, it would not matter what it was. She wondered where they would go, perhaps back to Germany. There were many places to live anonymously in Germany and elsewhere in Europe. They would follow his plan. And they would protect each other, that was the main thing. She thought of the money she had saved, the neat stacks of bills in the hatbox under her bed. It had never occurred to her to spend it, and now she was happy that she hadn't. It would be wonderful for them to have transportation of their own, perhaps a little red car. Then they could go anywhere.

Wolf was silent and his breathing was labored. A vein pulsed in his forehead.

She cradled his head in her lap. Outside it was gray, the morning so sudden. She wanted to make love again. She looked at him, his face drawn in the gray light. He was a handsome boy, his eyes closed now, his lips a thin hard line. She wondered what he was thinking. Was he thinking of her? She imagined herself in his thoughts. She imagined herself behind his forehead, being the blood rushing though his vein. Behind his forehead was a comfortable room, a pretty sunlit room with flowers, a place to live anonymously. She could see through his eyes; see, and not be seen. If he was thinking about her, what did he see? She kissed him on his forehead and his eyelids fluttered.

He whispered, The ambassador used to take me to the Department on Saturdays, when we lived in Washington and he was a deputy assistant to the deputy assistant, something like that. I was very small. He went to the office to read the cable traffic. To discover who's screwing up and where, he said. The office was quiet and I wondered whether the world stopped on weekends to give American diplomats a rest. There were always telephone calls to be made. At the touch of a button the ambassador could talk to other bureaus in the building, or with embassies abroad. He liked being in the office with the telephone and its buttons, and the switchboard that could link up — anywhere. And he had a picture on the wall, Lincoln. He took it with him wherever he went; it always hung on a wall close by. The ambassador's great hero, Lincoln. Lincoln and his mercantile war. Lincoln and his eman-ci-pa-tion proc-la-ma-tion. What a fucking fraud. Worse than Bonaparte.

She bent down so that her ear was next to his mouth.

He whispered, So now he does not know where I am, nor what I am doing. He does not know where I live. He knows no more of me than of the African he shot and killed. Yet I am an embarrassment to him, and in time I will be an embarrassment to the Department of State, to the government, and to the nation. He is afraid because he does not know where I found what I believe in; he does not know my antecedents. He is afraid because he does not know where I come from. I am like a foundling in the family. I was left on the doorstep, and he has a responsibility. Like Lincoln, he must try to hold the family together. But he cannot discover my provenance. I am like a code to which he cannot, try as he might, find the key. He has never known my heart. He does not know why I hate him so.

When?

He looked at her.

When was the first time you knew? She cradled his head, held him tight to her stomach, his beard scratching her belly. Knew their cowardice and corruption, their vanity. She held him more tightly, both arms around his head. She watched his muscles move in his arms and chest, his thighs. Her beautiful young man, Wolf. He uncoiled, his thighs parting.

They looked at him together. She wanted to jump out of her skin. She could not keep her hands off him.

Later, it was still raining. The sliver of sky that she saw from the window was pearly, the color of oysters. A soft Paris rain, benign and inviting, mixing with the smells of the street and their own sweet bed-smell. She closed her eyes, so happy, trying to hold on so that it would belong to her forever. She heard the high-pitched laughter of children on their way to school, and then a scraping in the corridor outside the bedroom door. For an instant, she held her breath; her eyes snapped open. *He* was there, prowling like an animal, listening. But her door was locked, they were secure. Max would never dare enter her room. After a moment, he went away and she was left with the sounds of the street and the rain, and Wolf rising, walking lightly across the room to the hotplate, carefully setting the kettle to boil.

He came back to bed with tea.

He said, I have been thinking about your question.

Yes, she said eagerly. She wanted to know everything about him. She wanted to combine their stories, his and hers, entwine them like vines so that there would be no difference between them. It would be the same story with different characters. In that way they would become one person.

He began to smile, bringing the tea to his mouth, holding the hot mug with both hands. She did likewise. He said, It was Thanksgiving 1975. The ambassador and Elinor had decided to have a family Thanksgiving, both sets of grandparents: everyone would come to Washington. He explained the American custom of Thanksgiving, its symbolism. Victory over the savages, thanks given to God.

3

H E MADE IT clear that the families did not get on. There
were cultural differences, and differences of taste. Some
small difference of politics. These were well known. It
was as if each set of grandparents was struggling for control of the
family: Elinor was an only child, as was the ambassador. The
grandparents disapproved of each other, as they disapproved of
the life their children had chosen. It was a replication of the contradictions of capitalism. It was a family in opposition.

They all arrived on Thursday morning, the Norths from Boston, the Ballards from Chicago. The ambassador had arranged for
identical suites at the Georgetown Inn, and once they were checked
in they all arrived at the house on O Street.

The atmosphere was badly strained, and to cover it the ambassador made a great show of making drinks. Everyone had a Martini, except for Grandfather North. When the ambassador asked
him what he wanted, he said it didn't matter. Anything. Anything
that was at hand, except he didn't want a Martini.

Well, the ambassador said, we have everything.

Perhaps some wine, Harry Ballard said. When I was growing
up, we always had Champagne at Thanksgiving.

You choose, Jerome said. It doesn't matter.

Sherry, the ambassador said.

Anything, Jerome said.

The women were in the kitchen. Elinor had made the ambassador promise to keep them all in the living room so that she wouldn't have to entertain her mother and her mother-in-law while she was preparing dinner, but the ambassador couldn't manage that simple task. So the grandmothers stayed in the kitchen while the men made small talk in the living room. The ambassador was nervous, trying to be solicitous of his father at the same time he was being polite to his father-in-law, knowing they both disapproved of him. Grandfather Ballard disapproved of his politics, and Grandfather North disapproved of his character. So they made small talk.

Gert said, Small talk?

Talk so small that it was almost invisible, Wolf said.

While the ambassador and Grandfather Ballard struggled to be polite, Grandfather North stood silently by, inspecting the premises. It was the first time he had been in the O Street house, and I could see him looking at the pictures on the wall and the books in the shelves, trying to simulate the ambassador's life from the evidence in front of his eyes. It was also true that the ambassador and Grandfather Ballard were smoking cigarettes, and the smoke hurt his eyes; so he stood apart from them, portly and meticulous in his dark suit, a gruff expression on his face. He watched Harry Ballard as he might have watched a dangerous animal. And Grandfather Ballard was hard to measure, being continuously in motion, his chin high in the air.

He and the ambassador had a second drink, and a third.

The women emerged from the kitchen, and they all stood in a tight little circle, except for Jerome. From time to time he would dab at his eyes with a handkerchief. But no one noticed, they were all talking at once, making such an effort with one another.

Elinor's face was flushed. I was on the top step of the stairs, watching them in the living room. I had gone around and shaken all their hands, Harry Ballard's dry hand, Jerome North's rough hand, the wet hands of the women; and then I had excused myself, to go upstairs on some errand or other. I knew Elinor had had a Martini before they arrived. For a week, she and the ambassador had talked of the Thanksgiving visit. An accident waiting to happen, she said. It is our business to make it pleasant, he said. As pleasant an accident as possible, he said, laughing. When we were alone that morning, I could hear her talking to herself. She hated Thanksgiving, the idea of it, and the food, stuffed turkey, mashed potatoes, creamed onions, and the rest of "the glop." She was careful to give me instructions, to be cheerful and polite, to talk to both grandmothers, to say please and thank you, to absolutely use no bad language, and, she added grimly, to keep my fingers crossed.

Grandfather Ballard held the floor. Elinor had asked him about the firm, how things were going, if he expected the market to rise. An unfortunate question, as it turned out, because the firm had just named a new chairman. There had been a purge. An aggressive, gauche, younger man. Unscrupulous. Jewish, he said, and then caught himself.

Very able, of course, he said. Very, very clever man; not an amiable man, but a clever man. Worked all day long. He turned to Grandfather North. It's hard when the young fellas come in, shoulder the old hands aside. When there's blood in the water it draws the sharks, ha-ha. Don't you think? When Jerome looked at him with no expression at all, he said, 'S matter of fact, this fella's from Boston, maybe you know him. Baum. His name is *Baum*.

No, Jerome said.

Smart little bastard, Harry said.

I expect he is, Jerome said.

He was a big shit in Boston, Harry said.

My goodness, Grandmother North said.

More like a little turd, Harry said.

Harry, Eloise Ballard said.

Why would I know him? Jerome asked quietly.

I don't know. Thought you might. Boston's small town, everyone knows each other. Isn't that right?

No, Jerome said.

Dinner's served, Elinor said.

Chicago, we all know each other.

It'll get cold, Elinor said.

You can all bring your drinks, the ambassador said.

But Harry was at the bar, pouring himself another from the

ambassador's silver shaker. When he turned around he spoke to the room at large, though he looked directly at Jerome North. He said, Mister Henry Fucking Baum doesn't like the way we do business. We've only been doing it for a hundred and five years, except for the war years when everyone joined up. European theater. We all went to the European theater, and the senior partner never came back. Interregnum then, we just closed up shop to win the war. We formed up again in 'forty-six, those of us who were left, been making money ever since. Profit every year, though last year'n the year before that a little down. OPEC, the god damned Arabs, and the scandal that you've got here in this town, the god damned newspapers. Business flat, the government's nose in everybody's business. The Grrrrreat So-ciety, started it all. That's way it is in business, up 'n down, down 'n up. Board looked around and brought in the turd. New blood. God damned right, it's new blood. But we'll see. Alla returns aren't in. We'll see about Mister Henry *Baum*.

Dinner's served now, the ambassador said.

And he's brought in his people, you expect that. New blood, new broom. Boston broom. Mister Benjamin Fucking Fein and one other. O'Reilly. Bond man in Boston. P'litic'ly connected, had some job in Washington. *You* probably know him, Bill. You know everyone in Washington. That's what my daughter Elinor tells me, when I ask her. There just isn't anyone who's anyone in the capital you don't know. Capital's right name for it, too. That's where all the money is.

The ambassador said, Name doesn't ring a bell.

He's a fixer, Harry said.

It still doesn't ring a bell, the ambassador said.

He fixes things. Things get bent out of shape, he fixes it. Thing's going in one direction, he fixed it to go in another direction. Fixes it so that his friends win and his enemies lose. He'n Henry Baum are *like that,* close as brothers, been working together in Boston for years. It's a sweet deal.

What's his name again? the ambassador asked. The women were at the door to the dining room, and beyond the door you could see the table and its candles, the turkey steaming on the sideboard. Harry Ballard hadn't moved from the bar, though.

Maynard O'Reilly, Harry said.

The ambassador turned to his father; really, it was a gesture of solidarity. He said, Wasn't Maynard O'Reilly a something-something in Treasury under Kennedy?

He was an assistant secretary, Jerome said. Johnson moved him out, put his own man in. Grandfather North hadn't budged either. It was a test of wills between the two old men to see who would be the last to walk into the dining room, sit down to the glop.

Baum, Fein, and O'Reilly, Harry said, making a little tune of it.

Dad, Elinor said.

And they've made their presence felt, first week. They've brought in a fat account, account we've been trying to get for years. Know how they did it? Maynard O'Reilly arranged to have some foreign aid money moved around. The account, the fat account, is a small bank in the Loop. Small, but profitable. It's money for the Philippines. The Philippine account. Doesn't sound like much, but it's quite a great deal of money. It's the money for the weapons. What the hell are they buying from us, Bill? Or are we buying from them? Everything's gone to hell in a hack since MacArthur died. You get my meaning?

Not exactly, the ambassador said.

Dinner's served, Louise Ballard said.

Maynard O'Reilly confided a few of the details, not all of them, 'course, because, Christ, I can't be trusted. I've only been a partner in the firm for forty fucking years, I'm this innocent who lives on the North Shore, votes Republican, pays taxes. I've never been indicted by a federal grand jury, for instance.

The ambassador turned to his father again. Was O'Reilly ever indicted?

There was some trouble in Boston, Jerome North replied. But he was never indicted, no.

He has pull, Harry said.

Jerome opened his mouth to say something, then didn't.

Anyway, the deal works like this, Harry said. It's the money for the weapons. Has to go somewhere. Money goes into this bank in the Loop, stays there for a few days, interest-free. Bank uses the money to factor. Swiss francs, Deutschmarks, fucking escudos. Then they send the money on to Manila or wherever it goes, and keep the profit. Risk-free. It's interest-free money, thanks to Maynard O'Reilly and his contacts at Treasury. Little favor we do our friends. And Mister Henry Fucking Baum and his fixer go over, have a cocktail with the chairman of the board of the bank in the Loop, first thing you know, we've got that account. They've got the money for the Philippines and we've got the account. That chairman's been in my foursome at the member-guest for ten years, but that's forgotten now because he can factor escudos for forty-eight hours, make twenty, thirty K risk-free, because it's a lot of money we're talking about, re-arming our plucky little democracy in Asia. Not that I'm against holding the line against the Commies —

Gert, Wolf said, and began to laugh, a kind of mirthless chuckle. *I was at the top of the stairs, listening to this, watching them. Grandmother North suddenly comes to the stairs, and calls for me, "Dinner's ready!" She looks up and there I am, listening. We stare at each other a minute. She knows I've heard every word. I smile, and she smiles back. Then she goes away, telling Elinor that I'll be down "momentarily." It's as if she wants me to hear them, uninterrupted, unedited, because they aren't ready to go in yet. Harry is making himself another drink, ice in the glass, gin over the ice, olive on top. Jerome still hasn't moved, he's stiff as an iceberg in the middle of the room. From time to time he brings the glass of sherry to his nose and sniffs it, like smelling salts. He's immaculately groomed, and he's wearing a thick tweed suit, looks to be about a hundred years old. Harry Ballard's casual, a bit disheveled, but with his blue eyes and light hair, his white shirt and his blazer and striped tie, he looks like an overage college boy. He has the kind of looks that are called boyish, but are really just unformed. A handsome man, but not a* mensch. *You know the difference, Gert. The worried ambassador is moving back and forth between them, father and father-in-law, trying to find common ground. It's shuttle diplomacy. The ambassador is trying to salvage the day. Meanwhile, the women are wringing their hands, except for Elinor, who's standing in the entrance to the dining room, looking at the ambassador. I know the look. I've seen it often enough. "I told you so." But she saw her father getting the worst of it, and she didn't like it. She didn't have much respect for him, but she didn't want to see him beaten up, either. The patriot's dilemma in any decadent nation. I came down the stairs halfway, the better to see the action. They had forgotten all about me. Where do you suppose they thought I was? It's disgusting.* Gert grinned, her eyes bright; she was avid for information of life in American ruling circles. How they fought for what they believed in.

You say he was one of Kennedy's people, Harry said.

Yes, Jerome said.

If he was one of Kennedy's men, how come he's got so much clout in the Nixon administration? I thought we had a two-party system in the United States, or am I wrong? Is it just the same people, no matter who's in the White House? His voice was truculent.

Men of that kind, they tend to know each other, Jerome said.

So do the fixers, it doesn't matter who's in or who's out. Whoever's in, they're in.

Gert, he said, *I could have laughed out loud. Comrade Ballard, meet Comrade Marx.*

Well, it depends, Jerome said.

I don't understand that, Harry said.

It's simple enough, Jerome said.

Maybe to you, Harry said.

Jerome looked up at that moment, Gert, and saw me on the stairs. A shadow crossed his face. I smiled, but he didn't smile back. He turned to the others, then looked back at me. "Hello, Bill. You don't have to hide. Come on down."

The ambassador didn't like it that I was there. He said, Go into the dining room, Bill. We'll be there in a moment.

But I didn't move, Gert. I stayed where I was, on the fifty-yard line.

Jerome said, Let him stay, Bill. Let him finish listening to our very interesting discussion.

Little pitchers, Harry said.

He's old enough, Jerome said. It's good for him to hear about the way of the world. I was going to explain about Maynard O'Reilly. I believe he knew some Californians who did business in Boston. Los Angeles interests, real estate, the entertainment industry. The Californians naturally knew Nixon, Nixon's people. Maynard O'Reilly was helpful to them in Boston, so they're helpful to him in Washington. It isn't politics. Politics doesn't have anything to do with it, except at fund-raising occasions. It's business. It's the way business is done. Always.

The ambassador shook his head, laughing. Chicago isn't Plato's Republic, Harry. I believe politics has been known to intrude in

Chicago business. Jesus Christ, don't tell me you're surprised.

Bill, Elinor said.

Let's go in to dinner, the ambassador said. But Harry didn't move, nor did Jerome.

It's not a question of surprise, Harry said. I'm not *surprised.* It offends me. The turd Baum and Fein, and the fixer. I think it's disgraceful. It's the way business is done, but I don't have to like it. He was talking to the ambassador but looking at Jerome. It was really between them, but the ambassador didn't see that yet. The ambassador with his great diplomatic skills. It was Jew and Gentile, and one kind of money and another kind of money, and how the ruling classes cut up the pie. Also, it was Jerome North's European nightmare and Harry Ballard's American daydream. And Harry had always figured it was *his* America, his and his father's and his father's father's and their friends, midwestern capitalists, Bourbons. They were people who had always met a payroll. They had the money and someone else could tote dat barge and lift dat bale. As for Jerome North, he was a cosmopolitan; his country was inside him. Wherever he was, his country was also. And Harry Ballard saw this; he did not see much, but he saw this. Who was Jerome North to tell him how American business worked? How long had Jerome North been a citizen of the U.S.A.? Moreover, Jerome North seemed to approve — of Baum, and of Maynard O'Reilly, and the Philippine connection. No outrage or disapproval in Jerome North's voice, his surface was as smooth and slippery as ice. Suddenly Harry realized he had been put at a disadvantage; he was losing the argument he had started. The old Jew was smarter than he thought — well, they were all *smart,* but more worldly, less emotional. And the ambassador, the bureaucrat his daughter had married, was laughing at him. So he thought he would up the ante. *He revved the engines, Gert, and ran the* Titanic *straight into the iceberg.*

It's sleazy business, he said.

It's business, Jerome replied. It's the way you've organized your country.

My country, yes. And yours also.

I pay taxes, I obey the law, I am a citizen, and if I went abroad I would carry the passport. I am grateful to this country, but it is not mine. My country disappeared in 1933.

This country has been hospitable?

137

Hospitable, yes.

Gave you citizenship . . .

Citizenship you earn, Jerome said.

. . . a good living.

You earn that, too.

Gert, the silence grew as they looked at each other, seeing for the first time the great gulf between them. It was more than Harry Ballard's suburban Jew-baiting, and Jerome North's German superiority. I allowed myself to look closely at my Grandfather North. His face was set hard as stone, and he communicated great physical strength, his shoulders and bald head, and massive hands wrapped around the sherry glass. If I had to guess his business at that moment I would have said gangster, a capo regime *of the* Cosa Nostra. *But he was not a gangster at all; he fancied himself a scholar, an educated man, and more dangerous by far than Harry Ballard, for he had no illusions. He gave the impression of a man who had seen everything, who knew how insecure things were, how on a knife's edge his own and others' existence. He was the sort of man who was always waiting for a knock on the door, poor bastard.*

At least we agree about that, Harry said.

And when I looked at Grandfather Ballard, Gert. I saw something new. He had pulled himself together; he was more resilient than I thought. But he was drunk, too, and angry. He looked like an angry child about to have a tantrum, and therefore unpredictable, like any child.

Dinner's waiting, the ambassador said.

That ended it for the moment. They trooped into the dining room, the table and sideboard laden with the essentials of an American Thanksgiving. The women tried to make light of things; the grandmothers were making a great effort with each other. But Elinor was glaring at the ambassador, and the grandfathers were silent. Harry had brought his Martini with him. Of course he continued to smoke at the table, ashes on his white shirt, and beside the dinky little ashtray next to his plate. But it wasn't ended. The silences were long, though the grandmothers and the ambassador tried to cover them. The ambassador's answer to everything is noise and more noise, aimless chatter, anything to avoid the truth. Which soon showed itself.

They want me to take early retirement, Harry said.

Is that what you want? Elinor asked.

No, it isn't what I want. Why would I want to retire? It's Baum. Baum wants me out. Baum wants to buy me out.

You should have seen him, Gert. He'd held it back as long as he could, then he had to let it out. He was purged, that was what he was telling them. It was Thanksgiving in a city he hated, and he was frightened to death. Fear and trembling. He'd looked around his warm capitalist aquarium one fine day, and saw he was face to face with a shark. Baum. The shark and the pilot fish, O'Reilly, running things to suit themselves. And he was out. Social Darwinism in Chicago. And there was no place to hide.

Is the price right? Jerome asked quietly.

Isn't a question of price, he said. I don't want to get out.

Jerome lifted his eyebrows, but said nothing.

I enjoy working. I have always enjoyed it, going to the office, putting a deal together, making money.

Yes, Jerome said.

Would you? Harry asked. Would you be bought out? A turd named Baum comes into your office, takes it over, decides to buy you out? Bye-bye, Ballard we've got other plans. Government money, a Philippine connection. The golf course isn't where it's *at*, Ballard. You wouldn't like it, you'd fight like hell. You'd go to your friends, fight like hell. Good, close friends, come to a man's aid. And that's what I'm going to do.

Friends, the ambassador said doubtfully.

Yes, *friends*. I suppose it doesn't work that way in the Department of State. Except I always heard it did, the Foreign Service Protective Association. Presidents come and go, the Foreign Service remains. You're secure, *perfectamente*.

I'm sorry, Dad, Elinor said.

This is real life, girl, Harry said. There's no security in business. It's not like the government or a university, the Civil Service or a tenured professorship. Or the fixers, on top no matter who's elected. This is free enterprise. It's the bottom line and only the bottom line, and whether or not you fit into their plans. Well, sometimes you can force it. With a little help from a few close friends, as the late Mayor Daley used to say.

Friends can be helpful, sometimes, Jerome said.

Harry's been worried sick, Grandmother Ballard said.

Shut up, Louise, Harry said.

Worried *sick,* she repeated. Insomnia, nausea —

Thanks, Louise.

It's *true,* Harry. You said the other night that it was worse than the Depression. She turned to the table and reminded them that Harry Ballard had saved his father's business. Drove from one end of the Midwest to the other, negotiating with creditors. And he paid them back, every penny. No one lost a cent. The first year we were married, she said, I didn't see him for six months. It was a very painful time. And of course in the end the business had to be sold.

Then I misspoke myself, Harry said. Nothing was worse than the Depression. The Depression was the worst time I have ever seen in my life. The Depression was a holocaust, that god damned Roosevelt. The only thing that got us out of it was the war. It was a hell of a high price to pay.

Well, the ambassador said, the Japanese had something to do with that.

We had warning, Harry said darkly. Roosevelt chose to ignore the warning. That's the most charitable explanation.

The ambassador offered more turkey all around, but there were no takers. No wonder.

Elinor said, What are you going to do, Dad?

Let's ask the ambassador, Harry said. The ambassador is skilled at difficult situations. What do you do, when things aren't working out? Well, we know what you do. You turn tail and run. You break your promises. A little heat in Washington, you just fold your hand. No matter how many've died, or relied on your *word.* You just let them walk in without opposition. I thought it was *disgusting,* the last days. That chopper on the roof of the embassy. Throwing people off so that the god damned *newspapermen* and their servants and mistresses got away. You should be ashamed of yourself. I'm ashamed, if you're not. Brave boys, dead for nothing. Brave ally, lost. Love your enemies, screw your friends. Christ, even Roosevelt wouldn't've behaved that way.

The ambassador was silent a moment. He looked at Grandfather North, raising his eyebrow in his characteristic way. He was very uncomfortable. Then he began to talk about the last days of Saigon, and the ten years that preceded them. He said something about a coherent strategy. You have to know whether victory is possible, he said. Sometimes it isn't. Sometimes victory is not possible, and then —

That's why half the world's Communist, Harry said. "Coherent strategy." Faint hearts. No balls.

The ambassador put the carving knife down, a clatter.

Then Jerome North cleared his throat. He was sitting at the table as though it were his office desk. His arms were resting on the cloth, his hands folded in front of him, just touching the napkin. His eyes were focused on the middle distance. He said softly, I have never found it wise to depend on friends, in the last analysis. Friends may be helpful in the beginning, until their own interests are at stake. It is asking too much of friends to put your interests above their own. And in extreme circumstances, it is very foolish. This is why I have always worked alone. I own a seat on the Boston Exchange. I do not even have a secretary, for my investments are few. Easy for me to keep track of them; and no one can keep track of me. Because of my method of operation, I have declined numerous profitable proposals; and I have losses of my own, of course. But I have found it imprudent to rely on friends or the government or any system apart from one's own appreciation of God's way. You would call this "the odds." These have rarely been in my favor. I suspect you have had better luck, but your temperament is more optimistic than mine, and your history more benign, with the exception naturally of the Depression. There was a depression also in Europe, though perhaps the surprise was not so great; we in Europe are accustomed to depressions. I agree with the poet who said that this is the worst century so far. I believe it is unwise to rely on luck, or on the experience of the past, if you have been lucky. Each day is new, like no other day; each day has its perils and requirements. Each day must be *lived*. You don't like me. I understand that. Perhaps I undermine your position. I have sympathy for your situation, and I do not envy you. However, the problem is larger than Baum. It isn't *Baum*. And it isn't O'Reilly. It's the — you would call them odds.

Harry Ballard was looking at his enemy with a fixed smile. He dropped his cigarette into the mashed potatoes, and reached across the table for the wine. His body arched, reaching; but his hand fell short, toppling a water glass. His face drained of color. Elinor and the ambassador looked away. Jerome did not move. Harry said, I think I'm going to be sick. And he left the table; and he was sick.

Ah, Gert, he said. *What a nest of snakes. Thanksgiving in the capital, the ruling class tearing and eating one another, and the ambassador, the host of the banquet, watching it all spin out of control while reciting his government's platitudes. I had some admiration for my mother, a woman who had clearly risen above her environment. And the ambassador? He did not know how to listen, and he would never learn. He did not know who he was, at that table. And the old men: neither of them lived a year. In a year they were both dead, victims of their own arrogance and greed. Vicious old men. Good riddance.*

That was the story. She listened with her whole heart. It had the enchantment of a fable. Varieties of American experience, the capitalist heartland.

That night she went with him to meet his friends, and the next week she left her father and the apartment for good. She said she was going to live with a boy and when her father asked for his name she told him Wolf. She believed he would hit her, but Wolf said he would not; Wolf would be close by to ensure that he did not. And in the event, her father was calm, almost nonchalant. She took her things, and her money, and left.

That was past, and still she lived inside Wolf's brain, behind his forehead. And Wolf lived in her, too. They had been everywhere in Europe, but lived mostly in Paris. It was easy for them to be anonymous in Paris, a beautiful young woman and her American boyfriend. Sometimes she pretended to be French, other times German. He was sometimes American, but mostly German. They pulled on identities like suits of clothes. They were fluent in languages and manners. They had found targets in Paris, Munich, and Rome. There were many enemies, dating from as far back as she could remember. Yet they were easily targeted, being for the most part unwitting. Always, however, there was meticulous preparation. Wolf insisted on it. Because of his obsession with security, the authorities had never discovered them. They remained free, masters of their own future, and she compared it to living in a dream, obeying no laws but their own.

In that way they — lived. They ate, slept, made love, went shopping, saw friends, took trips. The years passed. There was the rendezvous in Hamburg, where Gert was able to watch the ambassador and his wife. Gert and Wolf moved from place to place, settling finally in Berlin. They were waiting for something but she did not know what it was. She knew that Wolf was impatient, and it was in Berlin, sitting in a café on the Ku-damm one afternoon in October, that plans suddenly jelled. She was drinking coffee and watching the people; he was reading *Die Welt.* He muttered something in English, and then began to chuckle. He tapped her on the arm and showed her a short item on page five. The American diplomat, William North, would be delayed taking up his post as chargé in Bonn by an unspecified illness. Wolf tapped the paper with his finger, grinning. Then he moved to the rear of the paper, the television listings. Max Mueller the journalist would appear on weekend television, one of a panel of experts who would discuss NATO strategy.

Have you been thinking about him? he said in English.

She nodded.

How would you like to see him again, darling? he asked.

She shuddered.

I think so, he said. Yes.

4

THREE DAYS LATER they were in the open, on the street. Somewhere on the threshold of consciousness, Gert sensed a great mass of people. They were without recognizable faces or distinguishing characteristics of any kind. Anonymous urban life, faces you saw in a subway or supermarket, glimpsed and instantly forgotten. Gert scanned the wide boulevard, apartment buildings rising either side, high as the walls of a prison, and as bland. They were featureless brick buildings, shades pulled against the afternoon sun.

Wolf leaned forward, cocking his head, listening hard; there was music, an insistent guitar and hard bass, falsetto voices, modern Western music overhead, an angel's chorus. She turned and saw Wolf, the expression on his face one of radiant enchantment, as if he had entered a charmed circle.

Gert sensed the people inside the apartments moving restlessly, like rats in a maze. They would create a great pressure, their bodies bumping and sliding, tumbling down stairwells, falling over each other, scratching at the walls. There were more of them in the houses on the side streets behind the apartment buildings, far as the limits of the district, miles and miles, each house filled to over-

144

flowing; and everywhere a pressure to get away, to evacuate. They were unable to free themselves and each day there were more of them, younger and stronger, more determined and high-strung, pressing against the thick walls and shaded windows.

He felt the pressure inside his own skull and stepped back, away from the curb, giddy, a fixed smile on his face. Sunday in Berlin. A window slammed and the music stopped, midchorus. Up the street was a commotion.

Gert said, "Look."

All activity in the boulevard ceased, vehicles suddenly still. Gert looked at the faces of the occupants and could see they were terrified, their faces gray and drawn like the faces in church windows. What next? The light failed, as if a great hand had seized the sun, squeezing shut, releasing little lemon drop fragments of liquid light. An explosion crashed overhead, Boom! Gert did not flinch, and perhaps did not notice. Police appeared in their leather jackets and jodhpurs and steel helmets, dense with menace. It began to rain. Bells commenced to toll, and from the doorway of the largest building the rats began to pour. Gert watched them intently. The traffic waited as they scrambled out the door and into the street.

Gert continued to stare at the frightened faces.

Wolf stepped back from the curb, pulling the hood of his raincoat over his head. Gert shuddered. He knew she was suspicious; they had waited too long at the curb. He brusquely took her by the shoulders and moved her so that she was facing him. A raindrop hit her forehead and she blinked, surprised. He put his finger to his lips. Then he buttoned her raincoat and handed her a black plastic hat. Rain fell in huge fat drops, and thunder crashed once more.

"What?"

He said, "It's the church. Mass is letting out."

Her eyes narrowed, and she did not reply.

He took her by the arm and they walked quickly up the boulevard. The police had halted traffic, allowing them to cross the street to the church. Organ music, an exhausted recessional, filled the street. The priest nodded at them, but they ignored him. He hurried her along and at the next intersection steered her into a café. They stood at the bar and he ordered hot chocolate for them both.

He said, "Take off your hat." She looked at him and he nodded. She slowly removed the hat and let it fall to the floor, tossing her head as she did so, her dark hair swaying from side to side.

The chocolate arrived but when she moved to grasp the cup, he touched her wrist.

"It's hot, let it cool off. Let it cool." Her hand continued to move, as if she hadn't heard him. He said roughly, "Don't."

She stood on tiptoe and kissed his cheek, laughing gaily. He turned casually, eyes patrolling the room. An ordinary bourgeois café on a Sunday in Berlin, two couples at tables by the window, engrossed in conversation. An elderly bearded man drinking coffee at a table in the rear. The elderly man was looking appreciatively at Gert, admiring her profile. A teenager in blue jeans bent over the jukebox, punching buttons. He and Gert were the only ones standing at the bar.

She said, "What?"

He said, "It's hot."

"No," she said. "*What?*"

He said, "We wait."

She said, "It was the church."

"Yes," he said.

She bumped his shoulder and said deadpan, "Not the Rathaus."

"No," he said, smiling. Unpredictable Gert. She loved to make puns in English and German, and now turned the screw once more.

"Rats," she said, lapsing into baby talk so that it came out "Wats."

Outside the rain continued and Gert began to hum. It was the hymn they had heard on the sidewalk. He turned to look at her. Her head was moving slightly from side to side and she was smiling, her mouth half parted. She stood a little back from the bar, her coat open, its skirt swaying. She wore brown leather boots and black tights and a short sheath dress. Over her shoulder he saw the elderly man looking at her with open appreciation. In the dark light of the café Gert could have been almost any age, though in fact she was twenty-seven. In a certain light she looked forty, and in another kind of light sixteen; it depended on the light and her own mood. Her face sometimes went slack, the features thickening. She would pull her long neck into her shoulders and stare straight ahead, looking as if something momentous were about to happen. Now she moved from one foot to another, her hands in her pockets. She had drawn the attention of the teenager. Presently pop music filled the room, but she seemed not to notice; she was "in the zone," as she said, another pun. The light was flattering, and her head high and girlish as she continued to hum the Lutheran hymn.

The elderly man came up behind them, so stealthily that Bill did not notice until he heard his breathing, an old man's asthmatic wheeze. The elderly man bent down to pick up Gert's rain hat, smoothing it with his fingers, examining it, then looking her up and down, a caress, undressing her. He said, "Fräulein," handing her the hat.

She replied, "Thank you," not looking at him.

He said mildly, "You are English."

"No," she said.

"That is good. You are very lovely," he said softly. His lips hardly moved. "You are a very beautiful young German girl. Why do you not speak our language? I do not mean to be presumptuous." The elderly man smiled and gave a little bow and walked off, out the door and into the rain.

He had not looked up, not when the elderly man approached, and not when he departed. Now he said, "Fine, Gert."

She did not reply.

"Fifteen minutes more," he said. "Finish your chocolate." He glanced at his watch, it was noon. The café was beginning to fill up, pedestrians coming in out of the rain, laughing and complaining. The odor of chocolate filled the café. He offered her a cigarette and she shook her head. He moved close to her so that they stood facing each other, not speaking. Gert had withdrawn, way inside, back into a region of her mind where there were no people, only a stark and restless landscape, menacing in its simplicity. It was a warm day and a thin autumn mist covered the hillside. Running along the grassy ridge she could see for miles and miles, left and right. She could see to the very margins of an empty nation, a land without people. She felt that she was running along a knife's blade, one slip and she would be cut in two, sliced like a turnip. Birds wheeled overhead in a cloudless milky sky. Below in the valley there were sheep and shepherds' huts. She was crying. Her dress was torn and her face bruised. Her hands were bloody. The nail of her little finger was torn to the quick, and she tucked it into her palm. She stumbled and fell, rolling down the hillside, over and over, out of breath, her hands banging on the earth, her hair flying, tangled —

"Gert."

She turned to him, suspicious.

"Stop it now," he said, his mouth close to her ear, his voice very low but sharp.

"What?" She looked at her left palm, bloody where the nail had dug into it. He handed her a paper napkin which she pressed into her palm. The café was very crowded now, noise rising all around them. It was a neighborhood place, everyone knew each other. She moved closer to him. He said in a natural voice, "You've hurt your hand." But her eyes were far away and she seemed not to hear; at any event, she did not reply. He buttoned up the raincoat and put a bill on the counter, steering her out of the café and into the street. There was only a light shower now and she did not bother with the rain hat as she stood staring at the apartment buildings, no longer bland and featureless but singular and important. She dropped the napkin. He put his arm around her waist and they walked back the way they had come, past the church and across the boulevard. The elderly bearded man was ahead of them, strolling, looking into shop windows. They followed each other for a block, and then the elderly man crossed back to the other side of the street and they walked parallel for a while. There was very little traffic and no pedestrians. They were headed in the general direction of the Ku-damm. Gert pulled on his arm when they passed an art gallery. In the window were faceless mannequins, decorated with fruit and vegetables; apples for one, oranges for another, corn for a third. Gert looked at the figure with corncobs around its neck, and between its legs.

She said, "Soft-pore corn."

He smiled. All the while he was glancing across the street. The elderly man had stopped and now moved on, turning at the intersection. Gert was a few feet away, staring into the window of a sex shop. Women's undergarments in black and red, stiletto-heeled shoes, wigs, a leather chain. He said, "Here we go, Gert," and for the first time that day, she smiled.

They continued for another block, Gert striding out, leading the way. She began to hum. He was not familiar with the district, though he knew that the zoo was not far away. The elderly man was waiting for them at the stop light. When they were twenty feet away, still showing no sign of recognition, he quickly crossed the street and mounted the steps of a three-story apartment building, disappearing inside. They followed, up the stairs to the third floor. Gert took the stairs two at a time. The stairwell was dark but the third-floor door was open.

The apartment was light and pleasant, yet plainly furnished. It looked like a hotel room, with a threadbare carpet and nondescript pictures on the wall — a landscape, a pot of flowers, plums in a bowl — and no personal items of any kind except a pile of newspapers in the corner, and a copy of *Der Spiegel* on the coffee table. The elderly man was standing back from the window, looking here and there into the street. Apparently satisfied, he turned and took their coats and disappeared into the kitchen where, presently, they heard the banging of pots and china, and the rush of water. There were two chairs, one on each side of the coffee table. Gert took one of the chairs and Wolf remained standing.

The elderly man, beardless now and looking younger, returned with a tray, placing it in front of Gert. He said, "We were not more conspicuous than a battalion."

Bill said, "It wasn't too bad."

He put out his hand. "My name is Max."

Bill said, "I am Wolf."

Max raised his eyebrows, smiling, then sat down heavily, folding his hands across his belly. "Wolf? I know who you are, Herr North. There's no need for any of that here. We are quite safe." Then he turned to Gert, regarding her fondly. "How are you, darling?"

"Fine, Papa."

"You are looking very well. Isn't she looking well, Herr North?"

"Yes," Bill said. "I am called Wolf here. It is short for Wolfgang."

"Yes, of course. You are taking care of my Gert. Good care. You have a fine reputation, Herr Wolf. Pour the tea, darling."

Bill said, "You can talk German if you want."

"I prefer English."

Bill said, "As you wish." He moved to the window, standing back

149

from it as Max had done. The filthy glass reflected his own image, distorting it. He watched a Volkswagen accelerate and disappear around the corner, not fast enough. He said, "The boy in the café, the one playing the jukebox. The one watching me. He just drove by. What the fuck am I supposed to think about that, Max?" He turned from the window, facing the older man.

Max said, "He is one of mine."

"Not part of the arrangement, Max."

Max said, "Wait two minutes. He'll come by again, and park across the street. And when he does, I'll go outside and tell him to leave, if you'd like me to do that. I'll be happy to do it. The boy is a precaution. He has a device in his car that can signal if anything goes amiss. Awry. Just anything at all. He pushes a button on the little pocket calculator he has and there's a signal here." Max pulled a calculator out of his trouser pocket and placed it on the table. They all looked at it. "So we know if there's anything out of the ordinary on the street, a car that shouldn't be there, unfamiliar people. And the boy's clean, no worries about him." As Max spoke the Volkswagen reappeared, but there was no parking place across the street.

"Is he there?"

"Yes, but he can't park."

"You can always park in this street on Sundays."

"He double-parked."

"Ah, why can't things go smoothly, as they do in the cinema?" He laughed. "No one ever double-parks in the cinema."

Bill said, "Tell him to go."

Max did not protest. He rose and left the room. They heard him clumping downstairs. Still looking out the window, Bill said, "Is he as you remember him?"

"What?"

"Does he look the same?"

Gert thought a moment. "Yes."

He watched Max walk across the street and lean into the side window of the Volkswagen. Then the driver and Max looked up at him, grinning. The driver had an object in his hand. He made a sudden motion and Bill jumped back from the window. The little light on the calculator on the table flared, and went out. Bill returned to the window. The Volkswagen drove off. Max returned to the sidewalk, shaking his head.

Bill said, "He's a swine."

She said, "What?"

He turned to look at her, sitting so quietly, lost again in her own thoughts, staring at the tea things, her hands working in her lap. She was stroking the sore in her palm.

"Well," Max said, closing the door. "Herr *Wolf*. Give you a start, did we?"

Bill continued to look out the window, left and right.

Max said, "Yours is down the street, the Volvo next to the intersection." He settled into his chair. "The boy is very good, he made him right away."

Bill smiled. There was no one down the street, at least no one he knew. His group, what was left of it, was in Hamburg. He and Max would have to go around once again. "He's not mine."

Max said, "Look again. Look left. He's youngish, your age, perhaps a little older. Red jacket, blue jeans, no hat, driving a Volvo. It's a little peach-colored Volvo."

"We don't drive Volvos."

Max said, "This is exhausting."

"Perhaps your boy is mistaken."

"Perhaps so. He is inexperienced." Max sighed. "Darling, please pour the tea." Then, to Bill: "I am so pleased to see her again. It's been — years. I've worried about her day and night, as only a father can. But she has not changed at all, she is as I remember her, and as lovely as ever." He was talking to Bill as if Gert were not present. "And now she has a reputation as fine as yours. But of course it is sentimental for me, her father, to boast."

"It is not correct," Bill agreed.

He looked at Gert. "The poor darling. But it is good after all these years that we meet, you and I. We both have much at stake. Does she still speak of her mother?"

"No," Bill said.

"Her mother was a tragedy."

"In what way?"

"Ill so many years," Max said vaguely. "I was not able to be with her, owing to my own work."

"And where have you been, these six years?"

"Here and there," Max said.

"You were in America."

"Yes."

"And for a time in France."

"For a year only. It was very pleasant. The food and wine." He patted his stomach. "I have been trying to lose weight, but alas."

"And in Great Britain."

"You've been attentive."

"It's not difficult." Bill gestured at the newspapers in the corner of the room. "It's not hard, following your movements."

"So you've read the paper."

"Of course," Bill said.

"And Gert. Does she read the paper, too?"

"Sometimes I read it to her, if the dispatch is important or amusing. Or if it carries your by-line."

"In Washington I saw your father. A briefing at the State Department, something to do with southern Africa. A briefing for the European press, even the free lancers. I looked at him carefully, trying to imagine you."

"And was that easy to do?"

"No," Max said. "But now I can see the resemblance, you are tall, as he is. But you are sturdier, and the speech is very different. Perhaps because you have been in Germany. Is that it?" Max did not wait for an answer. "They say your German is excellent, a native's German. Of course your grandfather was a Berliner. What else is one to expect? Your father is thoroughly an American. He has a State Department face and uses State Department English, but naturally you know that. I listened carefully and at the end of the briefing — specially arranged for the foreign press, with drinks and a little food afterward, all very fraternal — I went up to him and asked a rude question, which he answered carelessly. I wanted to observe him up close, to see if he could be made uncomfortable."

"And could he?" Bill tried to imagine them together, Max and the ambassador: the rude question, and the bland institutional answer. The ambassador so tall and — contemporary, an inhabitant of the twentieth century, clean-shaven, good teeth, clear complexion, the evidence of a lifetime of wholesome nutrition. Max looking up at him as he asked his rude question and received his answer, the answer as smooth and neutral as oleo, nothing to grasp or to savor. Max so squat and contained, his face a mirror of central Europe: an old-fashioned face that an American might call "full of character," if by character one meant dolor. It was a face easy to overestimate — as the ambassador's was easy to underestimate. That was how the Americans had got as far as they had: always underestimated and misread. He wondered how Max had escaped detection all these years. He would have a dossier as thick as a telephone book, but the dossier would be disorganized, filed under half a dozen different identities — his Polish identity before the war, his Maltese, Greek, Rumanian, after the war. He would not have many years left because the computers would discover common facts, and sooner or later they would all lead to Max Mueller, foreign correspondent, veteran hack.

"He seemed to be irritated, no more," Max said. "I thought that through him I could see you. The son is always the shadow of the father, is that not true? But alas. These State Department people have no weight. And it was unequal, I had him at a disadvantage. I knew so much more than he did. I felt like a professor in the presence of a student. There was this familial link between us, of which he knew nothing: I was proud, he ashamed. And of that, too, he was unwitting. He was aware of nothing. He seemed distracted, bored with me, anxious to return to his office. He is not skilled at public relations, your father. He did not even know who I was! He had to look at my nametag, and even then there was no recognition: and I have been a foreign correspondent for thirty years. How simple it would have been to surprise him, to move him back a step, to interfere with his complacency. To watch his face when I said, *Herr Ambassador, let me bring you some news. Let me tell you about the children, who are celebrated in Europe. You and I, we have much in common. Your Bill and my Gert are lovers! They are the most dangerous revolutionists in Europe! And they are ours, yours and mine.* They are so smug in Washington, so self-satisfied. To have watched his face at such a time, it would have given me much pleasure. What do you suppose he would have done? Taken me off into a corner? Called the security guard? Perhaps both at once!

But I said nothing. I listened to his answer, trying to control my excitement. And then he looked at his watch, and was gone." Max paused, staring at the ceiling, then grunting as if struck by another thought. "And do you see anything of me in Gert? Not physically, of course. Physically, she follows her mother. The hair, and the way she carries herself. The shape of her body, her legs and bosom. But in the general way of things, do you see a resemblance? Perhaps she has my resilience and tenacity, my patience. It worries me, I don't mind telling you. It is only a matter of time before they have a picture, and then they begin the process of winding back. These people are worse than the Nazis, and I am covered and intend to stay covered. I am an old revolutionist, nothing more and nothing less. I am a living history of postwar Europe. Me! It is my life, and I am the last of my kind. And her. She is the first of her kind. Gert is my great legacy. She is my inheritance to the world. And as I look at her now, I see she is her mother's daughter. Her mother was the most beautiful woman in Berlin, it was well known. A beautiful, pitiless woman." He stopped abruptly, having said too much; or having said the wrong thing.

"I would have to know you better," Bill said.

"Which is impossible, alas."

"It is very unlikely."

"I want tremendously to be a grandfather. Does that surprise you?"

"No."

"It is time for me to be a grandfather. All my friends are grandfathers, those who have families, and are still alive. It is thrilling to watch them with their grandchildren at the zoo, looking at the animals, eating an ice." He looked at Gert a long moment, up and down. For the first time, she turned to meet his gaze, her eyes widening; it was an innocent look, without guile or complexity. They could have been strangers. She smoothed her dark hair with the palm of one hand, tucking stray curls behind her ears. Max leaned forward, and suddenly he looked very old. "It would be a wonderful thing, if you could make me a grandfather." Gert continued to stare at him, smiling brilliantly now, as if posing for a photograph. "Oh," he said, "I hope you are not barren. That would be a great pity."

154

She turned to Bill and said, "Dead men on furlough."

Max's eyes narrowed. "What? What did she say?"

"I'm surprised you don't know it," Bill said. "Comrade Lenin's remark. Surely you remember."

"I don't know it," Max said brusquely.

"Shall I explain it? Perhaps Gert will explain it."

Max stirred uncomfortably. "At my age, what good would it do?"

Bill said, "Shall we get down to business? My time is short."

"I thought we might come to know each other."

"Why?"

"It is correct."

"It is foolish," Bill said. "The situation is very tight."

Gert said, "Excuse me. I am going to the toilet."

Max said, "Through that door, darling, to the left."

"There has been a change this past week. The security people are everywhere."

Max watched Gert rise and walk slowly out of the room. He said, "I am surprised that she knew me. But I could tell right away, when I handed her the hat. I could see it in her eyes, that I had not been forgotten."

"Her memory comes and goes in bits and pieces. But you have not been forgotten, no."

Max nodded, apparently pleased. "She was that way from the beginning, you know. We were living with friends, and she was the first child born to any of our group. We were poor, living badly in a little town outside of Munich. We were underground, living in filth. We did not have experience with children, but still we knew. It was a difficult time for all of us, living that way. We thought it was inherited, her mother's brother was slow."

"Gert is not slow."

"The stories I have heard —"

"At your age, are you suddenly believing the capitalist press? *La belle dame sans merci?* Is that where you get your information, *The International Herald Tribune?*"

"Not only the press."

"Nothing you have heard is true," Bill said.

"How do you know what I have heard?"

"I know the stories, the stories in the press, the stories in the street. None of them are true. I am the one who knows the truth, all of it." Unsmiling, he looked down at Max. He had spoken the last sentence in German.

Max avoided his eyes. "I am her father, after all."

Bill said nothing, but moved so that he was behind Max, out of his vision.

"It was a noisy house. There were many arguments. Some people do not behave well when there is danger. But she was quiet as a child, always kept to herself. We were not young, her mother was thirty-eight and I was forty, when she was born. Her mother was gone during the day, working. I was often absent for other reasons. We all had our duties to perform, and we were under the strictest discipline. It was a difficult time, those years."

"You already said that."

"But exciting and passionate, perhaps a little different from now." He hesitated, thinking. "Some of what she remembers of that time, or thinks she remembers, is highly colored. Her imagination —" Max sighed and flopped his hands on his knees. The only sound in the room was the squeak of his wheeze. He said, "She was a very imaginative child, a romantic."

"Yes," Bill said. "And time's short. When I spoke to our mutual friend. And arranged for our meeting. He said you would be of help. So let's get down to business."

Max said, "I will try to be of help. I am authorized to be helpful, in what way I can. My information is, they have assigned Duer to investigate. That is a measure of the seriousness." He smiled. "You are public enemies, you and Gert. Duer personally is in charge."

Bill said, "Who's Duer?"

Max sighed again, shifting position so that he could see the younger man, and observe his expression. Everyone knew who Duer was. He said, "Very clever. He is a very clever officer."

Bill moved back to the window, looking left and right. The street was as before. "So?"

"They have a picture of you and Gert. The picture was taken in Hamburg, I don't know when or where. I do not know the circumstances, it could have been last month or last year. But Hamburg now is flooded with Duer's people. Do you understand?"

"I know that."

"A few years ago, your father was in Hamburg, Is this not true?" He waited for a reply and when there was none said, "In my business, the journalist's business, we say that silence is acquiescence." He smiled winningly, point scored. "So my sources of information are not so bad. They are adequate. I have been told to assist you. I have been told not to ask too many questions, that you are uncomfortable with questions, and suspicious. Your reputation precedes you. We are eager that you be satisfied with the arrangements, and that there be mutual confidence. I am told you are a paranoid young American, obsessed with security. Americans and Jews are known to be obsessed with security. And it is only sensible to be paranoid, so I do not object to any of this. It is normal. I understand it. But still. Here we are together. We must have an exchange."

She opened the bathroom door a crack, and peeked out. She could see Max in the armchair and Bill behind him, Bill framed by the window, his face in shadows. It was no longer raining, but the light was gray. She looked at Max, a wrung-out old man; red-faced, heavier, thicker around the middle, but she would know him anywhere. She had recognized him immediately behind the false beard. She knew him by his hands, thick with long heavy fingers, and his dark eyes. He frightened her, frightened her so much she could barely look at him; in the café she had kept her eyes averted, hoping he would not see her, but then the hands were holding her rain hat. She saw his knuckles, and the nails bitten to the quick, and the mat of black hair on his wrists. His eyes, black as night, seemed to drill into her person. Did he know what she was thinking? Could he see into her tangled memory, her life, what it was like for her? Could he see her wherever she was, in the tub, in bed with Wolf? Could he read her emotions? Yes, he could; he always could, wherever she looked there he was, big as a tree, big as the Brandenburger Tor and as indestructible. Watching him through the crack in the door, she began to tremble; she smoothed her mind, and tamped it down. She made it as placid and unreadable as the surface of a pond on a hot summer's day, thick and opaque as dark tea.
Pour the tea, darling.
Yes, Papa.

Isn't she looking well?
A tragedy.
Ill so many years.
Pour the tea, darling.

Wolf so good, betraying nothing. Wolf behaving as if it were normal, this reunion. Wolf so handsome and good, pouring the tea when he saw her hands shaking. She watched them now, through the crack in the door, her father talking in his deep guttural. She put her hands over her ears. It was correct that they were with her black-eyed father now, in this apartment. It was not his. She knew the way he lived, knew his bourgeois love of old furniture and thick carpets, his taste for the bourgeois commonplace, and he would never live in an apartment like this one. It was too — ordinary, with its blond wood furniture and glass-topped coffee table, the plastic tea service, the newspapers piled in the corner. Her father thought of himself *comme il faut*. And the district was conspicuous, near the zoo. He looked uncomfortable, as opposed to Wolf, who fit in anywhere. Wolf wanted something from him and he was reluctant to give it, whatever it was. They had discussed Wolf's approach and he promised he would be careful — circumspect, alert. Expect treachery, she had said. Watch him every minute. Watch his dark side. Treachery was typical of her father. It was normal.

She did not want to show herself. She would wait until they had concluded their conversation, making whatever arrangements they were making. She trusted Wolf. She had never found cause to regret living inside his forehead, imagining him imagining her, seeing through his eyes. She depended on him to arrange the future that she would secure, never having lost her early enchantment with his voice, as soft and sweet and full of promise and satisfaction as Mick Jagger's.

Wolf watched her open the door a crack. He could tell from the frightened expression in her face that she was not with them. She was way back in her mind somewhere, living in her vision of the future. Her mouth and eyes were troubled and he knew that had to do with Max. Max, a dark shadow from the first day they met, when he chanced to stop at the café in St. Germain to read the *Herald Tribune*. It had taken her weeks to speak a complete sentence, but it didn't matter because he thought he could read her mind; in those days, he had a belief in magic. *Why are you afraid of your father?* And he had hit home, as he knew he would. Everyone had a doppelganger, and Max was hers; as the ambassador was his. He knew her because he knew himself: looking at her was like looking into a mirror, and when he spoke he knew he was understood.

She opened the door another inch. It had been a calculated risk, meeting Max in the café; but it had been the safest of the available options. He wanted Max off-balance and if that meant Gert being off-balance too, well, it was unavoidable. Everything had its price. But she had done very well, with Max and with the boy, following the scenario to the letter, dropping her rain hat and remaining indifferent. She had not flinched when Max approached. She had not looked at any of them, and all the time they were undressing her; they stripped her naked. All the men in the café were staring at her — some openly, others not — but that, too, was unavoidable. On other occasions, it was useful. Her eyes were narrowed now, no more than slits. He tugged at his ear, a signal for Gert to stay where she was. He could not be certain she understood the signals. Gert was not always predictable.

She pulled back into the darkness, her face invisible now; he could see only the black toes of her shoes. Max was talking, a long reminiscence about the old days, the nineteen fifties in voluptuous Berlin. He and his friends had taken a little pockmarked house near the Dahlem, pretty little place with a garden in the back, on Sundays they'd take long walks in the Grunewald, it was there he'd met Gert's mother. . . . He listened with a show of interest, Max circling the target. He saw nothing of her in him, everything about them was dissimilar; his heavy build and bank clerk's face, and volubility. But there was no one like Gert, he had never imagined anyone like Gert.

"We were cautious in those days," Max said, smiling as if he expected a reply. When none came, he went on, "It was the effect of the war, and being on the run for so long. And we never knew the fine points of the program. We never knew the end point, the destination. Do you see? Everything was uphill. In those days, Berlin was the center of the universe. But" — he brightened — "many of us are still alive, and that's something. We are still around, here and there. Doing our jobs. Semiretired." He leaned forward, grinning, biting his lower lip, homing in at last. "My friend, tell me this one thing, now that we are together here. It would help me so much to know, and I am burning with curiosity. You remember Aachen?"

He nodded, knowing this was coming, expecting it.

"Aachen. It was about two years ago, that *aktion?*"

He said, "About that."

"Charlemagne's city, his court, before he became Emperor of the West. Was that Gert, in Aachen? I think it was. The newspapers said that a girl put the device in the *Damen*. The girl drank beer with the American soldiers, and the only thing the bartender remembered was that she spoke very little and seemed . . . distracted. He thought that perhaps she was Italian, something about the way she looked and moved. The soldiers gave a description, and naturally it didn't fit at all. Blond hair, short legs, jewelry, sneakers, a little red hat, a dumpy little tart. But I know that Gert has the ability to . . . change herself. She could have been an actress, my Gert. Mother Courage one night, Hedda Gabler the next night. She has range, do you not agree? There were two groups that claimed responsibility, and I knew that one was false. And I had never heard of the other. And when I read the account, I thought it must be her. It sounded like her, my Gert."

"No," he said.

Max continued, warming to the subject, "And the incredible thing, the girl leaves the café only minutes — seconds, according to one newspaper — before the device explodes. An act of daring. Looks at her watch. Oh, she says, I have to go collect my little sister, who is at school. I have to catch a bus for the school. I must leave right away. Don't go, Herr Hauptmann, I'll be back. And a few seconds later, when she is in the street, supposedly waiting for the bus, the device explodes. Except when witnesses are questioned, no one remembers a girl in a red hat waiting for a bus." He smiled. "How many killed?"

"Four," he said. "And a dozen wounded."

"I understand about the security," Max said.

"Gert has never been in Aachen."

"Nor does she have a little sister. As I say, I understand about the security. I understand about security, and anyone's natural reluctance to explain things. This is normal. But I keep wondering. I can't help myself. After Aachen, there was the industrialist in Strasbourg."

"Yes," he said.

"The industrialist was seen with a woman in a café near the cathedral. The woman was fashionably dressed, apparently a tourist. Their conversation was animated, according to witnesses. Then he vanished, no word at all for a week. Finally the family receives a letter, demanding money and the release of prisoners in — Chile?"

"Spain," he said. "Basques."

"Yes, of course. The letter allows forty-eight hours for compliance, obviously an impossible limit. No more messages, and a month later the body is found in a car near the Église Saint Thomas. The authorities believe the kidnapers, murderers now, were making a point: in the Église Saint Thomas lies the remains, the tomb, of Marshal Saxe. A neat twist. Kidnapers with a sense of humor."

"What was the point, do you know?"

Max grinned broadly. "And in the past two years there are perhaps three other *aktions* that I read about in the newspaper and say to myself, that *sounds*. Like Gert! That sounds like Gert and her American friend, although various groups claim responsibility. Muslims, Irish, Italians, Dutch. The *aktions,* with the single exception of the industrialist — whose name was not known outside Strasbourg — are always directed against anonymous people. Soldiers in a café, an obscure government employee leaving his home, a second-level police official. And now I wonder when I will read about someone conspicuous. Someone whose name will be recognized, in Europe and in America. I wonder when that will be. And I wonder whether I will be pleasantly surprised. Whether it will be a positive step, an advance on our long march. Helpful or not helpful. At the present moment, I have no way of knowing." He sighed, lifting his eyebrows, a bank clerk reviewing the paper on a bad loan. "So there is worry. There is concern about reliability. I mean the stability and integrity of your operation. One respects independence, that is foregone. It is a necessity. It is to be admired. But independence can become egoism, no? A group that operates without regard for comrades whose advice and counsel would be valuable — such a group is often a liability, because of the element of surprise. We are on the same side, after all."

"Security is necessary," he said.

"My people. They are smart people, they are not idiots. They have experience. They have knowledge that you, perhaps, do not possess. Despite your success. Perhaps because of your success. My people worry. They worry all the time."

He nodded, indicating the point was understood.

"This has nothing to do with security. This has to do with control. You can call it consultation."

"Well," he began. The fat fool. Control and consultation. When you had control and consultation, you had no security. When there was a bureaucracy there was insecurity.

"One last question. So that I am in the picture. I want to ask you about Munich. This is the Munich of October 22, 1983. Munich was a cause for concern. It was a broken operation, that was how we saw it. How we pieced it together. And if the authorities had not been so stupid. If they had only believed their own eyes, my Gert would now be in custody. You, too, in all likelihood."

"I am told there was bad timing."

"Bad timing, yes. Bad timing."

"Perhaps the watches were not synchronized."

Max shook his head. "She arrived at the hotel room at exactly the wrong moment. The security guard opened the door. She said she had knocked at the wrong room. And that oaf, that idiot, did not press. Did not ask her which room she wanted. Did not ask her for identification. Did not ask her to explain herself. Who are you, Fräulein? What are you doing on this floor? May I see your identity card? What is your errand, at two in the afternoon? And may I look into your handbag, please? No, none of that. Not one question. He waved her away, and so she was able to leave the hotel undetected, and unidentified. And unsearched. And it was only later, when the oaf was obliged to make a report —" Max opened his mouth, a soundless laugh. It was as if the fate of Europe had been decided that afternoon. "And you, friend. Where were you when my Gert was knocking on the door of room 409?"

"Synchronizing the watches," he said. Max had the story about three-quarters right. It was a broken operation, and they had been very lucky. Bad timing. Poor Gert.

"Not amusing," Max said. "And as it happened, the target of that particular operation of yours. That target was not the correct target. I tell you that in all confidence. And in all sincerity. If your operation had succeeded, it would have been a great embarrassment, a gross error."

That depends on who you talk to, he thought but did not say. They stared at each other, Max waiting for a reply. Bill thought, So this is what they are like, so formal, and so much withheld. But that was the essence of formality, after all. Well, he had longed to meet Max Mueller and now he had. The famous revolutionist: a man with hair in his ears and a weary voice. A European, he was certainly that: wary, pessimistic, conscious of form. He resembled a sentimental Bolshevik aristocrat, cranky, querulous, resentful that Stalin was dead, Trotsky forgotten, and party discipline obsolete. Intelligent, but very cautious, a man accustomed to following orders. His life would be a series of Chinese boxes, he would know the outside shape of things, but not what the boxes contained. A man who was perhaps not quite certain of his own place in the scheme of things. "My people." Who were they? East Germans, Bulgarians, one of those two; with the Soviets manipulating the wires. Max Mueller would not understand about free-lance *aktion*. He would not understand a campaign where everything was personal, including the discipline. He said, "That depends on who you talk to."

Max gave a little contemptuous wave of his hand, with a harsh sigh, *pah,* Maria Theresa dismissing a courtier's limp explanation.

Bill smiled. He was beginning to like Max Mueller. He said, "About Munich. There are one or two facts you don't know. Maybe your people know, though I doubt it. I don't have the feeling that your people go very far below the surface of things. For example" — he decided to throw one pebble into the pond, to watch Max react — "the oaf is not an oaf."

"It is not good to argue," Max said.

"It is a question of point of view, the selection of the target."

Max shook his head again. "A disturbing attitude, that is what I mean. That is what worries my people."

"Your people worry me, Max."

"Yes?"

"Their caution. Their insistence on discipline, but only their discipline. Their fondness for hired guns. Too many wheels within wheels, your people miss opportunities, on account of the bureaucracy. You're like the American Pentagon, you're muscle-bound. You're not flexible. You approach every operation like Desert One, and you fuck it up."

Max laughed, amused and amazed. "You are quite wrong about that. We would never, never have executed a Desert One. Never."

He said, "You never move at the propitious time, and at the other end of the scale — I take your point about Desert One, though you are wrong — you're terrified of failure. You won't move until the odds are one hundred to one and then someone says, Wait a minute. Too risky. Let's wait until the odds are two hundred to one. You want the error factor to be zero, and it never is. You have too many people and they talk too much. They talk to each other, and sooner or later the word gets around. Your people are dangerous. Dangerous to us, Gert and me. How do you think it is that I know about you. That I knew where to reach you, and how?"

Max hesitated. "From Gert."

"Not from Gert. You know better than that."

"Well," he said.

"Christ, Max. If you think that, you're really stupid."

Max colored, and raised a warning finger.

"Gert does not *understand*. She does not understand things in that way." He looked at Max, tense now. "Word is around, and I heard it. And I acted on it."

"I am in all the dossiers," Max said.

"Some, not all. And the information in them is wrong."

"Yes," Max said.

"Would you like chapter and verse?"

"No," he said.

"Your people are too old. No offense, Max. But your people do not understand the situation as I do. They do not understand the Americans, and how the Americans react to a breakdown of order. I could read you the new regulations from the Department of State. I have them in my possession. Your people would dismiss these regulations as of no interest, obvious, in some ways amusing. They have to do with personal security of diplomats. New procedures for the protection of embassies, the families of diplomats. Who is assigned bodyguards, who isn't. They know that these measures are cosmetic only, more irritating to them than to us. And the idea is to keep them irritated, off-balance, uncertain, weary, and afraid. And angry." As he spoke he paced the room. Max's eyes never left him. "Now we need help, Gert and I."

"I will have to know details."

He said, "No details."

"Not every detail. But I will have to know the main lines. Surely that is understandable. It is normal. What do you expect from us, a blank check?"

"Yes," he said.

"That is impossible."

"I need four passports, two for me and two for Gert. American and German for me, German and French for Gert. Expiration dates two years from right now. I need two cars, one with German registry, one with French, rental cars, Avis. They try harder. The German car I want to pick up in Cologne, the French in Paris. I also need money, but that's less important. One can always find money in Europe during the tourist season."

Max was silent a moment. "It takes time."

"Two weeks, Comrade. Surely you can do it in two weeks."

There was silence between them while Max thought, his eyes closed. He seemed almost to be dozing. "There was a report that you met your father in Hamburg, Your mother and father, a few years ago, that you met them and had a conversation. This is a report that we have and I must know if it is true."

"It is true," he said.

"You had them taken to your apartment?"

"An apartment. Not mine."

"Gert was there?"

"No."

"You talked for an hour, the three of you."

"Ninety minutes."

"Why? Why did you do this?"

"Why I did it is my business. Say I wanted to see them again. You can say that in your report."

"You see," Max said, "again. Again, this raises questions. It raises

165

questions about stability. Such a meeting was not wise. It was dangerous to do such a thing. And its purpose is unclear and that, too, raises questions."

"Everything worked out fine." He smiled. "We had a full and frank exchange of views."

"Herr North." Exasperated.

"And our security — my security, and Gert's, and the security of our people — is for me to decide."

"How many people are there. Under your supervision. Whose security is your responsibility?" There was no answer, as Max knew there wouldn't be. "What I am suggesting is that you are not an independent government."

"Yes, I am," he said. "That's the point."

"It is not good to argue," Max said.

He said, "Passports and cars."

"I must know the details."

"You don't want to know them."

"Those are my orders. I will speak to my people. I will tell them what has been said here. What you have said, and what you haven't said. That is all I can do. They will decide."

"How many people, Max? How large a meeting will it be? Two people, five? Ten? A ministry? And how many stenographers, and where will the transcripts go?"

"That is foolish," he said.

"Well, Max. I can get the goods elsewhere."

"Then why don't you? Why do you come to me, knowing that an explanation will be required? Surely you know that."

"I thought it was time we met. I thought it was time we sat across the tea table face to face, got to know each other. To see if there was mutual confidence, and understanding. Your experience has been very different from mine. I wanted to see if we were on the same side, given our different experience, our backgrounds. What is to be done? I wanted to see what you looked like, your manner. The authority that you have. The questions you would ask. I do not know very many from your generation." As he looked at him, he knew they could never work together; they were out of synch, and would always be out of synch. Perhaps it was a question also of nationality. Max Mueller had too much of the wrong kind of experience, too many failures, too many disappointments, too many after-the-fact justifications. Too much ideology, too little passion; too much history. He still distinguished between ends and means, failing to understand that the means were the ends; often the means were more expressive, more elegant, than the ends. Poor Max, he had ceased to appreciate possibilities, and his pessimism was infectious. He put his hand on the older man's shoulder. "And of course because of Gert," he said.

"I need to know the main lines of your operation," Max said.

He said abruptly, "Let's take a walk."

Max hesitated, then rose slowly. "What about Gert?"

He said, "I'll see to Gert. You wait." He smiled reassuringly and stepped into the bathroom. Gert was standing in the shower stall in the darkness. He could hear her breathing. He kissed her lightly and said they were going, would be gone for an hour, no more. They were taking a walk, he and her father. He and Max together, as they had planned. He repeated the words, and then he watched her nod. He lowered his voice and asked if she understood what she had to do when they left the apartment. She smiled brilliantly, and kissed him. He walked back to the living room.

Max was staring out the window, his expression thoughtful.

He said, "This room is stuffy, don't you agree? We need a walk outside."

"It's still raining," Max said.

"Only a drizzle."

"Gert will stay here?"

He nodded. "Until we return."

Max said softly, "You have a destination?"

He said, "No. I just thought, a little walk, a walk in the zoo."

5

ON THE STREET AGAIN, they both paused and looked left
and right. The Volkswagen was gone, and there was no
Volvo in sight. There were no pedestrians on the sidewalk, except for an old man and his dog. Max watched the old
man a moment, then they began to stroll through the rain in the
direction of the zoo.

He said to Max, "Did you know your father well?"

"Of course," he said, "he was my father."

Bill was silent. They walked on to the intersection. Bill said, "What
did he do? How did he make a living?"

"He was a factory manager. The factory made wheels for military vehicles, staff cars and troop carriers. My father used to say
that an army did not travel on its stomach, but on his wheels." He
smiled. "He died in 1928 when the factory closed. Everything closed
in 1928, the entire country closed down, the inflation, reparations
to the victors. The spoils of war. I was nine years old, but I remember him very well, he was an excellent plant manager. His plant set
records in the war, I mean production records. They gave him a
small pension when the factory closed, but still my mother sold the
house. We lived near Danzig."

"He would play with you as a child?"

Max looked sideways, puzzled. "Play? No, we didn't play. Why would we play? I played with my classmates." Up the street was the fading *waa-waa* of an ambulance siren. Max began to walk a little more quickly.

"You admired him?"

"A terrible injustice was done my father. The swine who owned the factories, my father's factory and other factories, simply closed them down. Put a padlock on the gate, and a sign: Factory closed until further notice. And went to live in Baden-Baden with his wife and his mistress. He was waiting, he told my father, for discipline to return to Germany. Still, my father could not bring himself to question what had been done, or to criticize. He had known the family for many years, the old baron as well as the young one. My mother was a vocal woman, in her opinions a radical. My father was always a company man, but then the company let him go. Because of his loyalty, he was a serf in their eyes. So I loved him, but I did not admire him."

They walked on, crossing the boulevard to the zoo. A group of children were waiting at the ticket window, spirits undampened by the rain. They stood in line behind the noisy children.

Bill said, "When did you become a Marxist?"

"I have always been a Marxist. From the earliest time that I can remember. Some of my friends when we were boys wanted to be army officers or lawyers or businessmen or civil servants. I always wanted to be a Marxist. I looked on it as a career, as my father looked on his career. Perhaps as your father looks on his career."

"My father always wanted to be a diplomat," he said.

"A reactionary."

"He would say patriot."

Max made a noise, and they both laughed.

At the ticket counter, Bill fumbled for coins and Max paid. The ticket seller looked naturally to Max and, as naturally, Max had the correct change in his hand.

"My father is in Washington now." They were looking at the zebras, who were huddled together in the rain. One of the children threw a piece of chocolate, and was admonished by his companions. "He is doing his patriotic duty in Washington. They have put him into a hospital. That is the last I have heard."

Max said, "He is ill?"

"I doubt it," he said. "My father has always been healthy."

Max said, "I know a little of his career, but not much." They were walking along behind the children. "I have looked at his C.V. But a C.V. conceals as much as it discloses, no?"

Bill said, "He has done their work in Africa, and also in Bonn. And in Madrid. I have watched him in his office, on the phone and talking to people, and at receptions. Very smooth and controlled. He is a very smooth American diplomat, good with languages. Often droll. Of course he is a company man."

Max said, "And the company will never let him go. No padlock on the gate. No sign saying closed until further notice."

"They might, depending on the circumstances. Depending on what happens. But they would let him go very quietly, and arrange for other work."

"Yes," Max said. "But he would have his pension."

"Oh, yes," Bill said. "They are very good about that." He paused and looked through the iron gates at the Cape buffalo, huge, horns the length of baseball bats.

Max said, "What would cause them to let him go?"

"Ugly creatures, aren't they?"

"A scandal, I suppose," Max mused. "A scandal of sex or of money. The Americans rarely have scandals of politics. I mean loyalty."

"He has never cared about money," Bill said.

"Sex then," said Max.

Bill shrugged. Possibly.

"Not loyalty, surely," Max said.

"He is an excellent diplomat. He has many commendations, including one from Bonn. He does their work expertly. Any ministry would be happy to have him. He is a professional in every way, and proud of his professionalism. Did you know he was first in his class to become ambassador?"

Max looked at him. "Class?"

Bill smiled, turning away slightly so that Max would not notice his amusement. He said, "Foreign Service class. He was the first of his class to become ambassador, and that was his ambition. Always had been. He was very young when he realized his ambition. It made him proud, naturally, he and my mother both. They felt —

vindicated. I suppose that was what it was. What do you think, Max? It must have been the same with you, so successful at a very young age, wanting terribly to do something, and doing it. Setting a goal and achieving it, as a young man wet behind the ears. But he had a great record, and he never turned down an assignment. You would understand that, Max. Wherever they wanted him to go, he went. He served the President, and it didn't matter which President." The Cape buffalo was standing motionless, staring at them. The children had moved off a little way, ignoring the animals, kicking a bright red soccer ball. Bill remembered the day the ambassador received word of his appointment. They had dinner together, the three of them. His father and mother drank too much Champagne. They were noisy and unbuttoned, congratulating each other, his mother so flirtatious, the ambassador so cute. They poured him a glass of Champagne but he did not drink it; he did not care for wine. The ambassador made a sloppy toast, and his mother laughed and laughed. Bill turned to Max, having one more thing to add, but the older man had stepped away and was standing quietly looking at the ostriches. The cries of children rose around them. "The ambassador is one of their prizes, Max. Always on display. Something about him reminds me of that creature," he said, pointing to the sullen Cape buffalo. "Very still, stupid-looking, large, dangerous."

Max nodded slowly. He had the air of a man who was listening carefully.

"So it is a fine career. He has seen the world. The secretary of state is his friend."

Max said, "The Americans are very successful at concealing scandal. The most successful of any country, and are the first to object to scandal elsewhere. It would surprise me if they let him go, a man first in his class. A man who is friends with the secretary of state. It would be an embarrassment to them. What would cause them to let him go?"

He watched the children skylarking, the ball passed and deftly kicked. One of the boys showed promise. He asked, "How did your father die?"

"He was tired. They called it a heart attack."

"Did he take a long time to die?"

"It was very quick."

"I would like his to be slow."

Max smiled, raising his eyebrows. He did not understand Americans. He did not understand what animated them. They had an insufferable belief in the rightness of their own actions. They had no discipline, and were never predictable; they were not patient. He thought of them in negatives, not this, not that. And of the American young, he knew nothing.

"Strike at the heart of things," Bill said.

"Yes," Max said nervously.

There was a sudden cry, and in a moment two boys were tugging at Max's sleeve. The ball had gotten away from them, it was Johann's fault, a mis-hit ball. Inept Johann stood to one side looking at his shoes. But there it was in the buffalo's cage, and what could be done now? Max looked at the boys and shrugged. He was deep in his own thoughts, wondering how far to push the American.

One of the boys said, "It's a new ball."

Max said impatiently, "Let's move on."

The boy turned to Bill, so tall, who was standing on tiptoe, looking into the cage, measuring the height of the iron fence. "My father bought it for me only yesterday, and now stupid Johann —" The ball had come to rest between the animal and the fence, a spot of brilliant color in the gray cage. The buffalo had not moved. He gave no sign of noticing the red ball. Bill took off his raincoat and handed it to Max, moving a few steps away, looking at the fence now at an angle. He looked around for a guard but saw no one. There was just him and Max, and the two boys, and Johann miserable on the sidelines.

Max said, "Don't be foolish." He slung the raincoat over Bill's shoulder. "This is not your affair."

"How high is the fence, Max?"

"I have no idea." He turned away, clenching his fists. "This is absurd."

"Do you want to make a bet, Max?"

The boy said, "It's only a buffalo, sir."

"How badly do you want your ball?"

"Very badly," the boy said. "It is new. My father will be very angry."

172

"Will he beat you?"

"Oh, yes," the boy said.

"With a strap?"

"His fists, sir," the boy said. He seemed about to cry. "He will beat me with his fists."

"You are a big boy, you could fight back."

"He is my father, sir."

Bill turned to Max and smiled sardonically. Then he handed the boy his raincoat and commenced to rock back and forth, heel to toe, practicing, finding his rhythm. He tucked his trousers into his socks, took off his wristwatch, and rolled up his shirt-sleeves. The boys moved back, looking solemnly at one another, very quiet now. Johann opened his mouth as if to say something, then didn't. One of the boys glared at him, raising his open palm.

"You can wait over there, Max." He pointed to a bench under a giant elm. "An innocent bystander, that's you. Give a shout if you see anyone." He kicked twice, very high, unlimbering. He knew he could scissor over the fence, had scissored higher many times in school and in college. But he had not jumped in a year or more, and then it was a makeshift bar in a public park, his audience Gert and two friends. He closed his eyes, recollecting the look of things when he was in college, the other athletes, the timer, the bar, the sawdust pit, the little knot of spectators in the infield. It was good that he was wearing sneakers. Suddenly he felt wonderful, exhilarated with a fine anticipation. He was concentrating now, deep-breathing, collecting oxygen. He took his belt in a notch and loped to the fence, stopping at the last moment. He calculated its height again, noted the place on the pavement from which he would kick off, and took a last look around. He walked back, his hands on his hips, his eyes on his shoe tops. It was all mental. Again he began to rock, breathing deeply, synchronizing his arms. He forgot about the boys and the rain, the red soccer ball and the angry father who struck with his fists. The animal was on the edges of his vision. When he began his loping run he knew that all the pieces were in place and when he jumped, sublimely airborne, he looked back to see Max stationary under the elm tree, his hands plunged into the pockets of his coat, looking like the unwilling subject of an old photograph, menacing, grainy, a souvenir from the last century.

He landed right foot first, slipping to one knee, then to all fours.

173

He gagged, aware at once of a thick animal stench coming at him in waves. Rising, he saw his sneakers were covered with black shit; his hands were wet where they had touched the ground. But the stench was the animal itself. The beast stared at him with brilliant dark eyes, still unblinking, but his right foot beginning to twitch. He had last seen buffalo in the bush of central Africa, bad-tempered, unpredictable creatures, deceptively clumsy. Great trophies, the ambassador had said, focusing his Nikon, clicking away from the safety of the embassy Land-Rover. The red ball was in front of him and without taking his eyes off the animal he bent to pick it up and in one loose motion threw it behind him, high over the fence. The animal lowered its head, and tapped the ground with its right hoof, a strangely dainty gesture. He could hear its breathing. Behind him he heard laughter, the boys chattering. Max said something and they fell silent. He did not turn around but moved crabwise, his hands at his sides, to get a sense of direction and the distance back to the fence. Six paces, no slipping in shit, no dry runs. The animal took a step toward him and he stopped, straightening. He could not remember about their eyesight, whether it was weak or strong; he thought weak. He remembered the guide moving the old Winchester off-safe when the ambassador got out of the Land-Rover to take the picture, focusing on a grazing sleepy buffalo. This one was not sleepy, nor in the wild. He stood facing the buffalo, his heart pounding. He felt a great surge, and stepped forward, standing now with his arms folded across his chest. His own eyesight was unnatural: he thought he could see into the animal's soul. Then he was talking, mouthing the words, directing his language to the animal. Come and get it, ugly bastard. Beautiful bastard. He knew the animal would not move, he could feel his own will overpowering it. He stood sideways now, between the buffalo and the fence. The animal snorted and shook its head, moving at last. But by then he had taken his six quick steps and lofted himself over the iron gate, sailing it seemed for minutes, scissoring over the spikes to land again on all fours, Max a few steps away. He noticed for the first time that it was raining hard. Rain dripped off Max's hat. There seemed to him an enormous silence, broken only by the drip of the rain and the pounding of his own heart.

He laughed loudly, clapping Max on the back. He could not believe he had done it. The older man was looking at him with dour amusement. He described the stench inside the cage, and hypnotizing the buffalo, staring at it squarely, not retreating, showing no fear. It was a spur-of-the-moment thing, and it had worked. A target of opportunity, seized at the propitious moment. That's the way you have to do it, Max. He laughed again, the tension all gone now. Then he craned his neck, looking around him. "Where are the boys?"

"They're gone," Max said, fluttering his hands. "You can see them go, there." The first of the boys was disappearing around the corner of the elephant house. One of them had the red soccer ball, and Johann had his raincoat. They appeared to be laughing, the scene reminiscent somehow of Mark Twain.

He said, "What the fuck."

Max smiled. "They were gone before I could do anything, and I must say I was transfixed, watching you and that creature. I was waiting for you to produce a red cape. But the boys were interested only in the raincoat. The ball was a bonus. Clever little devils. I dare say they knew their man."

He said, "The little shits."

"The young are not to be trusted," Max said blandly. "There is no respect, owing to the breakdown of the German family. Everyone runs wild. There is no authority. It is the American influence, everyone for himself. This is well known. And it's the same everywhere in Europe, France, Italy, the Low Countries. It's a scandal." He paused in his inventory of causes of the breakdown of family relations in Europe. "I assume and hope that there was nothing valuable in the raincoat. Nothing that could prove embarrassing."

He shot Max a sharp look. "The raincoat was valuable, it's the only one I have." He rolled down his shirt sleeves and pulled his trousers out of his socks. It was raining hard now. Inside the cage the buffalo was standing with its nose almost touching the iron spikes, its fur glistening in the rain.

Max said, "You do have a fondness for the beau geste."

He looked left over Max's shoulder to the zoo entrance, searching. But he saw nothing unusual, and no one familiar. A few families with small children were leaving, hurrying home. In the distance he could hear the gentle murmur of Sunday traffic. He looked at his wristwatch, thinking.

Max said, "Wouldn't you agree?"

"The little shits set me up."

"Yes," Max said.

"As you say," he said. "The young are not to be trusted."

"Quite a bag of tricks, it was neatly done. You have to admire them. In fact, their *aktion* required serious discipline. Meticulous planning and concentration, a knowledge of the terrain and the enemy. And most of all, good timing." Max unwrapped a fat cigar, wet it, and lit it, the match flaring. "They are good actors, those boys. They should be in the Berliner Ensemble, eh?" Grinning, he took a mini-umbrella from his coat pocket, opened it, and they began to walk back the way they had come. Dusk was falling; the zoo was about to close. What a lonely, strange, and sinister place it was, the Berlin Zoo at nightfall. From somewhere nearby an animal coughed, the sound drowned by the clatter of a passing train. In the darkness it was difficult to see the outline of the cages. Bill imagined himself in the bush, where when it rained it was unimaginable that there could be sunshine anywhere on earth. He and Max were walking close together, silent now, huddled under the umbrella. He turned away, the better to avoid the foul smell of Max's cigar.

"What happened to your wife, Max?"

"My wife?"

"Gert's mother."

"She died."

"How did that happen?"

"It was many years ago."

"Yes."

"She was not herself."

"Is that a fatal disease?"

They passed through the turnstiles and were now on the sidewalk. Max was allowing him the lead. Bill looked left and right, from the riotous fluorescence of the Ku-damm to the stately somber leafy darkness of the Tiergarten. They walked right. The streetlights winked on, dim in the rain.

He said, "Gert wonders."

"She was very young. We were living then in the east."

176

"Were they close?"

Max shrugged impatiently, a stupid question. "Of course. A mother and daughter."

He said, "Not always."

"I cannot believe that Gert has a memory of that time. What does she — say?"

"Gert doesn't *say* anything, Max. Sometimes she reacts to things that I say, or things that she sees, here and there, around. Songs that she hears. The songs especially upset her. Often she draws pictures, illustrations. They are pictures of that time, when you were living in the east and her mother was still alive. You'd be surprised, she's a very good artist."

"Gert?" Max stiffened, silent for a moment. He threw his cigar into the bushes, beyond one of the wooden benches that flanked the walk. The smell of tobacco was still around them. "That is hard to believe, my Gert. An artist." Then, "This is very interesting, but let us go back to what we were speaking of. Before. You spoke of striking at the heart of things. What did you mean?"

He said, "If I could give her an account of her mother's death, something plausible. Something that would put her mind at ease. Better I do it than you." Bill's voice was soft. "The truth would be a great joy. It would help her. Help us both."

"It's in the past," Max said.

"So is Gert," he said.

"She was sick," Max said.

"Yes, you said that."

"She wanted to leave, and so she left. It would be fair to say she abandoned me. She did not understand my work, and she did not like the east. She was always complaining. We were not suited, Ruth and me."

"She left, but Gert stayed."

"Of course. Gert was a child."

"She did not take Gert with her."

"That was not permitted," Max said.

"Who killed her, Max?"

"I do not like these questions."

"As you say, it was long ago. And it does not matter to me. It matters to Gert."

The older man sighed. It was somewhere between a sigh and a

snort. He did not say anything for a moment; the umbrella wavered. Finally, "I have no idea."

"Gert has always wondered, and at night she dreams. It is the missing part to her puzzle. I think that is so. How can I be sure? Gert lives in the shadows. She needs to know the events, what happened and why. Surely you can understand that, Max. You yourself . . ." He left the thought to hang. Ahead he saw a figure stumble, and collapse on one of the benches. A derelict, a man of the street; there were many such in Berlin. The figure curled up under a newspaper, its back to them.

"I want to return to your proposal."

"In a moment, Max."

"What's done is done, so far as Ruth is concerned. She was a disagreeable woman, thinking always of the present, her own comfort. Where she went when she left, what she did. It is impossible to say. You can tell Gert that it was a border incident. Or I will tell her. I can tell her in a sentence."

"A border incident," he said flatly.

"In those days there were many such incidents. Her mother was not well, and it was no one's fault. Perhaps she was lonely, too. She made a series of tragic mistakes. And we were not suited. I have nothing more to tell you about Gert's mother. It was many years ago, and I was never fully briefed. I had no need to know, and I did not want to know. She caused many problems. If Gert was one of the problems, so be it." He spoke with sudden violence. "Women like that, they leave a trail of misery. They are useless to themselves, and to everyone else. I know only that she is dead, and better off dead. It is better for Gert that she is dead. She received a proper burial. She left no estate. That is what I know."

"Who looked after Gert?"

"My associates."

"There was an incident," he said.

Max turned on him, his eyes hard. "This is not your business, you know nothing of our life then. I resent your questions. You spoke of striking at the heart of things. Wasn't that what you said, before the foolishness with the ball in the cage? We are conducting a business arrangement, isn't that so? That is why we are here. I have no interest in ancient history. And it is not your business, and not why we are here. You are here to confide details, and I am ready to hear them. Let us return to the facts: two passports, two cars, and money.

"An incident with one of your associates, Max."

"I know nothing more."

"One of your associates raped your daughter."

"That is impossible."

"No. It happened."

"It is a fantasy."

"And she killed him."

"A fantasy. That is Gert's fantasy. She had the same illness as her mother. It is a family illness." Max picked up the pace, and now they were walking rapidly through the Tiergarten. He heard the hum of traffic again. They were not far from the Philharmonie, and he wondered if there was a concert that night, von Karajan conducting Wagner or Brahms, ta-de-da, boom, boom, boom. He began to whistle a listless tune. Max was watchful under the umbrella. Their heads were close together, though the rain had moderated.

"No fantasy," he said.

"I think perhaps Gert should be in the Berliner Ensemble, too. Perhaps you also, Herr North. *Wolf*."

He was careful now, putting his hand on Max's arm, restraining him, slowing him down. He looked behind him; they were not quite alone. "We have so little in common, you and I," he said, speaking softly so that Max had to lean into him. "It is as if we come from different centuries. When you spoke of your father, I listened hard. I tried to recapture the time, 1928, and a man in charge of a wheel company, breaking production records. This was a time when my own father was not yet born, and my grandfather still in Berlin. Then, years later, your daughter is raped by an associate. Here we are, you and I, in the same line of work, so to speak. Yet our personal histories have nothing in common. I was interested when you described your own relations with your father. You loved him but did not respect him, and I thought that a strange turn. You loved him because he was your father, and for no other quality. It is not the same with me. I do not respect the ambassador, for his career, and his qualities. And I hate him."

Max seemed to relax. "You are too personal."

He said, "I'm going to kill him."

179

Max sighed, it almost sounded like a chuckle.

"That is what I must do."

"All right," Max said. "It is what you must do. But what happens then? What is the consequence?"

"I am not a fortuneteller. I do not read the future."

"But there must be a consequence. What is it? An ambassador is killed. His son is the suspect. What is the consequence of that? Why your father? Why not the secretary? Why not one of your father's associates? Why not a NATO general?"

"No," he said. "That's the point. Who knows what will happen? What is the natural consequence of the death of a father? The idea is to set an event in motion, and watch it spin. This event will be like a spinning top, now here, now there, finally spinning out of control." His fingers tightened on Max's forearm. Almost there.

"You're hurting my arm."

He said, "I will act in accordance with the laws of physics."

Max looked him full in the face, afraid at what he saw there. He wondered, Which law? Heisenberg, no doubt. They never grew up, the self-centered American young, natural products of an ignorant, arrogant nation, a nation without discipline or mettle. This boy was unpredictable and dangerous, and it was late. Max looked at his watch a long moment, suddenly nervous. He was thinking about the American ambassador. This was the end of it, though. He knew enough, he did not want to know more. He wanted to be quit of the boy and his patricidal schemes. Max said, "I want nothing more to do with it."

Turning, Bill relaxed his grip, grinning broadly. "Well," he said. "Here's Gert."

Max wheeled awkwardly, almost stumbling. His hands flew to his chest. For a moment, he thought it was someone else, a derelict in an oversize coat and heavy workman's shoes. But her eyes were unmistakable, so dark and fathomless. She was holding a small-caliber gun, a woman's gun no larger than a deck of cards. She pointed it at his chest. He had time enough to say "My Gert" before she fired twice. He heard both reports but felt nothing, no pain, no shock, not anything — before an oceanic weariness overcame him, and he fell.

*

Their room — rented for the night, paid in advance — was on a street off the Ku-damm. They lay in bed, looking out the window at the lights. From somewhere nearby, a street boy played the guitar, American folk music badly amplified. She buried her face in his neck, humming. Farther away was a jazz band, playing for pennies outside a record store. The street was filled with young people, Scandinavians, English, Germans, boys in jeans and T-shirts, girls in leather shorts and brightly colored hair. She had insisted that they stop and listen to the jazz band. Her feet moved with the music while she clapped her hands. He had whispered to her, and with reluctance she had moved along, down the side street to their room in the anonymous brownstone. He had looked back, anxious and fascinated. How different could it be from the 1920s, perhaps right now a young Franz Biberkopf was alighting from a trolley at Alexanderplatz in the distressed eastern sector, ready to begin again, wanting only to survive, adapting as best he could, getting in step. Getting back in line. Biberkopf, a humble workman, veteran of a violent episode, a common citizen without influence or grab, a Kleenex man: he will be the first to go. Lead him to the safe haven, let him sleep, let him be. Give him shelter, a thatched world safe for Biberkopf. Berlin, Biberkopf's center of the universe, the place where the top always spun fastest, raunchy, hilarious, psychotic, a scream of a city. Brother, can you spare a mark?

He thinks: I am yours till death.

She purrs, remembering.

A happy room, this one, filled with the brassy fluorescence of the district, magnified and concentrated by night mist, long Lang shadows, the fog of Europe. Wherever Europe is going, Berlin will get there first. The room is nondescript, charmless, their things piled carelessly on the chair, and on the high bureau his cheap brass traveling clock:

To Mel from Mom
Graduation 1975.

Complete, even to the period at the end of the thought. Mel had found it in his room in the apartment on Avenue A, the clock wrapped in tissue paper. Sent it to his friend, his only friend, at school. I have no use for it, man.

When he cranes his neck he can see the reflection of the throbbing strobe lights that had hypnotized Gert, and set her to dancing on the pavement. Pedestrians clogged the intersection, all of them on the search. In the streets were chemicals, weed, and powder enough to animate half the population of Europe. Berlin, showcase of the West, going for the gold. *Ja, Ich bin ein Berliner.*

She breathes in his ear and he smiles; her tongue tickles. He tells her of the encounter in the cage with the beast, its rancid odor and complacent face. He looks again at the clock, with him on all his travels, here and there across the boundaries of Europe, and begins to tell her of the night at Banker's Tower, Jack Horner and the girl weaving their way home from a party. Horner and Mel looking at each other, Mel's face freezing, remembering Horner's lecture that morning. *Jeez, Crown, this is pretty good. This is not bad. You're a talented boy, but it isn't done by magic. It isn't done by wishing. It's done by working, by attention to detail, each verb, each comma. The secret to writing is rewriting. So do it again.* Everyone looking at their hands, except Mel, who's looking at Horner. He'd written a story about his family, just laid it out for everyone to see. Not a story we were familiar with, not a story of suburban lawns and wine with meals. He'd written a story about the conditions of his life, his drunken father and junkie brother. He'd written all night long and I know because we were roommates, and I could hear him while he was writing. It was all *there,* you know, in one burst. And this asshole was making him chase commas. Cutting the grass of the battlefield while the dead and wounded lay about, screaming for the stretcher bearers. Horner's anxious to tell us how Henry James and Hawthorne did it, and how demanding it was, and how tre-men-dous the effort. *The secret to writing is rewriting.* He liked that concept so much he repeated it, handing Mel's story back to him. It's cluttered with notes, the son of a bitch must have spent as much time taking it apart as Mel spent putting it together. Except it's Mel's story, not his. It's Mel's life in America. Horner goes, *This is really verrrry good, but to make it excellent you're going to have to work on it, all right?* Mel didn't answer and when the bell sounded he left the classroom, went straight back to the dorm. I was going to follow, then didn't. He was really *hurt,* you know, insulted. He had given Horner a gift, and Horner had thrown it back in his face.

That night we went into the woods, drank some beer. Mel had a joint. It was late and no one was around. Returning, we saw the son of a bitch weaving across the common. He had a woman with him. Drunk, whistling to himself, his arm around the woman, nuzzling her. She was cooperating. He saw us and straightened up. We stood in the path so that they would have to go around us. Mel stood there, arms folded; then Mel began to advance. He called Horner an asshole, an ofay asshole. The woman clung to Horner and began to whimper. And that was when Mel hit him, first in the stomach and then in the face. Horner went down and Mel picked him up and hit him again. The woman had fallen and she was on her hands and knees, looking at Horner and Mel and then at me. She looked at me in a certain way and I recognized her. We locked eyes, she was looking up with — well, she was pleading with me. Horner told her to get away, "Run." And she did. She didn't even look back but took off across the common, and it was then that I put the name to the face. She was the very young wife of the dean of students, and she was as drunk as Horner. A whiff of scandal, and no matter that old Jack Horner was getting the shit beat out of him. She took off, a vanished witness. I thought about it and when I finished thinking I had a fresh understanding of their selfishness and instinct for survival at any cost, and the importance they attached to appearances, their hypocrisy and cowardice. Throw the weakest overboard. Of course that was why nothing much happened to me. They knew there was another witness, an oh-so-embarrassing witness, and that I knew who that witness was. And they knew that I knew that they knew, and that made them insecure. I had a hole card, and they didn't know if I would play it or not. It didn't matter about Mel. He was expelled at once, and no one would believe anything that Mel Crown had to say. Mel the charity case, the troublemaker, black Mel, Mel who refused to fit in. Naturally, I had no intention of saying anything. I was interested in watching them in their nervousness, listening to their official voices, lying to each other, to me, to the school. Quite a valuable lesson for a schoolboy.

So she fled across the common, never looking back. I heard a strange sound, at first I thought it was Horner. But it was Mel. He was crying. Old Horner didn't make a sound, except to grunt. That was all you could hear, his grunts and Mel's fists striking flesh and bone, and Mel's strange sounds. That night I understood how close things were to the surface, with people like Mel Crown. Horner didn't have a chance. Old Mel, he was fighting the human race that night. It was just a superb show. I thought he was going to kill the old man, but then the campus cops arrived and that was that.

You would have been proud if only you'd seen it.

What? She looks at him in alarm.

It's all right, he says. In the street he can hear the American guitar and another instrument, perhaps a balalaika. The players are dueling and the notes chase each other, faster and faster.

She gazes at him, her eyes glittering.

We did well today. He says in his conspirator's voice, We were in perfect synch. They won't find him until the morning. And they won't identify him for hours and hours. And then we'll be gone.

She burrows into him, reaching with her right hand.

He says, Tomorrow we leave for Bonn, and then Hamburg. Are you eager to see Hamburg again? It is nothing like Berlin. But we are lovers, we are lovers wherever we are, in whatever circumstances. Here, there, in the cage or out of it. And we are close to the surface, too. We are *that close*. He whispers, We are going home.

Reaching, she kisses him on the mouth.

He says, Hush. Listen to the music.

PART THREE

I

SHE WAS WORKING on the planes of Bill Jr.'s forehead when the buzzer sounded, softly at first and then louder. She did not hear it; or, more precisely, she did not notice it. She took a sip of cold coffee and, stepping back, appraised her work. Half his face was in shadows. She was talking to him under her breath, trying to get him to cooperate. She wanted him in repose in front of the window, Vineyard Sound in the background; only a suggestion of the water, and the white lighthouse at Falmouth. She moved her head left and right, trying to understand the angles. Awkward face, asymmetrical; his forehead was high and square, and she believed that if she could get it right, the eyes would follow. Her father's blue eyes, often cold, settled like big buttons at the base of his brow, wide-set. They did not give much away. The eyes disconcerted her; this was not her father's portrait, but her son's; it was necessary to take him on his own terms, not someone else's terms, not, God knows, her father's terms. Of course they were also *her* eyes, she had painted them. They were her creation, literally and figuratively. She took another step back, measuring. His forehead was furrowed as well as wide and square, reminiscent of Bill. She began to surface now. She became aware of the game on the radio,

the crowd's roar and the excited voice of the announcer, a long hit
. . . *way, way back* . . . She was listening attentively, imagining the
trajectory of the ball, the left fielder running, the crowd rising with
the ball, the ball getting smaller and smaller, the pitcher watching
it too, his back to the plate, trying to act nonchalant and not succeeding, like Bill watching a press conference on television, realizing that one artless word from the President could destroy a year's
work.

   . . . *going, going, gone* . . .

Baseball on radio was a tonic for the imagination, always forcing
you into the past; and whether the ball game was being played in
Memorial Stadium, Baltimore, or Fenway, or Cleveland Municipal
Stadium, the field in her mind's eye was Wrigley some time in the
late nineteen forties, the wind blowing out to left corner, an Em-
erald City of a field, the men in the crowd — and they were almost
all men — wearing fedoras and gray topcoats, and everyone smoking cigarettes.

She saw then that the light was failing, and she heard the buzzer.
Still staring at the canvas, she reached absently to turn off the timer.
She was concentrating on Bill Jr.'s shadowed brow, and its wealth
of associations. Then she looked at her watch, and despite the timer
she was alarmed to find that it was five o'clock, time to dress and
drive to the hospital. The game was over; it was Ripken Jr.'s homer
in the bottom of the tenth, so she switched off the radio: abrupt
silence, except for the hiss of the rain outside. She carefully cleaned
her brushes and took another sip of the coffee, dregs. She stared
out at the narrow street three stories below. There were only a few
pedestrians on O Street, all of them holding black umbrellas, proper
Washingtonians coming home from work, or on their way to the
last appointment of the day. The street had a European ambience,
with its Federal façades and tidy postage-stamp gardens, its cobblestones and shade trees and gas lamps, and thick curtains behind
wavy window glass. She watched the pedestrians for a moment,
thinking that there was no snap to their steps; they were tired,
poor babies. They were men who moved paper all day long; and
one young woman, very pretty with a discouraged face, who ducked
into the psychiatrist's house across the street: a painterly image
there, the girl pausing and collapsing her umbrella, and standing

a moment in the rain before opening the door and disappearing inside. Arrangement in gray and black, the girl so deft when she collapsed the umbrella, like a golfer addressing a putt, and so resigned when she opened the door; no doubt the weather would be worse inside.

She picked up the telephone and dialed his room. While the phone rang, she watched the cat rise from the chair and stretch, like a pitcher looking in for the sign, then stalk from the room. Five rings, no answer. Sometimes the boy answered if the phone was where he could reach it, and if he was in the mood. Most of the time he wasn't, and who could blame him. Then she remembered that Bill was seeing Hartnett and Carruthers, and hung up.

She covered the canvas and left her studio, closing and locking the door. The house looked unfamiliar to her, as it always did when she emerged from work; even her own paintings in the bedroom looked as if they had been drawn by someone else. The house was dark but she did not turn on the lights. She avoided looking at the photograph of Bill Jr., fearing that it would interfere with the image forming in her mind, and the truth of a photograph was momentary, accurate only at that split second when the shutter moved. She undressed and walked naked into the bathroom, quickly brushing her teeth. She stepped into the shower and soaked in hot water, tracing the outline of Bill Jr.'s forehead on the plastic shower curtain. She had gotten the shadow wrong, distorting him. The water was very hot and she moved the lever back a notch, too far; her stomach contracted in the sudden chill. She moved her finger back and forth across the surface of the curtain, erasing Bill Jr. The plastic misted over, and she tried again. She soaped with one hand and drew with the other. Then she turned to face the water, stretching her neck to catch the fine punishing spray, moving the lever back to hot, as hot as she could stand it. His face was there in her mind, then it wasn't. She forgot about Bill Jr.'s troublesome forehead and began to move the lever back down, lukewarm, then cold. She stood in the cold water for a year and a half, then banged the lever to OFF. Shivering, wrapped in a thick towel, she sat on the john and wondered what she would bring her husband. *Foreign Affairs*, the *Foreign Service Journal*, and *The New York Review of Books* had arrived in the morning mail. She could bring him those and something chewy from their library, the Waverly novels, *The Origin of Consciousness in the Breakdown of the Bicameral Mind, The Second Sex,* or *The Rise of the Vice-Presidency.* Jimmy Carter's memoirs? Mussolini's? How swell. Thou grand. She dried her hair slowly, taking her time, warming up. Bill would have a lot on his mind, after listening to Carruthers and Hartnett; they would stuff him like a Christmas goose. And the presence of Carruthers was ominous. . . . Perhaps, then, the Victorian Gentleman's memoirs or Anaïs Nin's or Joyce's naughty letters to Nora Barnacle, and her naughty letters to him, except they were unpublished, tied up in litigation of some kind, the scholars obsessed with Nora's underpants, believing that therein lay poor Finnegan's dirty little secret.

She was afraid he was going to die.

She sighed, the house was so cold and lonely, so dark and empty and creaky at night. She was frightened alone at night in Georgetown, the stately streets a magnet for violent and unpredictable children; and it seemed like only yesterday that they had left the house unlocked and the keys above the visor in the car. The neighborhood had not changed; the city had. The face of the street had not changed in a hundred years, and the most recent arrival the psychiatrist across the street; that was five, six years ago. Theirs was a street of lawyers and bureaucrats, two retired senators, and a professor emeritus at Georgetown. Old Halley Allen two doors down had been an economist with the Labor Department in the Hoover administration, and every succeeding administration until Ford's. Prices inflated and taxes rose but no one moved. No one seemed to die, either, a happy circumstance that moved Halley Allen to suggest that their block was bewitched, like that village in the Caucasus where everyone lived to be a hundred or more. It was the sort of block where you knew the names of your neighbor's children and their dogs. Strangers were immediately identified and sized up. Except it didn't help at night, with the spillover from Wisconsin Avenue and M Street. And what could you do about that, except write a Letter to the Editor of the *Post?* Still, Halley Allen's vision of their block as an isolated region of the Caucasus cheered her, at the same time reminding her to call the old man. He would want to know about Bill.

She folded the towel and hung it up, and returned to the bedroom, where she stood looking into her closet, wondering what she would wear. Something light and cheerful, of course, though she did not feel light and cheerful. Something sexy. The magazines were on the nightstand. She would bring him the magazines, *Billiards at Half-past Nine*, a carton of cigarettes, a tin of pâté, and a shaker of Martinis. That would irritate the nurses and give him much pleasure, reassurance that things had not changed after all.

And she could play the Samaritan and bring the boy one of her *Sports Illustrated*s. He never had any visitors. He was from Massachusetts and the current issue had a piece on the Red Sox. Then she remembered that his eyes were bandaged, and he couldn't read. Of course he could hear well enough. His hearing was first-rate. Poor boy, he was so young; and his girl was dead.

Elinor reached into her closet, searching for something light and cheerful. She started in the middle and worked to the left; each item carried its own associations. She was crying freely now. The room was very dark. She leaned against the closet door and hummed a few bars of the sweet melody from *Romeo and Juliet*. Of course everything had changed, every single thing. Her face and body were warm from the shower, and she seemed to burn from the inside out. She wished, how she wished, that Bill had a single room.

Thirty minutes later she stood in the corridor, looking through the open door of the solarium. The three of them were framed, as in a painting, something by Degas or Fantin-Latour, *The Hospital Waiting Room*, or *Lawyers Advising a Client*. Carruthers and Hartnett were dressed in dark suits, Bill in black pajamas and his white terry-cloth robe. He looked exhausted, his face drawn and his eyes sunken and colorless. Their end of the solarium was dense with smoke, most of it Bill's. Every few seconds he'd take a long drag, then blow smoke rings. The other two sat forward in their chairs. She noticed their trouser legs hiked up, revealing gartered shins; thin, white shins. She wondered why they wore garters. Bill didn't. Hartnett and Carruthers were both talking at once, explaining something to him; it was complicated, whatever it was. Their voices were very low, and she could hear nothing. Bill was sitting back in his chair, legs crossed, his right arm bent at the elbow and wrist like the gent in the old Man of Distinction ad. Except his left hand was inert in his lap. He was evidently bored. It was either boredom or fatigue. The hand that held the cigarette went to his forehead and she saw where she had gone wrong with Bill Jr. It was so obvious. Each side of his face was different, of course; all faces were. And the way she had set him up, on the deck of the Vineyard house, the water and white lighthouse in the background — it was all wrong. She had looked through her mind's eye and seen something else, seen what she wanted to see. It was Bill, not Bill Jr. It was his pose, not their boy's.

He looked up suddenly and saw her. His face betrayed nothing, was composed behind a slight wan smile. Nothing to attract the attention of the others. Carruthers was talking hard and Hartnett was listening. Bill placed his finger aside his nose, the con man's signal of Work in Progress. He wanted her to wait in the corridor a minute. She smiled back and nodded her head, but he was no longer looking at her; he was listening to Carruthers, and blowing a smoke ring.

She felt a hand on her shoulder and turned.

"Hello, Elinor."

She looked at him. "Brian." It was Bill's doctor.

They stood a moment watching the three men.

He said, "What is it, some kind of summit conference? I know Hartnett. Who's the other one?"

"State Department *consigliere*," she said.

"How long has he been out of bed?"

"I just got here," she said.

"That's a wonderful atmosphere for him. I'm surprised they didn't bring him a pitcher of Martinis."

She rattled her bag. "I've got those."

"They're bad for you."

"What are they, fattening?" She moved away from the open door and they stood looking at each other. She had known Brian Fowler for twenty years. Bill said he had the worst bedside manner of any doctor he had ever known, with the possible exception of Brzezinski. Brian Fowler was always harried, pleading overwork, though whenever you needed him he was at Burning Tree or in London for a medical conference, or on an island in the Caribbean with his thirty-year-old third wife, a former stewardess — "flight attendant," she styled herself — for Cathay Pacific Airways. He was a great favorite of the CIA, which was how Bill came to know him. He wore a beard in those days and was believed to use grass, very visible in Georgetown, a voracious womanizer. The deputy director had set up an appointment after Bill's African adventure. *Brian Fowler,* the DD had said, *best in the business, utterly reliable, discreet, thorough, and aboveboard. Let him check you out at Sibley, his connections are terrific. In matters of health, never trust the Jerries, particularly Jerries who practice on the Third World.* She and Bill often saw him around. He ran with agency and State Department people and he'd show up here and there, at a dinner party or embassy affair, usually on the prowl. One night when Bill was out of town — abroad, actually — she had allowed herself to be taken to dinner by Brian Fowler, and allowed herself to drink too much, and allowed herself to be charmed and offered a nightcap, knowing exactly where she was headed — and at three in the morning she found herself naked on his living room floor, him looming over her, a triumphant smile on his bearish face. Why? An accident, "a happening," as it was called then. He had thrown down a challenge and she had accepted it. A dare, in other words, and he was a man of some charm and not at all bad-looking, despite the childish beard. He liked women. And Bill was being a shit and her work was going badly and her thirty-fifth birthday was a week away and Bill could not, or would not, get back in time. So when Brian Fowler came sniffing around the drinks tray at the Brazilian embassy she sniffed back. It had been more fun than she thought it would, and they had a fling for a week. An overnight in Baltimore, lunches in Bethesda, dinner at his place. He was a wonderful raconteur, a connoisseur of CIA stories. That week he was treating a man for a strain of VD not seen since the fourteenth century. At the end of the week he announced that he had to leave for a medical conference. Raised eyebrows: CIA business. The next day, Bill returned, contrite; he hated missing her birthday. He had bought her a three-foot-high warrior's mask in Botswana, a peace offering; she hung it in her studio, where it remained, and would always remain.

She said, "What's new, Brian?"

"Nothing much. What about you, El?"

She said, "I mean Bill. About Bill."

He glanced in the direction of the solarium. "Can't you keep them away from him?"

She smiled. "No, I can't."

"He needs rest, some of the tests we're giving him are really — exhausting."

She said again, "What's new, Brian?"

"He's got something interfering with a nerve. That's what I came down to tell him. You want the technical jargon?"

She thought a moment, standing very still. It didn't sound too bad. It didn't sound like cancer. She said, "Without the jargon."

"Remember, couple years ago, we took a piece of iron out of his ass? The tumor we thought might be malignant until we saw it. And then when we analyzed it we found a chunk of iron, must've migrated. That shrapnel he picked up in Czechoslovakia."

"Africa, Brian." She wondered who it was that had taken shrapnel in Czechoslovakia, and when.

"Africa, that's right. We think he's got a piece of iron in his neck, resting inside the spinal column, on the spinal cord. That's what we think. Impossible to be sure. But we're going to have to go inside to find out. It's what the CAT scan says. But you never know. It's a tiny little piece, an itty-bitty thing, if that's what it is. Smaller than a pinhead. It's going to be a son of a bitch to get. The chief resident here is going to do it, but I'll assist." He opened his cigarette case, took out a Marlboro, tapped it, and lit it. He studied the silver box, weighing it in his hand. "He's got that stuff everywhere, it leaches out of him."

"I know that, Brian." When they were together in the shower she regularly picked pieces out of his back. They looked like little blackheads. "When are you going to operate?"

"Day after tomorrow, I hope."

She took a step back from him, to put some distance between them, and to see his whole body. "And what are the chances for success, do you think?"

He cocked his head, calculating. She had the impression that he was thinking of something else, searching his memory perhaps; she had not seen him in a year or more, and then it was across the room at a party. When she visited Bill, he was never around, she assumed by design. In any case he was not the man she remembered from fifteen years back, a week in which she had more fun than she thought she would. He wore his hair long now, carefully styled, and, she thought, dyed. It was attractive salt-and-pepper hair. The beard was long gone. Still, he was a good-looking man with an athletic appearance. He was the sort of man who looked ten years younger than his age; that is, he did not look forty but ten years younger than fifty. It was obvious he was fifty, or thereabouts. His neck gave him away. He took good care of himself, unlike Bill, who looked fifty-five, not a day younger; not five years older than his age. She had always looked her age exactly; she was now forty-nine, one more significant birthday in a month's time. But on this birthday she and Bill would be together. He said, "Pretty good. It'll work, don't worry. And don't let him worry. Useless emotion, worry. We have every confidence. When it's over, he'll feel a lot better . . ." The doctor let the sentence hang.

And she finished it, knowing exactly what he was going to say. "Until it happens again."

He shrugged. "It's possible."

" 'Pretty good?' Is that the official estimate, or the unofficial?"

"Better than pretty good. We don't know everything. There are not only the unks but the unk-unks." When she looked mystified, he smiled. "Sorry. That's airplane jargon. An unk is an unknown. An unk-unk is an unknown unknown, something out there in left field that you never knew about; it's impossible to allow for something you've never conceived of."

She said, "That's encouraging."

He dropped his cigarette on the corridor floor, and ground it under his heel. He looked at her directly. "What's your assessment of his mood?"

She thought that in Washington even the doctors sounded like public relations men. She said, "He's been better."

"Seems jumpy."

"He doesn't like hospitals, Brian."

"No. I think he doesn't like me."

"You're his doctor," she said, "not his buddy."

"Doesn't have to be that way, because a man's a doctor doesn't mean he's a shit. I always thought we were friends." He added, "Known each other a long time. Go back a long way." He waved

195

his arm. "Too old to make new friends. Got to keep the ones I've got."

"He's nervous, Brian. And when he gets nervous, he gets surly." God knows that was true. But she was nonplussed at this turn in the conversation. What was he trying to tell her? "What do you think? Maybe we ought to go in there, break up the summit conference." She suppressed a smile; his face was as troubled as a teenager's.

"It's important for him to go into this in the right frame of mind. He's got to feel good about himself."

She almost laughed out loud. The idea of Bill feeling "good about himself" was ludicrous. She wondered if he had told Bill to feel good about himself; she hoped not. She said, "Bill always rises to the occasion. He's very good in adversity."

"I asked him if he wanted a — Valium, or whatever, take his mind off things, and he said no, Christ, bit my head off, as if I'd offered him cocaine."

"He's never liked tranquilizers."

"They can be very useful, Elinor. Very useful, they're a tool, nothing more. They don't have a — moral weight."

"He likes to go into things straight."

"Bill's a snob. Do you know that? And a reactionary."

"Because he doesn't like tranquilizers?"

"Not only that," Brian said obscurely. "It's modern science, for Christ's sake."

"I think that's the point, Brian."

"That's exactly what I mean," he said. He nodded at a nurse passing in the corridor. "Well, they're here if he wants them."

"I'll tell him. But he won't want them."

He cocked his head again, distracted. "And you, El. How about you?"

"I don't use them either. I have an addictive personality and they frighten me." This was not true, but she wanted no alliances with Brian Fowler. The figurative nudge in the ribs, *You and I, we're adult, we understand the uses of modern pharmacology, morally impartial.* Her mood began to lift. The important thing was that it wasn't cancer, an enemy within; this was a foreign body, shrapnel or gunshot. Finite, specific. Bill would be all right after all, until it happened again; and there wasn't anything to be done about that, Africa's calling cards.

Fowler was shaking his head. "No, I mean in general. How are you getting on? What are you up to?"

She got it then, or thought she did. He had forgotten, the son of a bitch. In those days there had been so many women; that was his reputation, anyway. Fowler the Prowler. Probably he couldn't keep them all in his memory, like an expert bridge player forgetting a casual afternoon's rubber. It was extraordinary about men, the way they edited their memories. It must be wonderful living with an edited past, one triumph after another, never anything sloppy or cruel or stupid; it would be the reason men slept so noisily. Their sleep was important to them and a vivacious sleep depended on a virtuous past. Virtuous, error-free, seamless, and active. The thought amused her, and now she wondered how to answer his question. She did not want to discuss her painting or anything about her life, how she felt or what she thought about. So she smiled.

He looked at his watch, nodding, still distracted.

No harm in having a little fun, though. She said, "Brian? Bill likes you fine. It's just that he's nervous, not knowing what's wrong with him. It doesn't have anything to do with you." A double edge there, she hoped.

He looked up, a broad grin on his face. He truly did appear ten years younger than his age, and in Excellent Health. "Really? I hope so, El. We go back so damn far, way back to the Kennedys. Only a few of us still around." He had conjured an image of the tsar's household guard, valiantly struggling with the Bolsheviks at the gates. "Hell, that's so long ago, I was with the agency then, though I kept the connection pretty quiet. No one knew anything."

With his mysterious comings and goings he had been about as inconspicuous as Allen Dulles. She said ambiguously, "I know, Brian." It was a cachet, having been with the CIA in the nineteen sixties. It was like having been with Fitzgerald, Hemingway, and Stein in Paris in the nineteen twenties, raising hell. She wondered suddenly what had happened to the man with the fourteenth-century VD, if he recovered, or if it fell off, or what.

He said, "They were swell days, weren't they?"

"Dandy," she said.

They were silent a moment. The doctor lit another cigarette. She wondered if he had heard her sarcasm. Probably not. He was not the sort of man who listened carefully. He raised his eyebrows when he heard his name on the public address system. *Dr. Fowler . . . Dr. Fowler . . . Dr. Fowler . . .* He smiled apologetically. Time to go.

"I'll be back," he said. "I'll talk to Bill tonight. Give him the word."

"The sooner the better," she said. Then, "Tell him everything." She wanted to say, Tell him you haven't told me. But she didn't. An argument would delay him, and she wanted to see Bill.

"There's one more thing, El. Is he worried about Bill Jr.?"

"Why would he be worried about Bill Jr.?"

"I don't know. Maybe it was something I heard somewhere. Or something he said. Everyone worries about their kids."

"What did you hear, Brian?"

Perhaps it was something in her tone, low, serious, almost seductive, but he looked at her queerly, shrugging.

"About Bill Jr.," she said.

He shook his head, the memory apparently out of reach.

She said, "It could be important, the stories that float around this town —"

Fowler said, "It was something in my mind, I've got this ragbag of a memory."

She said, "Yes, you do."

"— here today, gone tomorrow."

She was silent, looking at him evenly.

"As I said, it's important for him to go into this in the right frame of mind. A confident, constructive frame of mind. I wish you'd talk to him about the tranquilizers. If something's bothering him . . ." He smiled and moved off, waving his cigarette like a wand. Suddenly he stopped and turned back to face her, his eyes changing expression, dark to light. He looked like a cartoon character who suddenly got it. She waited. "And did I tell you, El? You're looking marvelous. That's an exceptionally pretty outfit. Bill's a lucky, lucky man. I'd have to say. You don't look a day over thirty-five!" And then he turned, a kind of stately pirouette, and still smiling brilliantly — it was the smile of a film star, or male model, or talk-show host — strode away down the corridor.

"I didn't know what happened to you. When you didn't come in I thought you'd gone back home, that I'd pissed you off. That you'd said, Nuts to this. Nuts to husbands. Nuts to hospitals. Nuts to visiting hours. Nuts to us. Nuts."

They were alone at last, Carruthers and Hartnett having made their good-byes. There was no one else in the solarium. It was dark outside and the rain had stopped, but the atmosphere was damp. It was a dispiriting room, without heart; she closed her eyes, trying to revive her spirits. She emptied the glass ashtray, then spread a napkin on the low table and took out the pâté and the shaker, ice cold to the touch and sweating. The napkin was white with blue initials, a wedding present. Looking at it made her feel better.

"I was talking to your sawbones."

"Fowler the Prowler? Where is he now?"

"They paged him. He'll be back. He said he'd be back later on."

"He has news then?"

She struggled with the can opener until he took it from her, testing the blade with his thumb, then working it around the edges of the tin. The rasp of the blade was the only noise in the room. He looked ghastly, and the fluorescent light didn't help. He had lost his Vineyard tan. His skin had a yellowish look to it and he was breathing hard, levering the blade. She opened the shaker and poured gin into the two metal cups.

She raised her cup. "Confusion to the enemy?"

He looked at her and smiled. "Massive confusion."

"What did they say, those two? Carruthers looked embarrassed, as if I'd interrupted something. Or is he always embarrassed?"

"You did." He took a sip of the drink and sat back; the plastic chair sighed. "And I wish you'd come in sooner, if you had maybe they'd've stopped talking. Christ, I hate it when people talk at me. Got so I could concentrate only on the smoke rings, and when they saw that, it didn't make them stop, only try harder. They started talking at once, as if there were no time. Dumb of me. When I saw you in the doorway I should've waved you in. That would have stopped them, seeing you. It's a hell of a disadvantage, being in pajamas and a robe and feeling like hell when they're in suits and ties, feeling great. But they're gone now. And you're here." He paused and shrugged, as if he'd lost his train of thought; she observed him move inside himself, and wait. "What did Prowler say?"

"Says you have some shrapnel in your neck and it's pressing on the nerve. Says they'll operate day after tomorrow."

"Difficult operation?"

"Pretty difficult."

"Well, he's not going to do it."

"No. The chief resident's going to do it. Prowler's assisting. I was waiting for him to say that the chief resident was the best in the world or on the East Coast, but he didn't. He said he was good, though."

"That's not bad news. Could be worse."

"It's good news, Bill."

"I guess it is," he said.

"Except for the unks," she said.

He looked at her.

"And the unk-unks."

"Is that CIA horseshit or what?"

"Airline jargon. You want to hear more?" She explained to him about unks and unk-unks. It took a moment to get him laughing, but it didn't last long.

"Did you ever have days when everything stood still, no forward motion? Those are the days when the past catches up with you. You have to stand still to let it come alongside, and then you have to wait and listen to what it has to say. It's never what you expect. You start to walk again and it puts its dead hand on your arm. It's not finished. You damn well wait until it is finished. You're captive. Until it's ended, you can't move. It's all familiar; the thing has total recall. You try to jerk your arm away, but it won't let you go. More you fight, the stronger it gets. You ever have days like that, Elly?"

She said, "I just had one."

He smiled. "Don't tell me about it."

"I won't," she said.

"You've got to keep fighting it, though."

She thought suddenly that he was talking about something else. "Yes," she said sharply. "Yes, you do."

He leaned forward. "I'm happy with what I've done."

"Working for the government."

"Working for the government," he said.

"I don't much care for the past tense in that sentence, Bill."

He dipped his head, embarrassed. "Too much introspection today. Too much Carruthers. Forget I said it." He looked at her. "You get any work done?"

She said, "Some." She was angry with him.

"What was it today, hands? Eyes?"

"Bill Jr.," she said. "His forehead." She began to explain about the forehead, its planes and shadows. Then she described the girl with the umbrella, the image still stuck fast in her memory. In a moment they were laughing about the psychiatrist across the street. He seemed to have an inordinate number of female patients, so many of them young. He himself was not young but he had a pointed beard, very Viennese.

He said, "What else did Prowler have to say?"

"He thinks you don't like him."

"How could he ever have that idea?"

"It hurts him. He's pretty busted up about it."

"I'll have to watch my step, then."

"And he's worried that you don't feel good about yourself."

"Poor Prowler."

"You've got to watch it with the tranquilizers. When you refused the Valium, he took it as a slap in the face."

"Listen. You tell him I feel terrific about myself. I feel good about myself all day long, and him, too."

"He's an awful horse's ass, Bill."

"He's comic relief. I thought you liked him."

"I don't like him. He's a horse's ass. I think he dyes his hair."

"He does, definitely," Nodding agreement, smiling broadly. "It must be hard as hell to do, salt-and-pepper hair. Maybe he gets Julia Child to do it for him."

"He has a young wife."

"Maybe she does it. Maybe it's sexy, her dying his hair."

"I doubt it. I'll bet he keeps it a secret. Everyone has a secret, I'll bet that's his secret."

"I've known him a long time." He smiled. "This is one of those days I think I've known everyone a long time. But I'm not certain he wears well. I think I liked him better twenty years ago, when he was on the prowl. When he was physician-in-residence at Langley, a boy debutante, fresh out of Harvard Medical School via Yale, Exeter, and the North Shore."

She said, "Bill."

"What else did he say about the operation?"

"He says you'll feel better when it's over."

He wagged his left hand at her. "Restored to good use?"

"I didn't ask him, specifically."

"Say anything about convalescence?"

"He's coming by later tonight, give you all the details."

"I'd rather hear them from you."

"Bill, I'm sorry. I was upset."

"Look, Elly." He poured fresh drinks into both their cups. She thought his color was returning. That would be the vivifying qualities of gin. Gin and laughter. Droll stories. He looked at her and smiled sadly, and she knew that he had shifted direction. But when he spoke it was only to say "Thanks for the drinks."

"I bought you some cigarettes and magazines and *Billiards at Half-past Nine*."

"Do you know what I'd like? One of those cassette players, with earphones, so that I could listen to music at night, in bed. Some Brahms, and Wagner. Do you think you could find *Tannhäuser* on tape?"

She smiled. "*Tannhäuser* at half-past nine? Funny music to go to sleep to, Bill. It's not exactly a lullabye."

He said, "It's patriotic music. It's their version of a Sousa march. I figured that out the other day. I've been thinking a lot about patriotism lately. There hasn't been a hell of a lot else to think about so I've been thinking about that."

She was alert now. She thought of him as a pitcher in the ritual fidget before the delivery of the ball, scuffing the dirt, hitching his pants, correcting the bill of his cap, juggling the ball, looking in for the sign. It was up to her to give him the sign. She said, "I was going to bring *Sports Illustrated* to your roommate, and then I remembered that he can't see. So I didn't bring it." She told him about the ball game, Ripken Jr.'s homer in the bottom of the tenth.

202

She was giving him time to get together whatever it was he had to get together. It was not good news. Carruthers and Hartnett, god damn them. She should have walked into the solarium straightaway. But he had not seemed to want that. "The convalescence can't be too long, Bill. You'll get out of here, and we'll go back down to the Vineyard, hang out on the Vineyard until Thanksgiving." She looked at him closely. His eyes were closed. She took a deep breath. "Fowler said something else. He said that you seemed worried. He asked if you were worried about Bill Jr."

His eyes popped open. "Fowler said that?"

"I asked him where he got that idea, but he didn't answer. He said maybe he'd heard it somewhere or assumed it. He was very cagy. Said that everyone's worried about their children. I didn't like hearing it, especially from him. It made me think that maybe he knows something that I don't know."

"He still works for Langley, you know. Free lance, odd jobs, this and that." A ghost of a smile. "He's a character in *Tannhäuser,* too. One of the spear carriers, a second-rate baritone. But definitely part of the action."

"Well, no one ever leaves that place. You sign on, you're in for keeps."

"He likes it. It suits him."

"I know."

He looked at her. "So he's heard something, El. Word's around."

"What has he heard, Bill?"

He toyed with his cup, then took her hand. His eyes were bloodshot. She could feel his trembling and leaned closer, across the table. She kissed him. Rising, he shuffled over to the window. "You remember Warren Winston? They're worried about him, he and his committee have a fix on Bill Jr. and me. They know about Kleust, and what the Germans have, and when we saw him in Hamburg. It's part of Winston's committee's investigation, international terrorism and so forth and so on, ja-da, ja-da, jing-jing-jing. I suppose he thinks he's on the trail of Carlos or Abu Nidal, the trail that ends at Qaddafi's tent or a bomb in the nursery." He paused, noting that she had declined to smile at his sarcasm. He said, "Probably the committee has a line into the West Germans as well as the Department." He turned, his back to the window now.

"I'll probably be called to testify. Maybe you, too. It'd be executive session, probably. But you never know with those pricks."

She said, "Do they know where he is now?"

"I don't think so," he said. "But Carruthers didn't say, and I didn't ask."

"You should've asked, Bill." She took his arm. He seemed suddenly fragile in his pajamas and robe.

"Carruthers was cagy, but there's something new. They've got some fresh intelligence. He wouldn't say what it was. Maybe he didn't know. But he's a worried son of a bitch, because it could be bad for the Department."

She took her husband's dead hand, and squeezed it. She turned so that she was facing him. His face had gone slack, the color drained from it. His eyes were gray and dry as dust, infinitely serious. She said, "We have to find him. Us. We do. Before they do." She searched his face, and he nodded wordlessly. Yes, he was saying. Yes, we did. But she wanted him to know absolutely what she believed, and how she intended to behave. She said fiercely, "He's ours, he's our son, our responsibility."

"Well," he said, "it's gone beyond that."

"Not for me it hasn't."

"It's gone way beyond that, Elly. And they're going to want to talk to you."

She stared into his eyes. "Who is?"

"Carruthers. Maybe the committee will want you, when they've finished with me. If it ever gets that far. It may not. Carruthers is very clever."

"I don't know any more than you do."

"Tell them that," he said.

"I will tell them *nothing*." Then, softening, watching him as he turned from her to look out the window, she said wryly, "I'll plead the Fifth Amendment. No testimony, on grounds that it might tend to incriminate me."

He did not smile, but said in the same serious tone, "I want you to talk to Hartnett."

"Why?"

"He's a *lawyer*," Bill said, his voice sharp and exasperated. "Elly, for Christ's sake."

"I don't need a lawyer for this. Do you?"

He said, "They think he's coming up from underground."

So she would have to make herself understood clearly. She did not need a lawyer's advice. She did not intend to be cute or coy, modifying her statements, "to my knowledge," or "to the best of my recollection." She said, "Bill? Did you hear what I said? I said I will tell them *nothing*. I will remain silent." When he did not reply, she asked softly, "What will you tell them?"

"He's a dangerous boy, Elly."

"They already know that."

"I think they think he's going to try to kill someone."

She watched him carefully now. This was what it came down to, the two of them and their son, and the American government, and the loyalties each to each. The government was a personal thing to him. What had he said? *It could be bad for the Department.* Bad for everyone, bad all around, bad all day long. At that moment he did not much look like an ambassador. He looked sick and weary, and if she did not know him so well, frightened. A frightened old man who needed a haircut and a shave. And, apparently, a lawyer. His own wits were not good enough, he was walking through a minefield. But she could not believe that. She tried to imagine him at the witness table, Hartnett at his side, whispering into his ear, Hartnett's thick palm covering the microphone. It was the image of Hoffa or a crooked defense contractor, or the Watergate gang. But she knew how relentless the government could be, once its machinery was engaged, helped along by the sanctimonious boys and girls of the news business. The mediators. Avenging angels, they liked to think of themselves.

He said, "An American."

She put her hand on his arm.

"But it wouldn't matter, would it? A death, of whatever nationality. Is a death, after all."

"He's *ours*," she said.

"Do we protect him?"

"We don't give him up," she said.

"We let him do what he's going to do?"

"We don't put his neck. On the guillotine."

"But as you said, he's *ours*." He was silent a moment, looking out the window at the gray government buildings. "You're right about Hartnett," he said. "We don't need a mouthpiece."

She nodded.

"It isn't a question of avoiding anything. Or putting the best face on something. I think it's pretty much down the drain, anyway."

She tightened her grip on his arm. She did not understand what was down the drain.

She said, "It's us. We have to find him."

"We won't like what we'll find."

"No, we won't."

"But that isn't the issue. It never was. The issue is what we know, and what they don't know. What they need to know. We don't know very much about him, where he is and how he thinks. But it's more than they know."

She drew him to her. She was talking directly at him now. He did not blink or flinch. "It's a big government, Bill. They have resources. They don't need us. *We can't do it.* We mustn't. It would be a terrible thing, he's *ours*. We would be haunted always. We would be ashamed. We would be cursed." But even as she spoke, speaking with all the passion she could muster, speaking from the bottom of the thirty years they had loved each other, she knew she had lost. He felt, she knew, that he had a duty.

2

THE OPERATION was concluded. He knew that, in some accessible region of his mind. He remembered being wheeled into the operating room, a captive, already lightheaded, the bright lights above, nurses here and there, the odor of electricity, and Fowler's wink. Fowler's mouth and jaw hidden behind an aqua mask, but the heavy Rolex on his wrist and the wink unmistakable. Fowler had leaned down and said a muffled few words, something about Africa and the long migration of the fragment of a hand grenade. He was lying on his stomach and Fowler had to bend his knees to get close to his ear. He said, "Your misspent youth," as if Africa had been a pool hall. He looked straight at Fowler and was surprised to see contact lenses swimming on his irises. He smelled a leathery cologne, and noticed Fowler's immaculate manicure, a complement to the Rolex. Fowler turned and a nurse offered rubber gloves. Fowler winked at her, too. What could be worse than a vain surgeon? Except they were all vain. Why would a license to cut be an entitlement to egomania? What was their supposed pledge? *Do no harm.* Too modest a goal in the age of medical miracles. It would be just right for the Foreign Service, though. The chief surgeon put his hand on Bill's shoulder and said two words. We're ready. Then he nodded at the anaesthesiologist. Someone in the room was humming Mozart. He hoped to Christ that they had the anaesthesia right, that it wasn't someone's urine or meningitis virus or stale Coca-Cola. He smiled at the anaesthesiologist, wanting her to like him. All prisoners wanted to be loved by their jailers. He said, "What a swell job you have, putting people to sleep." She was looking at something and did not reply. He felt let down. The humming stopped. Curtly, she told him to count back from ten and at six it was lights out.

He felt no pain, nor any sensation. By the pale look of the sunlight he reckoned it was late afternoon. In the next bed he heard the boy sigh loudly, and shift position. Someone turned the pages of a magazine, fingernails on slick paper: Elinor. He listened without moving. He wanted to stay within himself a while longer, holding himself in comfortable suspension; he did not want to admit to anything. Inside, he was safe and without fear. He wanted to do nothing to draw attention to himself, and in that way remain invisible, yet sentient. He thought that if he opened his mouth his spirit would fly away out the window, out of control, perhaps lost forever. He was tempted to do this, there were so many spirits round and about. They were out of sight beyond the open window, but beckoning him. If he said anything his words would take wing, lost to him forever. His open eyes would provide an exit for his many important and individual thoughts and these, too, released, would vanish. Better to remain still, immobile in clean white sheets, listening to the rustle of the pages of a magazine.

He closed his eyes but still he could see the window and the light outside. He saw it in his mind's eye, so clearly that he could not swear to God that his eyes were closed, as he knew them absolutely to be; he had closed them himself and now was inside himself, safe. It was like being the man, the mirror, and the image in the mirror, all at once. The sky was very bright and the window was open. He could see the crowns of trees and a brilliant milky sky, of the sort observed only in the Southern Hemisphere. It seemed to press down upon the civilized earth like a great lid. In the Southern Hemisphere, of course, things were upside down; the seasons, the very sky itself, and the angle of vision to the rest of the world. When you looked north, it was as if you were looking down. The Cape of Good Hope was the top of the world; that was how it seemed, and that therefore was how it was, a continental perspective, the practical reality in Africa, and no great surprise because after all he had grown up in Boston, hub of the universe.

The breeze was hot, like an animal's breath, but light on his skin. It did not burn, it consoled. It was an African breeze, aromatic, redolent of the earth and its dense vegetation, its rot and exotic fauna: whydah birds, mountain apes, lowland crocodiles. It had come a long way, from southern Africa across the Atlantic. But it had maintained its integrity, collecting nothing from the sea; it was a pure land breeze. He was greatly comforted, for it brought with it the spirit of the continent, geologic time. All the emotions of Africa, his and the Africans', were carried with it. In Africa you were at ease with mystery, was that not so?

He knew that what he felt was miraculous, and not quite credible; but he did not let it go. He was awake and asleep at the same time, an ambiguous consciousness. He felt a sudden surge of ecstasy, as if all his African emotions were concentrated in a single place, a passionate kiss, a teardrop, an unexpected sighting, anything momentous.

He and Kleust in the overloaded boat, chased by a storm boiling up out of Zaire. Except it was not Zaire then, it was the Congo. It was Conrad's country. They had been hunting crocodiles. Kleust had a friend with a license from the government. The government permitted him to take five hundred crocodiles a year from the lake, transport the skins to the capital, and transship them to Paris and Rome for handbags and shoes. Everyone got a cut. Kleust's friend was on the run, there were references to a wife, and a police matter. The friend lived in a tent surrounded by ammunition cases, heavy steel boxes filled with paperback books, Gothic romances. On the covers of the books were English country houses, rearing stallions, women in deshabille, men in fox-hunting clothes. The steel cases were to protect the books from jungle rot. There were crocodiles everywhere. They hunted at night, shooting the crocs at will, eight, ten, in a single night. Kleust held the light, and the crocs' eyes lit up like the taillights of cars. The bay looked like a parking lot. They would bring them back to camp for the skinners to strip. They sat up late, drinking whiskey and talking. Kleust's friend said very little about the present, and nothing at all about the past. He and Kleust stayed for four days, then left; they were tired of killing. Early in the morning they departed from the camp. One of the skinners drove the boat, the sky above them wide and blue, and behind them great thunderheads, heavy with summer rain, black as hell; the bolts of lightning reminded him of the evil tendrils of a jellyfish, thick and white as milk.

We will outrace it, the skinner said.

I hope so, Kleust said. They both sat in the bow, eyes front, though every few minutes they would move their necks, bring their faces around in an arc, to observe the weather: the abrupt end of the wide blue sky and the beginning of the blackness, relentlessly gaining.

They were talking about Germany, what would happen to it; the weight of its past seemed a burden beyond imagining. And of course it did not need imagining, all you had to do was read the documents, the testimony, the memoirs, the daily journalism, and look at the films. It was the most documented horror in history, nothing left to the imagination except to wonder at the thoroughness of it all, and the enthusiasm the killers brought to their work. Brahms and Rilke in the morning, Zyklon-B in the afternoon.

A crisis in the humanities, Kleust said with an icy smile.

The weight of the German past was what had driven Kleust to Africa, wondering if in this new political environment things might be — chaste. However, Africa's politicians were fascinated by Hitler's new order, busy as they were in fashioning a new order themselves. An African way, Africa for the Africans. They did not understand the Third Reich, how it began, how it continued, why it ended. How did the Führer organize the state? Inspire such devotion? How did Dr. Goebbels develop the Propaganda Ministry? What was the role of education? The church? If the Germans — so intelligent, so civilized — adapted so readily to a one-party state, why not Africa? And what was it about the Jews? There were no Jews in Africa, except a few tribes in Ethiopia — Stone Age people, they said, sneering — and of course the Jews of European descent in South Africa. Kleust explained about the Jews, their role in history, their dispersion, their prominence in the cultural and commercial life in Germany, but still the Africans didn't get it.

Were the Jews like colonialists, then? Clannish, mysterious, racist, rich, taking what they wanted, promulgating their own laws, cuisine, clothing, religious customs, raping the land? Insulting the majority race! Could they be compared with the Indian merchants who held every African town and village in thrall — in a Hindu stranglehold? Kleust spent many hours late at night, explaining modern German history to the Africans, tracing the years from 1920 to 1945; only twenty-five years, but a political millennium. It was certainly an Era, beginning with Weimar and ending with the Thousand Year Reich, even shorter than the American Century. He was barely forty-five himself, and of course did not know Weimar; the memory of Weimar reposed in women, so many German men of that age were dead. Kleust preached the virtues of a benign anarchism, but the Africans were not impressed. They wanted control and authority, and there was also a thirst for revenge. The German model seemed convenient, so many lessons to be learned. Every nation needed living space, and its own identity. Kleust shuddered. We have washed our hands of Africa, he said.

Easy for you, Bill said. Not so easy for us.

You'd be surprised, Kleust said. Before his posting in Africa — this one, his second posting — he had been a functionary in the embassy in London, a city he despised, and a first secretary in Washington, a city that baffled and amused him. On the whole, he preferred Bonn.

Americans live in a dream world, Kleust said.

As opposed to Germans? he'd asked.

Germans do not live in a dream world, Kleust said. Germans live in a glass house, the world pressing in on all sides, everything visible.

They talked for a while about the European political climate, and the two Germanys, reunification, and what the future held. Ostpolitik was the symmetrical policy, though conducted with sleight-of-hand; its foundations had already been laid. Germans had long memories, history was with them every day; no day so bright that darkness was not visible. Everything in Germany was approached with profound ambivalence. Germans were afraid of themselves. Many Germans wished for a pastoral life, Goethe's "naturalness." Kleust waved his hand. Perhaps the harmless commercial activity of the Buddenbrooks. Tell me what is natural in our time. On the one hand Germans want to move their shoulders, gain room to live and breathe, influence the course of things. On the other hand, Germans want to disappear into Europe. Kleust fell silent. They were almost in the middle of the lake. Far in the distance a small fishing boat sat stationary.

Do you love your country? he had asked.

It is the Fatherland, Kleust agreed.

That is not an answer, he said.

It is the best I can do, Kleust said. I am a diplomat, like you. Germany is where I am at home. It is where I breathe easiest. At least in Germany nothing is withheld. Of course it is necessary to keep your eyes open, always alert. Every state manufactures its own propaganda. And it must be the same with you.

No, Bill said. I am at home anywhere. I am at home here, on this lake full of crocodiles, as I am at home there. Elinor and I, wherever we are . . . But I love my country, my dream of it. I love the freedom of it, its impulsiveness. The buffoonery, the instability, the romance of money, the loneliness, and the grab. It's a fictional country, arising deep from the imagination. In its reality, it is something else. We do not have identity cards in the United States. What I like most about it is that it isn't Europe.

Kleust cocked an eyebrow. Perhaps you are happier in this century than I am. Your country is happier, or luckier, than mine is. Well. It is supposed to be your century, is it not? Yet 'impulsiveness' is not the word I would have used. Impulsiveness is not to be admired. It is not an attractive quality, is it?

Call it spontaneity, then.

It's the same thing, Kleust said.

Bill laughed. It's a swell century, all things considered. The American part of it has been particularly benign, don't you think? In all its impulsiveness? And those of us who have played a part, wouldn't you say we had something to answer for? Then, after a moment's pause: Do you think you could commit treason?

I would not supervise a concentration camp, if that is what you mean.

It isn't, he said.

That is an order I would refuse to obey, Kleust said. I would not sell secrets to the Russian pigs.

He said, I do not mean refusing an order. There are orders all of us would refuse. And we have no secrets to sell, you and I, even if we were interested in selling them, which we aren't. I'm not interested in the betrayals of the past. I'm talking about the future. Tomorrow, the day after, next week, next year. I mean engaging in a treasonous act, a violation of our oath. Being forced to choose, and choosing an act of calculated treachery against the state. Harming the state. In my case, choosing against Lincoln. Your Goethe, my Lincoln. Telling Abraham Lincoln to go fuck himself, that it was in vain after all. *The union doesn't count.*

That's what it comes down to?

He said, Yes.

Kleust thought a moment. Kleust in deep thought, weighing his reply. When he spoke it was to slide off the point. He said, You mean "the government." Our experience with governments is not so good.

If we are not faithful, who will be?

We have a duty, Kleust agreed.

And our duty to the state is profound. We took an oath. We were not coerced to swear allegiance. At the least, we are like doctors: Do no harm. The state is in our care. We have an obligation to it.

Yes, of course, Kleust said.

In the instance of an American diplomat, it is the Constitution. The Constitution is the state. The state is the people. This is a great thing. Beside it, everything else is small. I'm in trouble, Kurt. As you say, Americans live in a dream world. What would you do, forced to choose between betraying your country and betraying your friend, or your kin? That's the measurement, isn't it? Isn't that the thumb on the scale?

Kleust said, What happened in Hamburg, Bill?

We met. We talked. Or he talked. We listened.

Duer did not interfere?

We were careful. Elinor and I know Hamburg well. It could be that he chose not to interfere, for his own reasons. And it could be that we lost him in Saint Pauli. I know he was on us in the beginning.

And what about Bill Jr.?

He shrugged. What about him?

Well, Kleust said. What did he look like? How did he behave?

He described his son's appearance, and what he was wearing. He said, He's a stranger, an exile. I had to remind myself, and keep reminding myself, that I am his father. *He is mine.* He owes his life to me, and I am responsible for him. He knows this, and it amuses him.

Kleust was silent.

I don't know why he wanted to see us. Maybe that was the idea, that there really was no point to it, that it was a bit of aimless theater. Maybe he wanted to prove he could get us to Hamburg. Maybe he wanted to show us off to his comrades. Maybe anything. He's far from home, Kurt.

Kleust framed his next question with care. Is he — unbalanced?

Is he crazy? Psychotic? He does not seem crazy. But he is not balanced as you or I would define balance. But our definitions are beside the point. He is furious, I can tell you that. He does hate us all.

Well, you learned something.

Nothing of value, And what I did learn, I would as soon not know.

Nothing that would help Duer? Or your own people?

Well, that's the point. That's exactly the point. Helping Duer, and my own people. But I can't inform on him, can I? Yet I must. I'm obligated to do it. I must either inform on him or take responsibility for him. And that is what I meant by my question, which you did not answer. What would you do? What would you do, forced to choose between betraying your country and betraying your friend or your kin? That's what it comes down to.

Bill, Kleust said.

I don't believe in making things easier than they are, he said.

Kleust smiled cynically, raising his chin so that he looked down his nose. He said, I shud rathah hope I shud have the cuddedge to betray my coun-treh.

Bill laughed, Kleust's imitation of an educated Englishman owed more to Heidelberg than to Cambridge. He said, Come off it, Kurt. You don't believe that Forster horseshit any more than I do. What a pretty sensibility he has. How learned. How humane. We don't have that luxury.

Kleust said, Maybe I do believe it. I think I do, as a matter of fact. It is not a convenient century we live in. It is a murderous century. It is perhaps the beginning of the end of everything. So given a choice, or forced to make one, I would choose that which is closest. Most precious. Most intimate. I would give my loyalty to that which is nearest to hand. Contemporary German naturalness.

And your heart? he asked. Where would your heart be?

The same place, Kleust said.

Bill shook his head. Not good enough.

Kleust said, I do not think you can choose an abstraction over flesh and blood. No, I do not think that. And you don't, either.

Bill nodded. The point stung. He looked back; the storm seemed no closer. He faced front, gazing now at the thick green water of the lake, wrinkled in the light breeze. He hugged himself, rocking back and forth. What if he were not a man, but a woman; and the betrayal not political but something else: sexual. One's wife or daughter become stupidly, joylessly promiscuous. Relentlessly, evilly promiscuous. A promiscuity whose object was pain and chaos; not light but darkness. He looked at the green water and tried to think it through. Well, it would not be a wife; it would be a daughter. And it would be a payback, a settling of scores. There would be a female grievance, some never-ending wrong, something she had taken deep inside her and resolved to purge. Good Bolshevik word, he thought. Stalin sending great Russians to the Gulag, or simply liquidating them. Well, who were you, then? The tsar? He tried to imagine a daughter, being father to a daughter who grew up hating him; as opposed to a son. A daughter he had grievously wounded, perhaps unknowingly. What then would be his responsibility? Speak, conscience. That was the trouble when you tried to think things through; too damn depressing. Well, it would never happen. They would be completely in tune, he and this daughter. Any daughter of his would be a Brownie and president of the student council while studying the cello with Yo-Yo Ma and physics with Richard Feynman between excursions to Pretoria to straighten out the Afrikaners on the question of apartheid and deciding whether or not to accept the invitation of the Cubs to try out at spring training and telling her publisher, sorry, she wouldn't be able to write her memoirs until 1990, earliest. Yes, that would be about it. Khrushchev had put the matter in perspective, replying to some proposal of Eisenhower's. When shrimps fart, he said.

Kleust said, Why are you smiling?

I'm thinking about female grievances, he said.

You don't have enough trouble?

I like to pile it on, he said.

Kleust said, You're more German than I am.

I wonder who she is, Bill Jr.'s *Kameradin*.

Kleust shrugged and shook his head.

They say boys like women who remind them of their mothers.

Maybe in America, Kleust said.

Probably skilled in weapons. Small-arms qualified. Wouldn't you say, Kurt? A nasty piece of work, mad as hell at everything. Except him. She wouldn't be mad as hell at him. Probably they're mad at the same things. It would be a fine love affair, mad at everything. Complete agreement on the things to be mad as hell at.

Kleust said, Forster still has a point.

He did not reply and Kleust looked away to the fishing boat a mile or so off the bow. They were at midpoint in their journey across the lake. The water was even greener now, thick with algae, and the other shore a thin dark line on the horizon. He wondered how Elinor would paint it, the green of the water, the dark line, the blue of the sky, and the black clouds astern. But she did not care for the pastoral; she painted people. He looked at Kleust, lapsed now into a gloomy silence. The curse of northern peoples.

He said, Sorry about the crocs.

Kleust said, It doesn't matter.

The hunt had not been a success, despite the etiology of their surroundings: they were less than fifty miles from the source of the great sickle-shaped River Congo, the very soul of Africa. They both felt it: they were Africa's guests, or its prisoners, obliged to tread lightly. Kleust had been upset by the crocodiles. The second night he declined to shoot at all. He had killed two the first night, and that was enough. He consented to go along and watch but he did not want to shoot. He thought the beasts had a strange powerful beauty, and it was so easy to mesmerize them with the lamp. Their eyes glowed hot and red as the morning sun. Of course they were man-eaters, but there were no men on this lake; there were only the three of them, the hunter and the two diplomats, and the skinners; but the skinners were not intruders. At dusk they stood on the shore drinking Scotch and watching the beasts float by, lurking, furtive. They talked shop: personnel problems, pensions, the change in administrations, the perennial menace from the right. On the third day he took the biggest croc of all, eighteen feet long; the head was the size of the hood of a small car. He shot him three times in the skull before he died, sinking to the bottom of the shallow lagoon. The hunter and two skinners had gone into the water to raise him, then manhandle him into the boat. One of the skinners estimated the beast's age at ninety, perhaps one hundred. Kleust had listened attentively, then observed that if the skinner was correct, the croc had been born about the time that Stanley had found Livingstone; and that place was not far from where they were. All those years on the same lake, eating and copulating, prowling. One of the skinners reached into the crocodile's scrotal sac and brought out its penis, enormous, heavy, ridged, gray as death. Kleust had turned abruptly away, muttering in German. The hunter had laughed, but he too was embarrassed. He nodded sharply, and the skinner stuffed the penis back into its sac. That's better, Kleust had said. That's much better. Let us show some respect for the hundred-year-old *Grossvater*. Let the *Grossvater* rest in peace.

He could smell land, and looked at Kleust, still lost in thought. He said, God, this is beautiful country.

Kleust turned suddenly, squinting into the sun. He said slowly, Is it?

He said, You don't think so?

Kleust shook his head. No, I think it is the edge of the precipice.

He did not reply. The sun was enormous in the sky, a furnace; its light glittered on the water, opaque with algae. The land smell was heavy in his nostrils. The sky was empty except for the sun; he did not look behind him. There were no birds about, nor any living thing. Yet he knew that beneath the surface of the lake there was life.

Kleust said, I am not like you.

He said, You're a good man, Kurt.

The German made a noise, a kind of scornful sigh. He unbuttoned his shirt, and flapped it against his sweaty skin. He said, I came in at the end of everything — true patriotism, faith, authority, integrity, purpose. German Expressionism, yes? Even the women are not what they were. They are not worthy. Everything has gotten worse, except the domestic life of the German people. Our economy is a wonder. It is because of the conditions imposed upon us: Mandatory restraint. Political reparations for our excesses. We lower our voices, we have no big stick to wave. We adhere to the Americans, the last colonial power. This is good. Who can doubt it? The rest of the world should be as restrained as we Germans. In this place, not your place, you look around you and say: What a beautiful country. You are entitled to say it, it is your American privilege. But do you know how bad Africa is? Have you *seen?* Have you left your compound, gone into the streets, traveled in the region? Have you traveled in the Madness Belt? The belly of the continent. Disease, famine, murder, ignorance, corruption, megalomania. It's grotesque. It pulverizes the imagination. Amin, Mobutu. They're little Hitlers, worse than Hitler, because they're exterminating their own people.

Jews were Germans, he said.

Hitler didn't think so, Kleust replied.

Their boat angled off. In the distance was the little dory with two fishermen. He and Kleust could vaguely see their rods pointed skyward; there looked to be four rods, the fishermen were trolling. It was a consoling sight, a sight almost from the century before, a peaceful scene from a painting by Caleb Bingham or Winslow Homer. If the sky were a northern sky, and the water choppier, it could be a seascape near Gloucester. Except they were nowhere near Gloucester. They were in Africa, on the edges of the Madness Belt, on a lake so remote it did not appear on maps. At the edge of the precipice, according to Kleust.

Off the starboard bow the dory rocked to and fro, shimmering in the heat. The storm was far behind them now; the skinner had been correct. They had outrun it. They were nearing land at last, smelling its thick milky smell, as if the earth itself were lactating. The skinner suddenly shook his head and sang something incomprehensible; it sounded like a dirge. He throttled back and they approached the dory slowly, circling it, staying out of range.

It was not a dory, and there were no fishermen with rods. He and Kleust leaned forward, appalled. What they believed from a distance to be a boat was a crocodile, dead and bloated, floating on its back, high in the water. It had taken sick and died; perhaps it had been crippled. Its fat legs pointed skyward, rocking gently as the croc yawed on the lake's surface. Its mouth was wide open, each tooth as long as a man's finger. The inside of its mouth was a ghastly pink. They idled a moment, looking at it. It turned toward them, moved by a sudden breeze or by something under the water. The skinner said, Female. The stench was terrible, curdled milk. They could not take their eyes from it, so unexpected an apparition. The tail has been eaten, severed at the base, ragged bits of white meat spilling into the water. He imagined the crocodiles tearing at it, hitting it again and again; the female too sick and terrified to defend herself, and finally giving up. Her belly was intact, though: smooth, creamy, swollen. The skinner throttled forward and their boat heaved, leaving the crocodile astern, swirling the wake. They watched it tip and bow, stiff and buoyant as a cork, obscenely inverted. It seemed to rush toward them, as if suddenly alive and giving chase. The dead eyes of it burned red in the sun. It followed a moment, then dropped back; something from below butted it, and the carcass began to turn, slow as the second hand of a clock. They accelerated, the skinner jamming the throttle all the way forward. They watched it recede, still rotating. As the thing receded, it resumed its former shape, an innocent dory, two fishermen in the dory, rods pointing skyward, a consoling picture.

Bill?

He turned, closing his eyes, feeling the African breeze on his face. He could not see Kleust's face. What had Kleust meant about worthy women? They had talked about everything but women. Perhaps he thought worthy women had died along with the nineteenth century. Poor Kleust, he had never married; he had no children. Instead of a family, he had his history, the modern history of the German people. He cared for the history as other men cared for a family; he had a responsibility toward it. He'd said, *I came in at the end of everything.* But what a sight it had been, that morning on the lake, the dory and the fishermen transmogrifying into the beast, and then back again. When the beast became a dory, they never looked back. The past was past, and they kept their eyes on the approaching shore, and the deserted village with the makeshift pier. They tipped the skinner, and thanked him; he departed immediately. Then Kleust remembered that there was a bottle of Scotch in the Land-Rover. They sat in the Land-Rover drinking Scotch and debating the various routes back to the capital. It was a two-day trip, hard country roads. Kleust insisted on driving. . . . He looked at Elinor, her eyes close to his.

Bill? How are you feeling?

Fine, he said.

Are you in pain?

No, he said. Was he? He didn't think so. It was hard to tell; he felt heavy. He came back slowly, by inches, as if from a long distance. Things did not look familiar. He was lying on his stomach, Elinor seated on a metal stool. He did not know where he was, and did not want to ask.

"Your eyes are so bloodshot," she said.

"Have I been drinking?"

She smiled. "Dear Bill. I don't think so."

"I've been dreaming," he said.

"What about?"

"Africa," he said, "Kleust. Remember, when we took that trip, hunting crocodiles. You didn't want to go. Kurt hated it. We shot that grandfather." He should have taken Bill Jr. on that trip, any boy would have loved it. But Bill Jr. was already gone, living somewhere else; living in Europe.

She smiled again. "I remember."

"He was here just a minute ago."

"No, darling."

"He's a good man, you know. We've had so many adventures together. He was here just a minute ago. We were having a drink, and trying not to talk about women." He hesitated, his vision suddenly cloudy. He said, "Where am I?" and as he said it, he knew where he was. The breeze died; Africa vanished. Kleust vanished. He forgot all about it. He gave himself up.

"Do you know where you are now?"

"I don't want to know." Making a joke.

She said, "You're with me."

"Well, it's all right then." He said, "My head hurts."

She said, "It's supposed to."

He said, "Jesus, it hurts like hell." He felt her lips on his cheek, smelled her familiar scent. He felt himself slipping, unable to concentrate. He had gone away, but now he was back, and wanted to go away again.

"Darling, the operation was a success."

"Is that right?" He remembered the operating room now, the bright lights, the doctors and the anaesthesiologist, and counting back from ten.

"A great success."

"Prowler came through?" The pain came at him in waves, centered somewhere in the front of his head. He wondered if he had shrapnel in his head, a chunk of iron that had been dislodged during the operation. He decided not to say anything about it.

"He came through. So did you. They said you're tougher than you look."

"I hope," he said. It was gathered right behind his eyes.

She said, "You were on the table for two hours."

"I believe it." On the edges of his vision, something moved. He did not know if it was the pain moving, or a person.

She said, "Does it hurt badly?"

"Yes," he said.

"I'll call the nurse."

"I want to go to sleep again," he said. The pain was a physical thing; it took human form. He could not see its face, but it was inside his head, talking at him.

"All right," she said. "I'll call the nurse." She put her hand on his shoulder, rising.

"Is Bill Jr. here?"

She said, "No, darling." He was looking at her thighs. He could not see her face.

He said, "I thought he was here."

She said, "No, darling."

He said, "You could never count on that kid."

She said something he did not hear, or could not understand. Her head was above him, out of sight. Then her face was very close to his. There was one thing that he wanted to say, but he could not remember what it was.

221

She said, "Bill?"

He was looking down a long tunnel, and beginning to fall.

She said, "I'll get the nurse."

He said, "No, stay. Stay with me for a minute." The pain lay stretched out beyond his eyes, grinning. It had a mean androgynous young face. It seemed to be challenging him, to fight or to consent; but either way there would be no winners. Moving again, fluttering its hands, the pain grew, swelling. He opened his eyes, and Elinor vanished. Why would she go, when he had asked her to stay? So it was just him and the pain, his dream world. Americans lived in a dream world; so he had been told. He felt his wife's mouth on his cheek again. She was crying. He had been talking nonsense, not knowing if he was asleep or awake. She kissed him again, spoke his name. He was so moved. The pain began to ease, rising, moving back into the shadows behind his eyes. Everything would be all right, if only she would stay. He said to her, "Stay." Then, what he had forgotten but came back to him now, he spoke without hesitation. "I love you."

3

BILL HAD BEEN READING a memoir from the Eisenhower years, and when the afternoon sun touched the top of the page he realized he had been dozing; that, or daydreaming. The radio hummed away at his elbow, Mozart. He came to. Perhaps he had transmigrated to the blue serge Washington of the nineteen fifties, to the Cabinet room of the White House, stuffed with businessmen, George Humphrey, Sinclair Weeks, Arthur Summerfield, and the others. He had been staring at the same sentence for minutes, perhaps hours. *The autumn of 1957 was portentous and impressive,* according to Boston's Bobby Cutler, Ike's special assistant for national security affairs. Gosh. All at once?

The music stopped and someone began to speak. A national hotline had been established for missing and abducted children, an 800 number, toll-free. There were pictures of the children in supermarkets and on milk cartons and if you recognized one you should call the hotline number. A million children each year, missing. That was a little less than one half of one percent of the population of the country, missing or abducted. How the hell could there be a million missing or abducted children? Maybe some of them just lit out for the territory, bye-bye Aunt Sally. He had run away from home once, got as far as South Station; it was more fun planning it than actually doing it. The voice on the radio had a portentous and impressive quality all its own, repeating the hotline number, emphasizing again that it was toll-free. Finger a kid, and it won't cost you a dime.

He turned off the radio and put the book back in the shelf, next to Sherman Adams, and called upstairs that he was going out for a walk. Elinor mumbled something indistinct in reply: Fine, don't be late, take it easy, whatever. He knew she was working, concentrating on her canvas. He could hear her radio in the background, rock music. Baseball in the summer, rock the other seasons. When she was thoroughly involved in her work she paid no attention to life outside the studio; it was as if there were no life outside the studio.

He stepped out the front door into O Street, surprised that it was so warm; the house was cool. It was early November and it might have been July. Washington's deceptive season. The trees, wonderfully red and gold, looked out of place in the lazy heat. Brittle leaves cluttered the sidewalks and gutters. He went back inside and removed his sweater.

He stood on the stoop looking across the street. A young woman was punching the code into the security system of the psychiatrist's house. Their eyes met, then slid away. She was dressed in black, black skirt, sweater, and tights, a thin gold chain around her neck. Black to match her mood, he thought, though she was an exceptionally good-looking girl, twenty or twenty-five years old. He wondered if she knew the reputation of the psychiatrist. Probably not, and anyway a psychiatrist's reputation varied with the patient. Or did they call them clients now? He glanced at his watch — ten before the hour — and when he looked up she had vanished, the door closing with a little audible click.

Bill walked slowly up to 34th Street and turned right. This was the part of Georgetown least changed over the years, at least physically. Pausing, he looked at the doors with their bright brass knockers, red security lights above the doorbells. All these houses had back yard gardens, flowering nine months a year, where the children played. There had been plenty of children in the old days, zipping up and down the sidewalks on their tricycles, as often as not supervised by a nanny or au pair. There were no children anymore, the neighborhood was filled with older people whose children were grown, or young professionals who did not have children. They had their careers and each other and the usual souvenirs, BMWs, houses in Virginia, money market accounts, caterers, expensive dogs, security systems. There was not a child in sight, and of course no one would dare leave a trike on the street; but if there were no children, there would be no trikes either. He had a moment of déjà vu, then realized that it was not déjà vu at all but an unconscious recollection that the brick and white-clapboard look of the street had not changed in thirty years; it had not changed since the portentous and impressive autumn of 1957. Except for the tricycles.

In the early 1960s they had lived up the street in a little narrow house Elinor called the vertical dungeon. Their neighbors were mostly young bureaucrats, lawyers, and newspapermen. In those days there were very few newspaperwomen. Women kept house and raised the children and (Elinor told him much later) made pacts among themselves: to stick it out, that life would get better, that the children would grow up and leave home, that their husbands would grow up and stay home, that there would be a reward at the end of the day. This was early days, before their community was truly a community: before the first inexplicable death, the first divorce, the first nervous breakdown, the first flower child. They were all married to boys apprenticing to Great Men. In time their husbands would be Great Men themselves, with public careers, rank and title, profiled in news magazines. The future was assured and it seemed altogether worthwhile, even morally superior, to be conspicuous in Washington as opposed to established in Lake Forest, Darien, or Sewickley, suburbs in which they had grown up and watched their fathers prosper. They never used the word, but the truth was they believed themselves patriotic, in government service. Even journalism was a form of patriotism, and later in the decade perhaps journalism most of all.

She had told him all this during their own bad time in the early nineteen seventies. He was astonished at how much he'd missed, at how much happened on 34th Street during the daylight hours, all the transactions in the park up the street, where the women went with their children late in the afternoon. She'd said that the women thought about sex all the time, sex being an undercurrent in Washington; sex in Washington was different, part of the city's cultural and political life. Everyone was in heat. It had to do with Kennedy and the people around Kennedy, and the careless atmosphere they created. Their husbands, being as personally conservative as they were politically liberal, refused to believe the gossip. It was the sort of conversation midwestern businessmen had in the locker rooms of their golf clubs. The women talked of little else. The men were interested in issues and answers, most of which were highly sensitive and therefore could not be brought home to the dinner table or the bedroom. At that time the city was filled with men who had outgrown their wives, giants married to runts. This was one of the hazards of Washington — so single-minded and hard-working, the stakes so high, the dangerous atmosphere reminiscent of wartime London, a *romanza*. It was a kind of epidemic, men outgrowing their wives, childhood sweethearts whom they'd married the summer after graduation, anticipating a pleasant commercial life in Pittsburgh or Chicago. But instead they came to Washington, were "lured," as they said, by the promise of involvement in the national life. The men went from success to success, and the women couldn't keep up. Nothing in their childhood had prepared them for the meritocracy and publicity of the capital, its high-mindedness and skullduggery, and their envious mothers were no help at all. Their mothers wanted the inside story of Jacqueline Kennedy's marriage.

They took themselves oh so very seriously.

Elinor's estimate of one Great Man who had left his wife of thirty years to set up housekeeping with a woman young enough to be his daughter: "I think he just wanted to get laid. He probably hasn't been laid recently. Probably he has never been laid properly. Look at his wife sometime. Of course he's no prize either. He is not one of the men that we think about when we think about sex. But he's on the front page of the newspaper, deciding the fate of the nation, and she isn't. So he gets the chippy. And she gets to go home." The silence that descended on the table that evening, the men so silent and embarrassed, the women aghast. Elinor had a way of going to the heart of things. He had delivered a long lecture to her when they got home. It was a lecture stressing the need for discretion, there were powerful people at the table. It was all right to think it, but it wasn't all right to say it. Really, she should have some consideration. People's lives were never what they seemed, and it was well known that the Greats had an uncommonly unhappy marriage, and he worked so hard. She had looked at him and giggled. Oh, come off it, Bill.

He was smiling now, remembering that; she didn't have to say anything else, and it was in the background always when he lectured her on the need for decorum and restraint. And the lectures were fewer, too; there hadn't been one now for years. Bill walked on, remembering the old days. He thought he would walk to the park — the park down the street from their old house, the vertical dungeon, where Elinor took Bill Jr. in the afternoons, to sit on blankets on the grass and talk with her friends and watch the children play — and keep an eye on the tennis. There was often quite good tennis. He paused at the corner, listening. From somewhere nearby he heard a violin. He listened hard, his emotions beginning to tumble. The music came from the second floor of the house across the street, he could see the open window. The notes hung one by one in the thick warm air, then a thrilling arpeggio, the last note traveling to the breaking point. He held his breath, the better to preserve the single note, and when it began to fade at last (he imagined it soaring to the heavens) the fault was not that of the musician but of his own concentration. He tried to imagine the violinist, practicing Baroque music on 34th Street on a warm Wednesday afternoon. The sound seemed to be for him alone, an audience of one. The street was empty, it could have been high summer, with everyone in the country or on Cape Cod or Long Island, the capital desolate.

He moved along, across the street. The music began again, fading at the sound of a motor. A helicopter overhead, and the sound of a horn on Wisconsin Avenue. A limousine slipped by, its smoked windows concealing the passenger or passengers within; it had official plates. Georgetown's narrow streets were not designed to accommodate twenty-foot Cadillacs, and this one navigated as carefully as a yacht approaching a dock. The limo stopped in the middle of the block and a woman with a briefcase got out. She paused to say something to the driver. The limo pulled away and she looked warily up and down the street before she rang the bell of the brick row house, and was admitted at once. He used to know who lived there. It was a senator from Pennsylvania. Either Pennsylvania or Michigan; he had been dead for years. The woman with the briefcase had the combative look of an attorney. But she had smoothed her skirt before looking up and down the street, raising her chin a fraction before taking off her eyeglasses. Not an assignation. She was dressed for success, not passion.

She had taken no particular notice of him. But neither had the troubled young woman across the street from his own house. They were both preoccupied, as self-absorbed as he was. He was anonymous, an invisible man, no threat or opportunity to anybody, an object of brief attention only because he was a pedestrian and there were so few pedestrians in Georgetown. The chopper had flown away and the street was silent again, stiff and formal as an old print. The violin music remained in his memory, however. He was suddenly depressed, walking lethargically toward the park, only a block away now. This part of town was a museum and he was one of the permanent exhibits, Stuffed Diplomat. He knew that he must look a very old man — hesitant, without vigor, not in heat, a convalescent. And truthfully, he felt cold and weary, without weight, slack around the edges, dull. An old fart out for an afternoon constitutional, when serious people were at their offices or arranging assignations. He flexed his left hand, and noticed that in the heat his wedding ring had become tight on his finger. His hand was alive, though, and there was no pain. It had been seven days since his release from the hospital.

"Sir?"

He turned, one more young woman walking toward him, looking at a piece of paper in her hand. She seemed in a great hurry.

"May I trouble you? I am looking for Dent Place?" Breathless, almost. She did not look at him, she looked at the paper in her gloved hand, a postcard from the look of it. She was smartly dressed in gray slacks and a sweater, ascot around her neck, tiny gold earrings.

"It's three blocks up," he said.

"Only three blocks?"

"Straight on," he said. She wore enormous sunglasses, of the sort that reflected your own image; in the mirror he appeared round-faced, almost healthy.

She looked at him at last, or over his shoulder; straight through him. She offered a brilliant smile, and thanked him, and hurried away, dropping the postcard after she had gone a dozen steps. Or not dropping it, throwing it to the sidewalk, as if it had no more use.

Careless young woman, he thought. People who littered, it was probably what she did in Paris or wherever she came from. She was much too chic for Washington, and she had an accent. He moved ahead and picked up the postcard, looking for a trash bin. It was a reproduction of one of Kirchner's lithographs, a street scene, Hamburg. And the card was from the Kunsthalle, Hamburg. There was nothing written on it He stood a moment, looking at the card, turning it over. The Kunsthalle, he knew it well, a great repository of the Expressionists. He had last visited it in 1979, with Elinor and Bill Jr. The street was empty now, the young woman gone in accordance with his directions. She had looked right through him, as though he were a pane of window glass. He put the card in his pocket and stood a moment, lost in thought. He turned, thinking he would go back home, share this news with Elinor; then he thought, No, and walked on. Perhaps it was dangerous news, and perhaps there was more to come.

Two young men in white were playing slam-bang tennis, serve and volley. At the far edge of the park a woman walked her dog. He looked left and right, like a general surveying the battlefield, then sat on the wooden bench under the shade tree and watched the tennis players. The bench was covered with initials. He ran his hand over the grooves and wondered if somewhere there were Bill Jr.'s initials, or Elinor's. Perhaps the women had carved the names of real and imaginary lovers two decades earlier when they gathered in the park to talk about sex, giants, and runts, and what the future contained. He traced a heart with an arrow through it. Populated with ghosts, the park seemed alien to him, a zone of insecurity, not at all what he expected. His forehead was beaded with sweat, and he thought of Elinor cool in her studio, listening to music, rock and roll or Mahler, "I have become a stranger to the world." His mind raced, remembering the old days; the past was close enough to touch but the future seemed out of reach, obscure and inscrutable. It couldn't even be imagined, even if he had the strength to try to imagine it. Trying to connect this to that, he foundered, his thoughts incoherent, and he was sorry now that he had left the house, and the safety of the portentous and impressive autumn of 1957. Things then were near to hand. He stretched his legs and closed his eyes, hearing the thump of the ball and the grunts, *unh-unh,* as it was served and returned. He tried to concentrate on a single thing, to take his mind off the young woman and her dropped postcard, Kirchner, the Kunsthalle at Hamburg, the mordant message from his son, if that was what it was, and he couldn't imagine what else it could be.

Of course he would choose that bench, it would be familiar to him. Always, people returned to that which was familiar. It gave them a sense of security, the past being inherently more stable than the present. He watched the ambassador's fingers move over the rough wood of the bench, tracing initials. Everything in the park was familiar, the swings and teeter-totters, the tennis courts, the baseball diamond, all of its ringed by low row houses, obscenely expensive, houses of the *haute* bureaucracy. Their reward for the burden of public service, sigh. The trees were bigger and leafier than he remembered, but it had been a few years. The light was so fine and golden, it glowed with well-being, a spirit of public happiness, autumnal, an agreeable middle age; that, too, was familiar. He looked at the diamond, the dusty infield and wire backstop, and remembered a long-ago baseball game. He was nine or ten years old. He was playing third and someone hit a high pop fly. He went back and back, and when he looked up the golden sun blinded him. He flung up his mitt hand to block the sun and the ball fell into it, plop. People clapped and cheered. It had been the play of the day.

Bill Jr. drummed his fingers on the dashboard of the car, a Japanese sedan with tinted windows. Easy to see out, not so easy to see in. He had watched the ambassador's progress up 34th Street, watched him give directions to Olga, watched Olga drop the postcard, watched the ambassador pick it up, look at it; watched his head tilt, his hand go to his chin; watched him squint at the card, watched the light bulb ignite as Olga hurried away. Olga wiggling her ass just a little bit more than was necessary, not that the ambassador would take notice of *that;* the ambassador looked a little bit beyond *that.* Olga adjusting her big sunglasses, turning the corner and breaking into a run. A young girl running to an appointment, running to catch her bus, meet a lover, whatever. It was ludicrous. God, he looked old as he stood swaying in the street. His clothes didn't fit properly, and he needed a haircut. He looked a hundred years old. And he was pale, the ambassador who had always had a ruddy complexion. He looked as if a breeze could blow him away. He had watched the ambassador hesitate and turn, as if to retrace his steps, go back to the house on O Street, cry on his wife's shoulder, then decide against it; decide, perhaps, that the afternoon held promise, that there was an act yet to come, that if he went the last inch — why then, the drama might reveal itself.

Whose phrase was that? It was the egoist Solzhenitsyn, the Vermont squire. A dying man was obliged to go the last inch, to fully feel and appreciate the magnitude, the momentousness, of death. Otherwise it was just another event in a life. No poison, no bullet in the brain, no matter how painful or squalid the disease. It must be felt, or it was meaningless.

Christ, this was nerve-racking.

Bill Jr. watched the tennis players in the distance; young men from the look of them. On the edge of the infield, a woman walked her dog. The ambassador was sitting slumped on the bench. He looked almost to be dozing, except from time to time his hand would go to his chin. So he was not dozing, but thinking; and his eyes would be wide open. But the question was, How much would he see? What would he recognize? Bill Jr. reached over the back of the seat to touch the package on the floor. A plain brown paper bag, the sort of bag that might contain a bottle of wine. The ambassador was not being watched; he was certain of that. The tennis players were intent on their game; they had been playing for an hour. The woman with the dog was — a woman with a dog. At the last moment, Bill Jr. had trusted his instinct, that the ambassador would go to the park, and choose the familiar bench, the one with the carved wood, and the convenient trash barrel beside it.

A young woman in black crossed the street in front of the car.

She reminded him of Gert. He watched her walk into the park, and stand a moment in the sun. She moved aimlessly, as Gert often did. He looked away then, sad beyond measure; he felt tears behind his eyes. He wanted her now. He worried about her, where she was and how she was keeping. Well, he knew where she was; she was well looked after by people who liked her and were kind to her, but he worried just the same. Gert was unfathomable, and that was part of her allure. But sometimes she went so far inside herself that she became lost, as anyone would in an uncharted ocean. When she was lost she panicked, terrified. Her instinct was not to retreat, but to advance. He feared always that she would disappear, and be lost to him forever. And he could not live without her, literally; she was his other half, his secret self. She defined him. Without her, he was just another abandoned American boy. If she were lost, she would never be found; and he would break down. Up the street, behind the maple tree, was the little house, the first homestead; two stories high, twelve feet wide. The Bertram stories, Dr. Seuss. People in and out of the house, friends. He tried to imagine him and Gert living there, sleeping in the front bedroom with the rattling air conditioner, cooking outside in the back yard on warm evenings. What was the life they wanted for him? He would be a second-generation Washingtonian, a certified cliff dweller, involved some way in the government. Government business, the family firm. He stared at the house. It had a new coat of paint, but it did not look lived-in. He imagined Gert at the second-floor window, looking out at the park, remembering Germany, trying to fit that into this. She would look into the park and see dead men. She would watch a simple baseball game, see a little boy go for a fly; and she would hate him. She would despise all of it, and one day she would wander away and never return.

He shuddered; shook his head to clear it. The woman in black was circling the park, staying in the sunshine. She had a free and easy gait, a kind of sexy swing, a young woman alone in a public park on a lovely afternoon in early November, unseasonably warm. She cast a long shadow that undulated over the brilliant leaves. The ambassador was watching her or seemed to be. Sexual thoughts creeping into his dead head? A little stirring of the groin, thoughts of the way things used to be? Doubtful: he was so out of it. She moved around the perimeter of the park in the direction of the tennis courts. The boys in white were beginning to slow down, it had been a long game. Something about their movements on the court suggested European tennis. They tended to stay back, and their footwork was unusual; perhaps there was something about their outfits, too. Hard to know. Hard to know exactly what it was that alerted him. Bill Jr. looked left and saw a black Mercedes slip down 34th Street, pause, and pull into a parking place. A Mercedes on 34th Street, and a limo idling on the other side of the park.

Too many questions, too many things seen, all at once.

So it would be later. He had a plan for that also. Bill Jr. put the car in gear and drove away, a little faster than he needed to, not so fast as to attract attention. His eyes were on the rearview mirror, but Volta Place behind him was empty. No one followed. He had not been seen.

Mordant messages. Maybe she was listening to rock, maybe to Mahler. Bet on Mahler. *A stranger to the world, I have become.* That one. Oddly, for the alto voice; one would have thought a baritone. But Mahler was always evenhanded. Women got out of joint no less than men, when the world got up and wandered away. Perhaps women did not mind it quite so much, having a more complete inner life. It was hard to imagine a woman lost inside herself.

He crossed his legs, idly watching the tennis players. He touched the postcard in his pocket. A tangible clue, evidence for Carruthers, for Dunphy and the committee, dapper Warren Winston. He could approach them voluntarily. I am an officer of the government, and this is my full disclosure. On 34th Street, Northwest, at four in the afternoon, she was an attractive young woman, enormous sunglasses, slender and chic. Foreign, French from the sound of her accent. A professional approach. If he had neglected to pick up the card, she would have tried again, some other way; or someone else would have. He knew every question they would ask. He was one of them, after all. They thought alike, government men; he had been one his entire working life. He was more a part of them than Elinor was. Elinor had looked at him and said: *Nothing, give them nothing.* So the world had wandered away, but he had wandered away, too. Elinor remained where she had always been. And the boy? He was to the back of beyond.

Well, the world was neither coherent nor consistent. You played for time; time was the prize, though not always the prize you wanted.

His vision blurred but he made out, across the park, the young woman in black. Her hour had run its course, and he wondered now what had taken place between her and sensitive Dr. Bixby, the Talleyrand of the female orgasm. Nothing good, from the look of her slow step, arms at her sides, head down; she looked like a priest advancing on the altar, a vivid figure, black against the red and gold of the trees. Probably she too was a child of the Establishment, perhaps consoled by its moral disarray. *What is to be done?* No doubt Bill Jr. had asked the same question, already knowing the answer. He was not interested in the next question, *What is to be done after we do what we have to do?* First things first. Bixby would be a big help. After a glance at the clock, he would lead her back over the difficult terrain of the past, the past imperfect, mommy, daddy, nightmares, daydreams, the shadow of love, the absence of justice, the day the dog died. Christ, it was such a sham. He imagined Bixby leaning forward, so solicitous, staring into her dark eyes as she unraveled. You'll feel better with your clothes off, my dear. By God, she was a good-looking young woman in black. All afternoon, surrounded by young women; and he had not felt the slightest sexual urge. He had no desire. Maybe somewhere in Georgetown there was a female Bixby, who for a hundred dollars an hour could coax him out of his shell. Make yourself comfy, put your feet up. Have a cigarette. Like some warm milk? Tell me your dreams, Bunny.

"Hello, Bill."

He turned, startled. He shaded his eyes from the sun, burst suddenly through the trees. Turning, he twisted his neck and the pain shot into the small of his back. For a moment, he didn't know what to say. He waited for the pain to ease, and when it didn't he turned away, groaning, gaining time. The tennis players had paused in their game and were watching him. He felt a great rush of gratitude, why he couldn't say; this visit was nothing to be grateful for. He rose slowly and they shook hands. He said, "Hello, Kurt. Take me home."

4

KLEUST SAID, "The car's over here."
 Standing, lightheaded, he was conscious of a stillness in
the park, a cessation of movement. The young woman in
black had disappeared, and the tennis players had abruptly finished their match. They were sitting on the grass, breathing hard.
One of them was smoking a Gauloise, the unmistakable raw French
odor saturating the air. He and Kleust walked in silence to the car,
an old black Mercedes sedan with ordinary DC plates. Bill got in,
stumbling once, then leaned back against the leather cushions and
closed his eyes. The leather gave off a wonderful oily smell, the
rotund atmosphere of a gentleman's club. Old Kurt, looking stiff
and formal as a line of German script, while he himself felt like a
child's hand, erratic, vague, hard to decipher. You have me at a
disadvantage, he thought.

He said in German, "What a surprise. The day is full of surprises. How did you know where I'd be?"

Kleust said, "I guessed. It wasn't hard. They told me you took a
walk in the afternoon."

He opened one eye, and looked at Kleust. They?

Kleust said, "You look half dead."

"And everyone says how well I'm getting on."

Kleust smiled. "They're lying." Then, "We have to talk, Bill. I don't have much time."

"Are they yours, the Hitler youth on the courts?"

"Two boys from the embassy. They play every afternoon."

He said, "Christ."

"They're nice boys," Kleust said.

"The woman in black?"

He said, "Bill," reprovingly.

"The dish in the limo?" It was parked up the street, the chauffeur leaning against the hood smoking a cigarette. While they watched, he flipped the cigarette into the street, got into the car, and pulled away. Kleust laughed, and put the key into the ignition. He started the car and let it idle, the engine quieter by far than the Beethoven quartet on the cassette. After a moment, Kleust cleared his throat and put his hand on Bill's arm. "Look," he began, but Bill shook his head. Later, when they were at home, when Elinor could join them. When he had taken a pill, and had a drink in his hand, and was in his own house, safe.

"You might want to hear this first, old friend."

"No," he said.

Kleust looked closely at him. "God almighty. What did they do to you?"

"Cut my neck," he said. Then, smiling: "Successfully."

"Shrapnel?"

"That's what they said."

"If that was a success, I'd like to see one of their failures."

He laughed. Old Kurt, he had a great bedside manner. "Well, fuck you, too." Christ, he was tired; tired and slow, moving as if he were under water.

Kleust said tentatively, "Bill —"

"Funny thing, I was just thinking about him."

"Who?"

"Bill Jr. That's why you've come, isn't it?"

Kleust put the car in gear.

"Well, then. Let's go home." They rode in silence to O Street, where, miraculously, there was a parking space in front of the house.

Elinor was downstairs. When she saw him, so obviously out of it, she gave a little cry. When Kurt came in the door behind him, she recoiled; there was none of the usual banter of the unexpected visit. Where had he come from? One look at the two of them told her it was bad news, and when Kurt held out his hand and kissed her on the cheek, she pulled away in confusion. They stood awkwardly in the vestibule, embarrassed as if they had a secret between them. Bill asked her gently to bring in a drinks tray. She listened for a signal but his voice was neutral, perhaps with fatigue. He and Kleust went into the study.

He took a pill. The house was cool after the heat of the park. He noticed that Kleust was wearing a tweed suit, and sweating freely; probably he had just gotten off the plane. Elinor came in with the drinks tray and some peanuts and cheese. She poured Scotch for them and Coke for herself. Then, on second thought, she added rum to the Coke. Her hand was shaking but she was certain they didn't notice, they were so caught up with each other, and whatever secret they were sharing.

Bill took a long drink and felt better at once. "You just got off the plane?"

Kurt nodded. "From Frankfurt."

Bill smiled sadly at Elinor, then said, "I've got about thirty minutes of concentration."

Elinor said quickly, "Do you want to stay for dinner? We have plenty, I'd just have to set another place." She knew what was coming and didn't want to hear it. She pulled both legs up under her on the chair, both hands around the glass in her lap.

"I've probably got to get to the embassy."

She caught the ambiguity in his voice and nodded. They could decide later.

Kleust looked at each of them in turn. "We have word about Bill Jr."

She murmured, "Thank God," and put her face in her hands, the glass cold against her cheek. "Thank God, thank God." She reached across the table and took Bill's hand. "I thought he was dead. I thought Kurt had come to tell us he was dead. All this week I've thought, 'He's dead.' Something kept pushing at me, telling me that he was dead in Europe. I haven't been able to get it out of my mind. Every time the telephone rang —" She put the glass down.

"No," Kleust said. "He's alive. He's in Germany."

She turned away, her glance falling on the photographs in the bookcase. The three of them ten years ago, Bill and the boy demarcating her, like a picture frame. They towered over her, though Bill Jr. had yet to reach his full height. They looked so young; they looked like the product of Picasso's early years, a family portrait before the Blue Period, before Cubism, before things got so fantastically complicated. She turned to Bill, staring silently into his drink. She said, "How do they know where he is?"

Kleust said, "We have reliable information." He put his hands out, palms up.

Bill said, "His name is Duer."

"Well, who's Duer? I don't know any Duer."

Kleust said, "He's one of our people, Elinor. He's very reliable."

She turned to her husband. "Do you know him?"

"I met him in Africa, remember? I told you about him, Herr Duer. He was the one who had the photographs, Bill Jr. and the girl in Hamburg. I didn't like him."

"I don't know him," she said firmly. "I don't remember Herr Duer."

Kleust leaned forward, speaking quietly as if fearful he would be overheard. "They have been tracking Bill Jr., and his group. One of them, a young woman, flew from Hamburg to Munich to Rome. And from Rome to Montreal. By train from Montreal to Burlington, Vermont. And by air from Burlington to Washington. They are very thorough. That was last week. She disappeared in Washington, so easy to do despite the assets we control. It is easier to disappear in Washington, D.C., than in the Amazon Basin. Your government does not control its own borders! We are certain she was here yesterday, but perhaps she has flown away again."

Elinor said, irrelevantly, "All that travel. It costs a lot of money."

"Yes," Kleust agreed.

"Where did she get the money, Kurt?" Bill wanted to get back to specifics.

Kleust smiled. "They kidnaped a child in Munich."

Bill raised his eyebrows.

"A banker's daughter. The banker paid, immediately. A half a million Deutschmarks, cheap at the price. And the banker actually got her back, which isn't usual."

"Was she hurt?"

"No, she wasn't hurt. She was hysterical, but not harmed. They told her to say nothing, or they would return and mutilate her. They made her believe it. They were very persuasive. The entire transaction was over in twenty-four hours."

"All right," Bill said. "And what else?"

"That's where the money comes from," Kleust said.

"I know that," Bill said.

Kleust looked at his drink, picked it up, and took a sip. He spoke slowly, choosing his words with care. "The question is, Why is she here? What does she want? The evidence that we have is not a hundred percent conclusive. But we believe she is here because of you. She wants to make contact. She is carrying a message, to be delivered privately. A message to be delivered to you alone. They would suspect a telephone tap, and suspect a mail cover; so it would not be a phone call or a letter. We believe. *Herr Duer* believes. They want to arrange a meeting." He had been moving his eyes back and forth between Bill and Elinor. Now he looked only at Bill.

He said, "She has been in Washington a week?"

Kleust said, "Yes."

"But you think she may have gone?"

"Only if she has made the contact."

Bill was silent.

"Has she?"

Elinor put her hand on Bill's arm. "A meeting. For what purpose?"

"We are not sure," he said evasively. Then, "But they killed a man in Berlin. Bill Jr. and his girlfriend did."

Elinor said, "I don't believe it."

"Who was he?" Bill said.

"I don't believe it," Elinor said again. "Were there witnesses?"

Kleust looked at Bill. "There is evidence."

"Who was he?" Bill asked again.

"We're not sure."

"*Kurt,*" Bill said.

The German looked up with sudden understanding. "It wasn't an American. No one connected with your government. Or ours." He added, "I'm not at liberty to say who it was. We are still waiting

239

for positive identification. I have instructions. I am going by my instructions."

"This is an official visit, then."

Kleust said, "No, Bill. There will be one, no doubt. But this isn't it. This is private."

Elinor began to speak. She was looking at the portrait, suddenly rearranged in her vision. Bill and Bill Jr. looked misshapen to her. She was trying to connect then to now, but it was all now. She realized she was incoherent and shut up. Bill listened a moment, then rose and went to the window. O Street was brilliant in the fading yellow light; it was almost dusk. He looked without seeing, imagining the girl somewhere nearby, perhaps the park or on the crowded Wisconsin Avenue sidewalks; perhaps she was in a singles bar, listening to the chatter. It would encourage her, evidence of decay from within; Marx confirmed in Clyde's. But it was a large city, she could be almost anywhere. No doubt she had already left, as Kleust suspected. Bill knew now that it was important to betray nothing. He looked left and right at the people in the street, his neighbors returning home from work. Then he stood by Elinor's chair, listening. The postcard was in his pocket, and he restrained an impulse to touch it; to check on it, as one would check on a sleeping infant.

He said, "What else, Kurt?"

Kleust put ice in his glass, and Scotch on top of the ice. He was entirely American in his drinking habits. He said nothing for a moment, stirring the drink with his index finger. They could all hear the ticking of the clock in the hallway.

Elinor said, "Why is she here, Kurt?"

"She hasn't been in touch, then?"

"No," Bill said. Elinor glared at him: *Nothing* meant nothing, not no, not yes, not maybe.

Kleust caught the look and said softly, "You're certain?" Then, realizing suddenly where he was and with whom he was talking — a colleague, one of his oldest friends — he looked at the floor, understanding that he'd caused offense. "I'm sorry, Bill."

"You've had a long day." He placed his hand on Elinor's temple, caressing her. He touched her neck, and placed his hand flat on her shoulder. She was cool to the touch, but he could feel her trembling. She was trembling inside. Probably she had it now. "And it's not over, is it, your day?"

"No," Kleust said.

"Why do you suppose he didn't come himself? My son."

Kleust shook his head. "He is careful."

"He's waiting in Hamburg," Bill said.

"Probably in Hamburg," Kleust said.

Bill leaned down and spoke only to his wife. "I'm the next target, El. That's why she's here. That's what the hugger-mugger is about, her setting up a rendezvous. Except I'm not supposed to know that. I'm not supposed to know what'll happen at the rendezvous. I'm such a dumb son of a bitch. He thinks I'm so stupid or ignorant or arrogant I'll miss that." He took his wife's hand. God, he was tired. He was only fifty and he felt at the end of the road, out of gas, the last ambassador. He held her hand more tightly. He had to fight, but he didn't know if he had the strength. He had the will but not the strength. He wondered if Bill Jr. knew the difference. Probably he did. The lad was quite a military historian, and would know the example of the Battle of Hamburg. Bomber Command under the authority of Air Chief Marshal Butcher Harris deciding that the war could be won by terrorizing the civilian population of Germany. Hamburg was convenient in 1943, as London had been convenient in 1939. Destroy the morale of the people of Hamburg and you've won the war. This, a virtue of necessity; Bomber Command did not have the skill to destroy military installations, the precision bombing of the penny press being in reality bombs dropped out of planes helter-skelter. Forty thousand men, women, and children dead in a single night of firestorm, five thousand more in the next month. July 1943. Christ, he thought, what an attractive analogy, though not without edge. The ambassador was as irrelevant as the Hanseatic League. And the boy every bit as brutal and careless as Butcher Harris and his German opposite number. The strategy worked, too. Hamburg's spirit was destroyed and driven mad, as any would be under merciless medieval torture. Hamburgers called the events of July 1943 *Die Katastrophe.*

Elinor looked at Kleust.

"That's what we think," Kleust said.

"And what do you advise, Kurt?" Bill rose, swaying.

"Don't do it." He smiled helplessly. "And keep me informed."

"What does Duer think?"

"They have killed once. Probably more than once. Almost certainly more than once. As for Herr Duer, Herr Duer has other priorities."

"I'll bet he has," Bill said.

"He has his own job," Kleust said stiffly.

"Duer," Bill said. He put his glass down. He thought he was going to collapse. He said, "I'm going upstairs to rest. Call me in ninety minutes. We can have dinner together after all."

"Please stay," Elinor said.

"Do. I'm bushed, but I'll be all right after a little rest."

"You're sure?" Kleust said.

"Yes," Elinor said.

Walking upstairs, putting one foot laboriously in front of the other, he paused and leaned against the wall. He knew that Elinor was at the bottom of the stairs, watching him. Ahead of him was one of her pen-and-ink portraits, an old man behind a desk; he thought it was a drawing of his father, though she denied it. Generic old man, she said. He worked his way down the corridor, her pictures on the wall, either side, and entered their bedroom and lay down on the unmade bed, not bothering with his shoes, though his feet hurt, and he hated to dirty the spread. The room was dark and cool. He felt the presence of the girl outside, sensed her as he had sensed the hot African wind. The girl was waiting for him, just out of reach; she would be in the shadows, waiting. He stared at the ceiling, absently flexing the fingers of his left hand. He knew Elinor was at the door and he wanted to make some reassuring gesture, a wave or a wink, but instead he said, "El? What do you suppose my father would do?"

She smiled wryly, as if about to make a smart remark. Then she shook her head. "I don't know, baby."

"I don't either."

"He didn't like it when you joined the Foreign Service."

"Hated it."

"But he didn't think it dishonorable."

"No," he said. "Not dishonorable."

"And you didn't threaten him."

He looked at her a long moment, wondering; threats came in various guises. His father was skeptical of diplomacy — it had not been a conspicuous success in the Second World War, not even in Italy, where it was invented. However, it would be a struggle, as one hears struggle in Beethoven or Brahms. The old man had had a turbulent history, very much of the Old World, not an optimist. He felt the necessity of making himself obscure, half visible. Bill said, "I think he was frightened of America. America's potential, its reach, its *grab*, its ignorance of the dark side of things. America had no understanding of true malevolence." That was what he thought about in the evening, studying his texts. The notion that God had a special place in His heart for the American continent seemed to him fantastic, ludicrous, and dangerous.

"I've got to see to Kurt," she said.

"He thought, you know, that I'd find anti-Semitism in Washington."

"Yes," she said. It seemed to her so long ago.

"He thought the Foreign Service was like university presidencies and New England banks."

"I know," she said.

"He said, 'You'll have to lie low.' "

"I know, Bill."

"And I said I wouldn't have to because things were changing. In Washington no one gave a damn, except some of the old farts and they were on their way out."

"Go to sleep," she said.

"I saw the prettiest girl today."

"Goodness," she said with a broad smile.

"She was gorgeous. Sexy, too."

"Young, I suppose. I suppose she didn't have a gray hair in her head."

"She's the one who sees Bixby."

"I've seen her. She's a very pretty girl. Too young for an old fart like you."

"What about Bixby? He's older than I am."

"It's part of the therapy."

"Maybe we can have some therapy tonight."

"I'd love it," she said.

"Who was the one with the orgone box?"

"Reich," she said.

He patted the bed. "Orgone box, right here."

"Dear Bill," she said. "What a good idea. It's been weeks."

He said, "You go, look after Kurt."

"All right," she said.

He said, "I'll be down in an hour. I'm not so tired anymore. Thinking about the therapy."

She smiled. "Pretend you're in Back Bay."

He laughed. "God, all those ghosts."

"Sleep for an hour, Bill."

"I'll think about the Back Bay, be asleep in seven seconds." She left, closing the door behind her. The golden sunlight stirred his memory. It was reminiscent of Marlborough Street in October, and when he closed his eyes he could see his father, expressionless, so still in his heavy dark suit, the light coloring his bald head pink. They lived on Marlborough Street, but the old man had never left central Europe. He had a ghetto mentality, always apprehensive, fearful of the future. The old man had not chosen Marlborough Street; his wife had. It was a Gentile street in a Gentile city, and she had to convince him. She had to convince him of its anonymity and privacy. She had to convince him that she knew best, being both a Bostonian and a Gentile. But he could never refuse her, she understood him so thoroughly, and loved him without reservation. They loved each other and their music, and their privacy. In time he came to cherish Marlborough Street because it reminded him of a residential district near the Grunewald, big, heavy houses, a district that seemed indestructible. In the street there was always the sound of German music, Bach, Brahms, Beethoven, Schubert. And the same was true of Marlborough Street, in the 'forties and 'fifties. Gas lamps, narrow streets, and the Public Garden two blocks away. Walking distance to Symphony, the Goethe Institute around the corner. People kept to themselves, it was almost a condition of residence. The hurly-burly of political Boston was infinitely remote; it might as well have been taking place in Dublin. The old man came to understand that on Marlborough Street he could be as inconspicuous in Boston as he had been in Berlin, even after

244

the advent of the National Socialists. And with a Gentile wife, he remarked drolly, he was covered. She always surprised him. He was surprised when he married her, surprised that he wanted her so; and surprised that she wanted him, a European refugee, tormented sometimes beyond understanding. Of course he had no immediate family that would object, not that he would have respected their wishes. Some demands you had to refuse, no matter how painful; and without pain, life was not life. The old man thought that to be invisible was to be secure, or less insecure. For that reason, among other reasons, he hated New York. Or was it fear? He guessed it was fear, though the old man had never said.

That afternoon, so long ago. In fact it would have been the portentous and impressive autumn of 1955. They had been talking about Washington, the Presbyterians, and the meritocracy. Bill had said that the center of the nation was shifting from Wall Street to the Federal Triangle. This was obvious, anyone could see it.

The old man had said, And this is a good thing?

Bill remembered gesturing with his hand, brushing the comment aside. This was not something you could observe from Marlborough Street. Good or bad, he said, it's what's going to happen.

It might not be so good, his father said.

One more example of the old man's hopeless provincialism. Boston had always been a backwater, a distinguished past, no future. In that way it was identical with central Europe, a regional museum. He remembered his excitement, describing the surely imminent demise of the old Establishment. You could hear the death rattle. The government was filled with old, tired men, mired in the past, obsessed by it. The country yearned for a new beginning, for freshness and change, and action. The country was falling behind.

There wouldn't be any room anymore for anti-Semitism.

The old man moved, the chair creaking. He lifted his head, his eyes focused on a far corner of the dark room. He said, "What do you know about Jews?"

In the dizzy silence that followed, he suppressed an urge to cry out. He felt his face grow hot. The dark room, with its residue of absolute authority, discouraged any challenge. He could have been standing in the Oval Office of the White House.

He'd said, "I know enough. I'm your son."

The old man looked at him oddly, up and down, but did not speak.

He thought, Perhaps that doesn't count. To a man imprisoned in the past, obsessed with texts, with the history of a tribe, their relations with God; perhaps, to such a man, paternity was only a detail, an accident. It was not the fact of birth, it was the experience of life; once a Jew always a Jew, except it did not mean that you automatically knew the territory. To know the territory you had to work the territory, understand the terrain, survey the various battlefields and holy places (sometimes they were the same). But he was not interested. Let the North family silver stay buried. He remembered bending down close to his father and saying quietly, "There's more to the world than this house and Back Bay. More to humanity than the Jews. More to us than just us. We're cosmopolitan people, isn't that true? We've been cast out, isn't that true? We're wanderers and we have a conscience and we know there's justice to be done. We know that better than anyone. Who would know it better than we? And aren't we under an obligation?"

"An obligation?" the old man said dully, turning again, his hard glittering eyes fixed on a far corner of the room. He was looking at his texts, the wisdom of the Jews, which covered, the wall, floor to ceiling. When he turned back he seemed to look straight through his son, though his eyes were moving up and down, appraising the wrapping — polished loafers, gray flannel trousers, nubby sweater over a blue buttoned-down shirt, a tweed jacket with patches on the elbows. He had always thought he had a New England face, a stranger might think his forebears were seafaring men and the stubborn women who saw them off at the docks and waited ardently for their return. A coastal face, windblown, not a face of the interior; a well-made face, and at odds with the soft flannel and tweed —

"Yes," he said.

"Do you mean an obligation to God?"

"From God," he said, then stepped back, surprised; the words had popped out. The room, so familiar in the dark afternoon, seemed to beckon him. It seemed to pull him into the ambiguous darkness at the edges of the light. Surely there was a loyalty higher than a family, or a tribe, or history. He thought his father wanted to bind him to a dead European culture, a culture of the discredited past; an odious past; a holocaust, in fact. Sometimes it was necessary to banish memory, as a government sent an agent provocateur into exile. He waited, trying to find voice, wanting to speak of America's position in the world, the importance of a vigorous and rational foreign policy, the necessity of exposing the brutishness of the Soviet system without rocket rattling. . . . Well, he didn't want to talk about Jews. All this time his father remained motionless.

In the light of the reading lamp he was as conspicuous as an actor on stage. A vein pulsed in his temple. He said, "We cannot always remain apart, our bags packed, ready to move on."

"We *are* apart," the old man said. "It is a fact of history."

"It is a state of mind."

He looked at his son, but did not speak; his expression was one of infinite weariness. He did not have to speak, for his son could sense the names forming in his mind: Auschwitz, Treblinka, Belsen, and all the others. And there was no answer to that; there never is. It is as conclusive as the final sentence of the Old Testament, the Book of Malachi: *And he shall turn the heart of the fathers to the children, and the heart of the children to the fathers, lest I come and smite the earth with a curse.*

The old man said, "William."

He said, "I'm sorry, but it is what I believe."

The other nodded, his eyes far away.

"Daddy, we must *move on.*"

After a moment's pause, gesturing at his texts, the old man began to speak of his early life, his childhood and young manhood in Germany, his residence in Berlin, where he had gone in 1925, believing the family safe, so excited by the ferment in the most cultivated city in Europe. . . . Then he stopped and lifted his eyes. He stared at the ceiling, clasping and unclasping his heavy hands. At last he said, "I want to tell you a story. You won't like it. It concerns your great-uncle, my father's brother. You met him once, many years ago. Perhaps you will not want to claim him, so if you want you can think of him as one of our tribe. He was in the camps. He survived his camp, four years, and made his way to Chicago. I wanted him to come to Boston, but his wife's family was in Chicago. His wife had not survived her camp, and he wanted to go to Chicago. A year ago he was walking to work when a car sideswiped him, knocked him down, hurt him. A cab driver, a Negro as it happened, stopped to give assistance and stayed with him until the police arrived. Whereupon my uncle accused the cab driver of being his assailant, the driver of the car that ran him down. The police took the cab driver away, and my uncle was satisfied, very happy with what he had done. Now there was someone to sue."

He had glared at his father, the anger rising. "That is an evil story."

"Yes, it is."

"It is slanderous. Why would you tell such a story? Such an ugly story."

"It is not slanderous. It is true. And it has a moral."

"Does it?" He was disgusted.

"And the moral is this. *Life in the camps does not make a kind, loving, generous, forgiving soul. It does not make virtue. Good does not arise from evil. It is not a romance.*" He paused, breathing heavily, then spoke loudly. "It terrifies a man for life, and in the case of my uncle a man who wanted two things only: security and revenge. Can you understand that?" He paused again, the silence lengthening. They stared at each other a very long time, and when his father spoke his voice was almost a whisper. "You don't know anything. You don't know anything about it. You must read and read and read, and listen. You must study. You must think. You must know everything, and you must never forget. You cannot *move on.*" He snapped his fingers, the noise loud in the dark room. "Like that."

He turned away, as one would turn away from a blow. He was appalled. How had this begun? They had been talking about Washington and the Presbyterians, and what he wanted to do with his adult life, and in the bat of an eyelash God and Auschwitz were in the room.

And the old man was not finished. "I worry about your loyalties, William. You speak of change, but I don't know what change you have in mind. I mean the specifics, you who want to involve yourself with the government. You who don't want to be on the inside with your own people. What is it? Do you think we have fallen behind, that we are irrelevant in America? Do you think we have nothing to offer? Do you want to join their clubs?"

He remembered looking at him and deciding not to argue about who was inside and who was outside; who was where, us and them. Who was exclusive and who wasn't. Refusing to argue was itself a statement. They were like two hostile nations, and it was necessary for the son to see the father in a certain light in order to rally his own forces.

"So tell me," the old man said. "What are you, then? Where does your heart lie?"

He wanted to say "With Lincoln." But he did not. Lincoln would have no meaning. And he wanted a contemporary word, a newly minted coin, a word not found in the Old Testament. He said, "I am a pragmatist."

"A pragmatist!" the old man said, shuddering, then laughing out loud. "A prag-ma-tist!" He looked away to his bookshelves, and his texts, and the volumes of Kant, Hegel, Heidegger, Freud. Still laughing: "Is that what you get from your mother?"

"What do you want me to do?" he shouted, angry now. The old man's sarcasm was humiliating, but he thought he knew what the trouble was and went straight to its heart. "Do you want me to hang a sign around my neck, Half Jew?"

The old man shook his head. Staring up at him, he looked more than ever like a medieval woodcut, a Dürer masterpiece. He cleared his throat before he spoke, ending the conversation. "But that is right. You are."

He moved to the door, his feet silent on the thick carpet. He had never until that moment been able to judge the depth of his father's bitterness and disillusion, and infinite sorrow; he atoned in his own way. He knew absolutely that they were of different, and competing, nationalities. His father was a German, in all but passport. He was a German of the nineteenth century and a Jew of the twentieth. He thought then that his father wanted to destroy him, as a symbol of the assimilation he loathed; the father saw the son as a monstrous rebuke. Standing at the door to the study, he said, "I am going to join the Foreign Service, and I am going to become an American ambassador." He remembered hesitating, waiting; he thought that his father might respond after all, and offer his blessing. The old man was staring off to one side, his face as hard as oak. He could have been dozing, except for his eyes. The younger man thought he had an advantage, and pressed it: "I am going to Africa, and the Middle East, if I can figure a way to do it, and I know I can. And then, some time in the future, I am going to serve in Germany. I am going to know Munich, Heidelberg, Cologne, Hamburg, Berlin. Especially Berlin."

But the old man continued to stare off to one side, and he knew he was in another realm. When he opened the door, he heard the old man rustle, and finally speak, his voice dry as dust. He spoke in German. "Those are only names. The cities are dead. They have been dead for a long time."

He remembered the conversation as if it were only the other day, yet it was thirty years ago. He thought of his father as very old, but he was only ten years older than Bill was now. He remembered closing the door behind him and hurrying down the stairs and through the front door into the open air. It was dusk and the lamps along Marlborough Street winked on. Such a handsome street, one of the great city streets in America, though he did not think so then. He walked quickly to Clarendon and then turned left to Commonwealth. People were walking their dogs. He recognized most of them, older people with small, bad-tempered dogs. It was the neighborhood where he had played as a child, though he had few friends; and his parents had none. He remembered pausing, the silence drawing away from him. He was standing below the heroic statue of William Lloyd Garrison, the thrilling message chiseled boldly on the plinth.

> *I am in earnest — I will not equivocate — I will not excuse*
> *I will not retreat a single inch — And I will be heard!*

He stood in front of the statue, worrying the scene with his father. And he recalled standing in the snow and telling the old man about Garrison. He was in the fifth grade and his civics class had spent an inspiring hour on Garrison, great Boston abolitionist, pamphleteer, conscience of free men. The civics teacher admired Garrison and for several years after he harbored a desire to become an influential newspaperman. Paine, Garrison, Marx. He remembered talking excitedly to his father about Garrison and his father nodding politely, listening, and finally smiling and seeming to agree.

And muttering under his breath, *"Shlenter."* His fifth-grade self took this to be a compliment. His father often used Yiddish words as compliments (this was before he discovered that few such words exist in Yiddish, it being largely a tongue of insult and invective). Until one day he asked someone — in fact a friend of his father's, who had used the word in what seemed another context altogether — and the friend had laughed and laughed and said it meant con man. "A fast talker, William. A bullshit artist."

He stood a long time in the dusk, looking at Garrison's statue. It began to snow, large soft flakes. He decided to return to Marlborough Street, to apologize to his father, so gravely offended. He would apologize for his arrogance, his zeal, and for his brutal remarks about the old country. But he would not retreat from his decision to join the Foreign Service. He trudged back to Marlborough Street, but when he got in sight of the house, he began to run; he had a premonition that the old man was dead. A heart attack brought on by his only son's disrespect. The study door was closed, and he could hear the sound of Beethoven inside; of course he would die to Beethoven. He raised his hand to knock, fearful, terrified as the Hindu son obliged to light the funeral pyre of his father — and heard the murmur of voices, and laughter; it was his mother's soft, ghostly laughter. Then the rumble of his father's voice, and her laughter again. He had the fantastic idea that they were making love. He backed away from the door, his hand still raised, like a character in a comic. He remembered thinking that there was a part of their life that would always be concealed, beyond the reach of his eyesight or hearing, beyond the reach of his heart, and that he was an outsider. They lived in some self-created Shangri-la. He waited an hour in the living room, a room so formal it might have been the chamber of an Old World grandee, and he a subject come to request an audience. Then he went to his own room and packed to return to school. He thought about leaving a note, then decided against it. What would he say?

She watched her husband turn his face to the window; and the nicest smile lit his face. He looked years younger, and she wondered what occasion he had recalled; well, he was thinking about sex. He might say it was Back Bay, but it was sex.

Downstairs again, she poured fresh drinks, and handed one to

Kleust. The German said nothing and she knew he was embarrassed for them. She so slow to get the point, Bill so blunt, then giddy as exhaustion overcame him. Poor Kurt, he had found himself in the middle of their private life. She, Bill, Bill Jr., and Kleust, a man of heavy black lines, so angular. He could have been a portrait by Max Beckmann, a *Selbstbildnis*. At any event, it was not the family group she would have imagined.

She wondered if, really, the girl had made contact. The way Bill behaved, she must have done.

Kleust turned to her then, clearing his throat. "Do you know anything that might help me?"

She said, "I can't help you."

"It's very dangerous for you," Kleust said.

"For Bill," she corrected. "But it's the same thing."

"Do you have any idea where he might be?" He waited, allowing the silence to gather. "We know so little about him, actually. We know our own, not yours. I have been allowed to read everything we have on your son, and we have more than you might expect. But. It's one piece of paper after another. Herr Duer has been thorough, conducted the necessary interviews, discovered the relevant documents. You'd be surprised, how easy it is, to gather it. Bill Jr.'s school transcript was particularly helpful, to the degree that anything was helpful. He was not well liked at school, you know, though he performed beyond expectations, and was never in trouble except for the incident in his last year. The assault on the teacher. He and the other boy."

"I wonder what happened to him," she said.

"Yes, of course. That is what we are wondering."

"Not Bill Jr.," she said. "The other boy."

"He is in the penitentiary," Kleust said.

"You found that out?"

"Yes," Kleust said. "He killed a man."

"My God," she said.

"We tried to talk with him, but . . ."

She looked at him. "But what?"

"He refused to see us. It was his right, under your law. They made it difficult for him, and still he refused to see us."

"I don't understand. How can the West German government —"

"We were working with your people, of course. It was a strange incident, the one with the teacher."

"Yes, I suppose it was," she said. And refused to say more on that subject.

"We have some of his stories from that period, the instructor is still at the school. He was able to find them in his files, and was happy, more than happy, to give them to us. Happy to do anything to help us. They are strange stories, though quite artful. The instructor said that in his class the boys would typically write stories about young children, and the girls about young adults; the girls seemed to want to go forward, and the boys backward. Bill Jr.'s stories were always about middle-aged men whose lives ended badly. Of course, at that age. One always believes the lives of middle-aged people end badly."

"Don't they usually?"

"Always in Bill Jr.'s stories there would be a compromise of some kind. He was quite politically aware, you know. So there would be a compromise, and consequences. And the hero of his story would end badly. Except the hero was never a hero, but a villain. His stories were without heroes."

"That's very interesting, Kurt."

He stared at her a moment, sipping his drink. "It's quite a dossier, but it's incomplete. There's a missing part, and perhaps he's the only person who knows what it is, the part that's missing, that gave him the belief that — his father is an enemy to be destroyed. It's all there somewhere." He thought it was like trying to recall a vanished civilization, the Hittites, the Etruscans, one of those. "The missing part is important to us because it could give us a clue to his behavior. We are not at a point where we can predict what he'll do, or how he'll do it. He does not seem to have a pattern. Herr Duer calls it 'grammar.' He does not have a 'grammar' that we can parse."

She said suddenly, "Are there ever any women in his stories?"

"No," he said.

"Never? Not in any of the stories?"

"We wondered about that, too."

"Bill and I —" she began.

"Yes?"

"Nothing," she said. "Nothing, nothing, nothing. I can't help you. And if I could, I wouldn't."

"We were hoping," he said patiently. "We are looking for a clue to the pattern."

"You'll have to find that yourself," she said.

"Elinor," he began.

"Bill and I love each other very much," she said.

"Yes, of course," he said.

"It's important to understand that."

"All right, Elinor." He filled his glass with ice, and Scotch to the brim. He knew what she was saying, but he didn't see how he could put it to use. And he was not sure he believed her, that the boy was a consequence of her happy marriage. She and Bill, who loved each other very much. That fit no pattern he knew of.

"Tell me about the girl," she said softly.

"We know very little about her. We think she's retarded. Autistic. Slow, at any event. A young woman who lives inside herself. We have found out that much. We know very little of her former life, except that in Paris she worked in a dress shop. He is kind to her."

"And is she kind to him?"

"It would appear so."

"And what do you know of their comrades?"

"Nothing. We think Bill Jr. and the girl move around, now with a group in Munich, now in Hamburg, now in Berlin. It's a culture. It's an entire culture in Germany. They despise Americans, which makes Bill Jr. very unusual. Very, very unusual."

"Tell me about them," she said. "Yours. This culture that my son and his girl have joined. Or that has joined them."

"Good haters," he said. "They've been stunned, by the memory of the Nazis, and the advent of the Americans. They see the Americans as barbarians, the great colonialists; people like me are weaklings and traitors, American puppets. Fausts. The governments of Europe are only the creatures of the Americans. American money, American culture, American CIA. They see a world out of control and want only to hasten the process, start it spinning faster and faster until it — melts." He leaned forward, smiling. "Like your own children's story, Sambo, and the tigers turned into butter. A kind of Sambo as if it were written by the Brothers Grimm. Except they don't know what kind of butter they want. They don't think about that, and I imagine it doesn't interest them. It doesn't *animate* them. To deracinate, that's what interests them. They have no ideology except that of the young Marx." He made a face, indicating a furious, uneducated, adolescent Marx. A Marx who had not yet written anything of consequence. Who had not *thought*. "Destroy what is destroying you, destroy it completely and forever. And then decide what is to be done." He said, "We live in a dream world. The trouble is, so do they."

His soft, cultivated voice seemed to fill the room. He had a mid-Atlantic accent, only a trace of German guttural; what gave him away was the formality of his diction. Elinor thought it was an easy voice to listen to.

"What does she look like?"

"She is a good-looking young woman, slender."

"Fair?"

"Dark."

"A German?"

Kleust nodded. "She is German, yes."

"Stylish?" Elinor asked. "Is she stylish or dippy?"

"Stylish in the way of European young. She is well groomed."

Yes, Elinor thought. That was what she wanted to know. "You said she is — retarded? It's hard to believe. Bill Jr. . . ." She shrugged.

"She is slow. She rarely speaks. But perhaps that is only her way. Perhaps there is something in the background of her life. Perhaps it is an act. These things are hard to know."

"That's it, then," Elinor said.

"What's it?"

"It's an act, a masquerade. She's playing a role of some kind. She's not retarded."

"How do you know?"

"My son hates imperfection. It offends him. He likes things to be complete and faultless. Quite the idealist, my son." She said, "And they killed someone."

Kleust nodded.

"My son and the girl you think is retarded."

"Yes."

"Who was the man they killed?"

"Please," he said.

"Who was the man they killed?"

Her voice, so loud in the quiet study, startled him; it rattled the glassware. He waited a moment before replying, and when he did it was in the same easy manner. "I won't tell you, Elinor. I can't. I have been instructed to say nothing about the killing, where it happened, or the identity of the victim."

"Why?"

"Security, I suppose. I don't know why," he said. "They didn't tell me *why.* I have no need to know *why.* That's the truth."

"Was it a cold-blooded killing?"

"Yes."

"Who pulled the trigger?"

"Does it matter?"

"It does to me, Kurt." She tried to imagine it, the location, "the scene of the crime." Was it a crime *al fresco?* Or indoors. Perhaps at lunch or over drinks. Perhaps after a quarrel, angry words, and an impulsive solution. She wondered if they took him unawares; perhaps his back was turned to them. Then she realized she did not know if the victim was a man or a woman. But she wanted to know, and would keep asking questions until she found out. She wanted to know everything about it, *them.*

He tried to avoid her eyes. He could not connect the son with the mother, they seemed to be of different species. But Americans were always difficult to connect, one to the other, husbands to wives, parents to children. In Washington, everyone came from somewhere else; and they never returned. They seemed to create themselves, with no reference to their forebears or place of birth. They seemed to be without definition, so unpredictable. He remembered Elinor and the boy together, years ago in Africa; the boy was stubborn, she was just as stubborn. They were always locked in combat. So they were not of different species after all. He looked at her now, her eyes hard as granite. She would follow the road wherever it led, an admirable woman; she was a woman who liked the truth. He said, "I will tell you what we think, and then you must ask me no more questions. Is that agreed?" She nodded.

"There is some evidence that the girl pulled the trigger, but we are not sure. And it does not matter. Truly it doesn't, except in a court of law. That is not an issue here. In the terms we are discussing, it is only a detail."

"Thank you, Kurt."

He said drily, "You're welcome."

She said, "I had to know."

He reached across the table to touch her hand. She reminded him of a woman he had known in Hamburg, after the war, the athletic daughter of a merchant family. He had fallen in love with her, and with her entire family; they had endurance. They had lived through the worst days of the war, managing somehow to maintain themselves, the personality of the family; she was a lovely girl, married now, living somewhere in the south of Germany, politically active, he seemed to remember. He remembered, irrelevantly, the family's house in Hamburg, in the pretty Uhlenhorst district, near the little cul-de-sac canal. They had lived — been born in, had died in — the same house for three hundred and fifty years. The house had been rebuilt many times, and passed down as one would pass down a family Bible, because it was a family Bible, in a way, the structure that contained the family's spiritual history, with all its parables and lessons and laws. The house was damaged in the war, but not destroyed; many family members were killed, in Hamburg and elsewhere. Now he remembered about the blond-haired daughter, she was a Green. In his mind's eye Kleust saw the daughter and her father, old Croner, stiff as a ship's mast, marching along the canal in the evening with the family Weimaraner. . . . Then the image vanished, as quickly as it had come. He released her hand and said, "Do you see what I mean, about the danger to Bill and to you?"

She looked at him, surprised. "I have always seen it," she said.

"Well, then," he began.

"Tell me what to do," she said, leaning forward, her chin resting on her knuckles. It was a simple question, and then her voice began to rise. "Tell me what you would do in these circumstances, if you were Bill and me. What would you have us do?"

The glassware trembled again, and again he waited for the noise to recede so that he could speak again in his soft voice. "Tell me everything that you can about him, anything at all that you can think of, that might help us. Friends, places that he used to go."

She looked up, offering him the slightest of smiles. "I don't know anything, Kurt. I know nothing about him, nothing that would help you or help us. I know nothing that would allow us to — predict. Where he is, or what he'll do."

He said, "My colleagues and I, we are at sea."

"Yes," she said.

"Perhaps when the young woman makes contact —"

"If she makes contact," Elinor said.

After a moment he said, "How long have you lived in this house?"

She hesitated, considering. "A long time. Twenty years? I guess it's twenty years. My father and Bill's father lent us the money to buy it. Otherwise . . ." She shrugged, sighing, inspecting her hands.

Kleust waited for her to continue and when she didn't looked over her shoulder at the books, floor to ceiling. Bill's books, shelf after shelf of lives of Lincoln, and of various American statesmen, the Roosevelts, Wilson, Truman, Eisenhower, Hull, Stimson, Dulles. And the wars, Revolutionary, Civil, One, Two, Korea, Indochina. Congressional directories, beginning with the Eighty-sixth Congress, first session. He smiled. The library was recognizably a Washingtonian's. She was watching him and he said, "Who was Gaston W. Means?"

She turned to look at the books. "A thug. A private detective who wrote a book about Harding."

"Harding?"

"One of our Presidents. Between Wilson and Coolidge."

"Yes, the Washington Conference. A limit to the world's navies."

She smiled. "I don't know about that. When we think of Harding, we think of Teapot Dome."

He said, "It's a fine library."

"My library is upstairs."

"Yes?"

"Novels, books on art. Narratives and pictures. Women's things. Tell me a story, draw me a picture, Kurt."

"Your boy is out of our orbit," he said. "That is what Duer thinks, and I agree with him. If this were Germany, I would have an idea. Like Inspector Maigret, perhaps; the crimes he solves are always very *French*, don't you think? Something would present itself, a bouillabaisse without rascasse. But in this country —" He gestured at the books, and let the sentence hang. "Our own crimes, and those who commit them, are German. Do you see? Products of our own culture, which they seem to love, hate, and fear all at once, and without discrimination. In any case, they see it being destroyed. I think they see it as already moribund, Europe as a museum for the pleasure of American tourists. America's attic. A theater of American operations. For the next war, an American battlefield."

He heaved himself to his feet and stepped to the window, looking out into O Street. The streetlights had blinked on, but the sidewalks were empty; it was such a warm night, how strange that no one was about. "Good burgher children, brought up during our economic miracle. That was what we thought it was, a miracle, a testament to the resilience and energy of the German people. A triumph of the German *culture*. To them it's ashes. They think it ashes, for which their parents and the friends of their parents are responsible. The rulers of Germany. They rule the world, or anyway that part of the world that the Americans don't rule. Destroy the rulers and you destroy their world. Make them frightened, make them want to fight back, the more vicious and the clumsier, the better. Kill one man, frighten a thousand men. Cause their world to creak and groan. Inspire nostalgia. This will take a long time, the longer the better, because this is what they *do*. This is a way of life. They are patient, they are tough, they are ambitious, they are unbalanced, and they don't believe in miracles. In their way, they are realistic."

She had moved to the door and stood there now, nodding. "Come upstairs, Kurt. You want grammar. I'll show you grammar."

She had never invited a friend into her studio. Kurt stood shyly to one side, as if he had entered her bedroom. She turned on the bright overhead lights, then walked to her easel and positioned it so that he could see it clearly.

She said, "My son."

A small canvas, at first look a thicket of black lines, in disorganized opposition to themselves. Then the trees became a forest. Kleust saw the face, then lost it, and found it again for good. She had used the blackest pigment, and as the German stared at the portrait he thought of Conrad's Congo jungle in motion, seething and deadly at dusk. Malignant but alive, he thought. He looked at the canvas and thought of the beginnings of things. This was young Bill as Elinor saw him: a face in the jungle.

"It's good, El."

They turned. Bill was in the doorway.

"It's just damn good, don't you think, Kurt?"

"Yes," he said unconvincingly.

"Looks just like me, don't you think?"

Kleust smiled. "Did you have a good sleep?"

Bill looked at Elinor, raising his eyebrows. "Grrrrreat," he said. They heard the ring of the telephone downstairs and Bill turned, moving out of the doorway.

She put her hand on his arm. "I'll get it. You go downstairs with Kurt. Make us drinks. Big ones." She went quickly down the stairs.

"You do look better," Kleust said.

He repositioned the easel, then turned off the lights. He was so preoccupied that he did not think to agree, to say the natural thing: Yes, I do. I needed to lie down. Sleep works wonders. All I needed was a good sleep.

Wisconsin Avenue seemed narrower than he remembered it, but it was not narrower, only more crowded. Lights flashed and throbbed, and the smell of food was everywhere. There was noise also, music and traffic and chatter, the American young on the prowl, having at each other in Georgetown. Here and there a matron or bureaucrat walked quickly, homeward bound, blank-faced; hear no evil, see no evil. Bill Jr. stood on the sidewalk in front of the drugstore and watched them; there were all the elements of a European circus. A faggot pranced by with two sleek Afghan hounds. Two dazed teenagers with backpacks pointed at him and giggled. A girl with her right breast exposed strolled by. Three black boys followed the girl, jiving, talking at her. She slowed and moved to partly cover her breast. He thought that compared with this, the Hamburg waterfront was almost demure.

He watched a patrol car, two bored officers in the front seat. Bill Jr. watched them carefully, but they kept their eyes front, like soldiers on parade. One of them appeared to be asleep. When the patrol car stopped in traffic, the black boys began to hiss. *Hisssss.* But the windows were up and the air conditioning was on, so the police didn't hear anything, and it wouldn't have made any difference if they had. The girl went into a leather boutique, but the boys did not follow; a security guard was at the door, conspicuous with billy club and holstered revolver. Packages to be checked at the door. Shoplifting punished to the fullest extent of the law. No smoking. No bare feet. No food. No drink.

American young: empty vessels, you could pour anything into them, chemicals, melodies, basketball scores, a war. But not a revolt. Not an upheaval. Their delicate systems would reject it as completely as salt water. They'd vomit it up, retch it into the gutter. Too much *trouble.* Who needed the hassle? Who *needed* it? Where's the real action, man? They were as useless as the tsar's household guard, lazy and drunken and without fiber. What control the authorities had, to so demoralize and undermine an entire generation. Never underestimate them. Never underestimate the tenacity and cunning of the American ruling classes. He had said it over and over again, but the comrades refused to believe it. Better believe it, he said.

A derelict in fatigues was pulling at his arm now. Bill Jr. had wheeled at the touch, and the derelict did not know how close he came to a broken wrist. A buck, he needed a buck. He was scarcely coherent, unshaven, stinking of wine. His hands shook. One of the veterans no doubt, they were everywhere. One of the comrades had said Washington resembled Berlin in 1920, American streets similar to the noble George Grosz canvases. The derelict stepped back, his hand out, palm up. The security guard was watching them, alert to anything that could interfere with commerce. Then the derelict seemed to lose interest, ambling off; he looked suddenly frightened. At any event, he did not want to push too hard. The man in the leather jacket and blue jeans might push back, and then where would he be? Better to keep to the straight and narrow. Better to ask, not demand. Better not to be too insistent. Better to take what is given, and be thankful. And if nothing is given, that was anyone's right. One had no claim, really. Bill Jr. watched him go, the encounter already forgotten. The derelict in fatigues was standing in the middle of the sidewalk, making pass after pass with his hand; he looked like a vagabond matador, old, overweight, out of touch, out of it. But no one noticed. Passersby passed by, their eyes on the middle distance, up; the old soldier was invisible. But Bill Jr. noticed that as the people passed, swinging their arms, they checked their billfolds, the men patting their rear pockets or their coats, the women squeezing their purses, holding them a little more tightly. Everyone did this. No exceptions.

He stepped back into the shadows and checked his watch. Not much time. He looked left and right, and across the street. A woman interested him. She was walking with a man in a Borsalino hat; they were both carrying briefcases. They were talking animatedly. The woman was wearing very high heels and he fancied he could hear them, even across the street above the noise of the traffic and the music and chatter. Click, click, click. The man was good-looking, no doubt her husband or lover. Bill Jr. quickly crossed the street and fell in behind them, ten feet or so behind, other people in between. She was familiar, a face from his adolescence. What was her name? Wendy? Wanda. The wickedly wonderful Wanda. He and Mel Crown had discovered her in New York; it was some weekend or other. She and Mel had smoked grass and they had taken turns screwing her. She had loved to play games in bed; had been happier, he thought, with Mel than with him. Mel Crown was soooo black. Bill Jr. scrutinized her, noting the changes, a little heavier in the rear; her step didn't have quite the bounce it once did. Her father was a congressman, now she looked like one. The man with her was a lawyer or influence peddler. Possibly a journalist. It was all the same thing. He stopped and let them advance. At Q Street they turned left, and disappeared from his view. They had had a raunchy time that weekend, he, MC, and WWW. She had taken them out for lunch on Sunday, a last meal before they returned to school. An expensive New York restaurant, she had paid with credit cards. She had opened her purse and the cards fell out, one card after another, American Express, Visa, Master Charge, Diner's, Hilton. Brooks Brothers, Bloomingdale's. Hertz, Avis. She was laughing, dumping the cards on the table in a rattle of plastic. Mel looked at her, spoke his favorite word, and left the table. Mel was always quick to identify the enemy. Now

Mel was in Attica, she looked like a member of Congress, and he was on the run. Varieties of American experience. He wondered if she knew anything about him. Or if she ever thought about him, where he was or what he did. What ever happened to Bill North, you remember him, the quiet one, the one who never said anything, always glowering and sarcastic, so dissatisfied with things? Probably her father would know, would grunt and say something like "The North boy went off the deep end, and I feel so sorry for Bill and Elinor, such terrific people." He felt a sudden tug on his arm. The derelict had followed him across the street and stood there in front of him, his hand out, eyes averted. A useful reminder. Time was short.

Bill Jr. crossed the street again and hurried back to the drugstore. He had been stupid. Wanda was trouble, always had been. It was stupid, hanging around Georgetown, anyone could recognize him; he had changed his appearance, but his walk or his posture could ring a bell. And the bell could be an alarm. This fat, dumb country always lulled him. There were too many faces from the past, too much history. It was time to go home, time to return to Gert. He fished in his pocket for a coin and stepped into a telephone booth, closing the door. He dialed and waited. One ring, two, three.

She said, "Hello."

He pressed the palm of his hand over the mouthpiece so that she could hear no sound. He listened to her breathing. He was concentrating, needing to hear everything.

She said again, tentatively now, "Hello." Then, very clearly, as if she wanted someone to overhear, "No, I'm afraid you have the wrong number." And then another long silence.

He hung up and left the phone booth. He was smiling. Why had she lied? She had lied because someone was there, Herr Kleust no doubt; his Mercedes was still parked in front of the house. So she did not want Herr Kleust to know that he had been in touch, that perhaps — perhaps! It was so difficult to know, with the clear overseas connections — he was even in the United States. And that lie meant that they would go to the Kunsthalle.

There was one last souvenir to deliver. His car was parked on 28th Street near P. He drove quickly to Q Street and across Wisconsin Avenue and left on 34th Street to the park. He waited for five minutes, watching for any unusual movement. But there was no one about, either in the park or on the sidewalks. It was drinks time in Georgetown. He left the car and walked in the darkness to the bench near the baseball diamond. He stuffed the paper bag into the trash can.

Back in the car, he checked his watch. An hour to Dulles, and seven hours to Geneva. Geneva to Copenhagen, and by car from Copenhagen to Hamburg. At about the time he was leaving Geneva, the bomb would explode. It would be five in the morning, no casualties, a bench and a trash can destroyed, windows shattered nearby. The fact that it would be five in the morning, and that there were no casualties, would be an ominous message all its own. It would give those terrific people a little something to think about. How vulnerable they were. How easy it was for him to move in and out of his native land. How simple to obtain and transport the materials for an explosive. How far off the deep end he really was, and how necessary, therefore, that they journey to Hamburg for the last act, if that was what it was.

Crossing Key Bridge to George Washington Parkway, he realized that his breathing was shallow and that he was sweating. That was the thrill of it. The doing of it, with no errors. The movement back and forth, the package, the bomb in the package, the timer in the bomb. The danger, the mystery, the unknowableness of the present moment. Coincidences, unexpected sightings. Standing motionless on Wisconsin Avenue for thirty minutes, watching the parade. The telephone call, her breathing, her voice, so brittle, so familiar. And to have control, meaning to have it all in your own hands. Go or No Go. The thought always that you could do this forever, take it to whatever point you wanted. There was uncertainty in everything. At the last minute, there was no reason not to back away, save the last act for another day; the important thing was that it was always there. You never ruled it out; you never signed the treaty renouncing the use of force. It was just a little bit like the Cold War itself, an infinite number of possibilities, meaning calculations and miscalculations. Wasn't that what the old men meant when they talked about the balance of terror? It had been nicely balanced since the end of the Second War. It wasn't only the weapons, fascinating as the weapons might be, it was the calculation of intent, and not only the intent of the venerables in Washington and Moscow, but the intent of younger, harder men in capitals no one ever heard of.

He began to laugh. The beauty of his plan was that it could go either way with no loss of tension or menace. They would always be at the edge of the precipice. His plan was a replica of the time. *The threat was always there.* Kismet.

PART FOUR

PART FOUR

I

THEY SAID that a cancer cell was a cell that went haywire. One minute it was good, the next it was bad; one minute normal, the next wild, momentous, and out of control. They did not know why. They could observe it under their microscopes, but were powerless to do anything about it. *Tant pis*. Except for a final solution, kill it or it kills you. Take no prisoners. The medical equivalent of the neutron bomb, leaving the body's skin in place but everything within dead. No halfway measures, no patient negotiations. Yet there were decisions to be made. Life was precious, but was it *that* precious?

That's *very* cheerful, Hartnett said.

We are not a witty family, Bill replied.

Hartnett thought that an odd reply, and said so,

They were having a drink in the first-class lounge at JFK. Elinor was at the newsstand, buying the papers and a magazine. Bill had been talking about his father, in response to some question of Hartnett's The old man had been dead ten years, cancer, acute lymphocytic leukemia. That was the time, Bill said, when the only possible reaction to anything was — a kind of caustic benevolence. The old man had reserves of courage and patience that were as-

269

tonishing in the circumstances; they were his weapons in the final quarrel with God.

Hartnett sipped his drink, not wanting to hear it, but listening anyway. When Bill North had a story to tell, he told it.

They had a program for him, Bill said. A protocol, they called it, an inventory of chemicals, seven specific drugs that acted in concert. This was the strenuously named Regimen B maintenance schedule. I was there when the doctor explained it to him. Doctor was about thirty-five, nice-looking fellow, thin as a pencil, very intense. He had a rubber band he kept winding around his fingers while he talked. No promises, he promised no promises; this was experimental treatment. Might work, might not. He watched my father as he spoke. The old man's eyes never wavered, he never looked more like a woodcut. The doctor started out talking rapidly but he eventually slowed down, and began speaking in complete sentences, often clearing his throat. There were seven drugs and I can remember their names even now. Daunorubicin, vincristine, prednisone, L-asparaginase, 6-mercaptopurine, cystosine arabinoside, methotrexate. He did not rush over the names but enunciated them carefully, the old man nodding as if they were euphonious Old Testament prophets, Jeremiah, Micah. The doctor said there were dangers which every patient should be aware of. The drugs were toxic and had side effects. The old man had not said a word until then. He raised his index finger and said: "Explain them." Well, the doctor said, each drug had its own specific side effect. Daunorubicin caused bone marrow depression, which often resulted in infection and bleeding. There was also hair loss. Reversible, he said. Also, possibly, cardiac toxicity. Vincristine caused hair loss, tingling of the fingers and toes, muscle weakness, and loss of reflexes. And, frequently, a mild form of bone marrow depression. Prednisone often caused fluid retention, diabetes, skin rash, high blood pressure, stomach ulcers, and curious changes in appearance, which included a rounding of the face. L-asparaginase often caused nausea and vomiting, diabetes, abnormalities of the liver, pancreas, and serum proteins; mental changes and anaphylaxis. (He told me later that it was difficult for him to maintain a straight face. Mental change as a side effect! And if there were no mental change, would that be considered normal? Perhaps that would be an anaphylaxis of its own, a severe allergic reaction, though seldom fatal.) 6-mercaptopurine also caused bone marrow depression. Similarly, cytosine arabinoside. Methotrexate typically caused sores of the inside of the mouth and the lining of the gastrointestinal tract, and hair loss. When it was administered into the spinal fluid, headaches or fever were common. That was pretty much it, the doctor said, not a pretty inventory, though every human being was different and reactions varied, they could be worse or they could be better, that is, milder, but that was what Mr. North could expect, pretty much. The doctor used the collective pronoun "we" when describing what could be expected, "we" being the medical profession, medical science, chemotherapists. At the end, God bless him, he told my father that he was very gravely ill and that the prognosis was not "positive." The old man listened to this, lying in bed, his hands folded on his stomach (only once did he look at me, and that was at the third or fourth mention of hair loss, the old man being bald as an egg, a condition that the doctor did not notice, being so concerned to get the protocol in its proper sequence). He did not look gravely ill just then, his complexion was still ruddy and his belly round and full. When the doctor had finished, he nodded slightly and glared at the bureau. His Hebrew texts were piled high, eight, nine books, heavy, thick tomes that he had brought from his library. Also Nietzsche, *The Birth of Tragedy from the Spirit of Music.* The doctor looked at me and I made a sign to stay put; my father was thinking. He had been told all he wanted to know, and now he needed to think about it. But the doctor had one thing to add, it was the question he was always asked, and now he moved to anticipate his patient. He said, "You'll be wondering about the odds, in treatment of this kind —"

My father shook his head. "No, I'm not."

"You're not?"

"I know what they are, without hearing them from you." He continued to think.

I sat quietly, looking out the window. The doctor wrapped and unwrapped his rubber band, impatiently turning the face of his wristwatch, pursing his lips; the old man had him spooked. I turned away so that my father could not see my tears, though of course he knew. Twice I had to blow my nose. It is not possible to weep in silence. I admired him so: he had been given a sentence of death, which *might* be spared by torture. I think my father was looking into his own soul, into the marrow of his bones, to calculate the time; to figure the odds in his own way. At last he shifted, sitting up on one haunch. He put his hand out and the doctor shook it. He thanked the doctor for explaining things so clearly. Of course he had done some reading himself, on acute lymphocytic leukemia, and other, related, matters. But he would not agree to the protocol. He smiled sadly, as if distressed to disappoint medical science. "I would rather struggle with God," he said. And he was dead in three weeks.

"The doctor, poor son of a bitch, thought he'd failed."

Hartnett put his arm around Bill's shoulder.

"The unspoken thought was that the old man's body could be of use. They might learn something from it, its reaction to daunorubicin, vincristine, and the other toxic prophets. But he didn't see himself as a gerbil. One to be experimented upon, the results tabulated and published. I think that brought forth other memories, and a precedent that had already been set, that he did not want to see reset. He was very much of the world, and of his books. At the end all he could think about was Auschwitz."

"My God," Hartnett said.

"God, too," Bill said. "God and Auschwitz."

"Did you ever have second thoughts —" Hartnett began. A lawyer's question.

"All the time. One thought after another. And third thoughts, and fourth thoughts. But he didn't."

"Tough man," Hartnett said.

"Not at the end. At the end he wasn't so tough."

"No, of course not," Hartnett said. He was unnerved. He could not imagine the situation, he who prided himself on being able to imagine anything. Caustic benevolence, indeed! He thought to say, "And your mother?"

He remained at home, Bill said, until the very end. She cared for him, fed him, washed him, injected him. At the very end he went to the hospital, where we had our last conversation. He was very sick, in and out of consciousness. He was lying on his side because his stomach hurt. I sat next to the bed, and told him how worried I was about Bill Jr. This was about a year after the incident with the English teacher. I said that the boy had grown away from me, from us both, Elinor and me, and that he seemed to be far from home. The old man listened to me, breathing very heavily, trying to concentrate. I said that the boy was consumed with hatred, and that I was afraid. I was afraid for all of us, perhaps because things were the way Nietzsche said they were, that God was dead and that we had killed Him. To a son, a father was God. There was some ritual killing that had to take place, everyone knew that; it was normal. A boy had to find his own feet. I looked at my father and reminded him of our own bad time; perhaps we had never completely settled it. He and Mother were so close, as Elinor and I are close. I said that I felt the darkness closing around me — and at that he turned, looked me in the eye, and smiled. It was the only time that night. I was flustered, but I went on. I felt that I had to tell him everything, that I could confide in no one else. I was incoherent, but there seemed so much to say and so little time to say it. I found myself talking about true faith, and that led naturally to my oath of office, "true faith and allegiance . . . that I take this obligation freely and without any mental reservation or purpose of evasion, that I will well and truthfully discharge the duties of this office . . ." It sounded like the marriage vows from the Book of Common Prayer. I was drawn back into the Constitution and from the Constitution to the government, and all this was *us;* him and me, and me and my son. This seemed to be all I had to go on; my true faith and allegiance, and of course Elinor. But somewhere with this boy there had been a profound disappointment, some monstrous evil. I did not know where it began, but I thought I knew where it would end, hence my fear. There was nothing I could do about it.

He said, "William," his voice soft as cotton.

I said, "Probably you were right."

He murmured, "About what?"

"The government," I said, and then knew I didn't mean that at all. I said, "Moving on." But I didn't mean that either, and what I did mean I could not find voice to say. I meant to tell him that what he had said so long ago was correct. There was only us after all. There was not more than just us. We were what we had, and we had our history also. We need not neglect or despise others, but they were not what we had. However, that was too much for this old man in extremis. I did not think he would find the thought consoling.

He smiled a kind of cracked half smile. He said, "You're a good man, William."

I lowered my head. I was staring at the threads of the bedsheet. He had never said that to me before, and now I wanted him to say it again. "Do you think I am?"

He said, "Yes." And then something seized him because he moved, groaning. He turned his back to me, seeking a more comfortable position. I put my hand on his shoulder. We were both trembling. I wanted his advice. I wanted him to tell me what to do, and how to do it.

I said, "Can you tell me —"

But he shook his head before I was finished. He had something that he wanted to say. "The boy," he said.

I said, "Yes."

"Your son," he said, "my grandson." There was a very long pause while he shivered, his teeth rattling. I could feel his muscles and bones move under his skin. I rose to lean over the bed to look at him. He was crying freely but the tears seemed to arise from some ghastly, equivocal joke because he was smiling, too, and when the words came they were droll indeed. "He needs someone to sue."

He closed his eyes and the trembling ceased. The painkilling drugs took hold and he fell into a deep sleep. I knew it was a coma, and that it was the end. I remained at his side for a very long time, thinking about his life, and mine, and our life together. And who would he sue, given the chance? I left the room and stood in the dark corridor a minute. A bright light at the end of the corridor announced the nurses' station. I moved along the wall slowly, the wall supporting my body. I told the nurse that my father would surely die that night and that they were to make certain that when he did, he was comfortable, and without pain. They would see him struggle but there was nothing they could do about that. And I left the hospital and four hours later he was dead.

"Bill," Hartnett said.

"I'm the fellow with the deep pockets," he said.

"For Christ's sake, Bill! Stop it!"

"All right," he said. "I'll stop it."

Then Elinor was at their side, carrying three newspapers and a magazine. Bill brightened, seeing her. He made a joke, they finished their drinks, and walked to the gate.

Hartnett said, "Good luck."

Elinor said, "We're lucky to have a week before we report. We're going to have a nice relaxed holiday, before Bill gets down to business in Bonn."

Hartnett said, "I'll let you know what's happening at this end. I'll have the committee report by next week, the draft version. The one that'll call for hearings or not. We're clear for a while, anyway. They won't do anything for the next few weeks. Have a good holiday. Do you know exactly where you'll be?"

"Here and there," Elinor said.

Bill smiled and stuck out his hand. They shook hands and embraced. The line began to move. Not very many people bound for Hamburg on a Monday night in November, so he and Elinor would have an easy trip, able to stretch out. Hartnett took her hand and bent to kiss her.

He said again, "Good luck."

She said, "Take care. Thanks for coming down."

He said, "Will you let me know?"

She said, "We'll call you in a week, Dick."

"And I'll ride herd on the committee."

Bill said, "Fuck the committee."

Hartnett said, "Telephone me next week."

Bill said, "Don't forget Richard." He hoped that Hartnett would keep his promise to visit the boy, and stay in touch with his doctors. He knew more about Richard than about his own son, and felt closer to him.

Hartnett looked at him, having forgotten all about Richard; and then, remembering, he nodded. The lawyer watched them go. Bill had his arm around Elinor's waist, was whispering something into her ear; she turned and laughed. How extraordinary they were, Hartnett thought; they were perfectly complementary pieces of music. The lawyer moved to go, looking around him, noticing suddenly how shabby JFK had become. The international departure lounge was dirty and poorly lit, without cheer or festivity. He had known it when it was Idlewild, and the most modern airport in the world, always exciting, always filled with a fine edge of anticipation.

They had a drink and dinner, not talking much, and now she was sleeping. He stared out the plastic window, watching the moon glitter on the surface of the North Atlantic. He had ordered a double Cognac after dinner, trying to chase his depression; no luck. No wonder. He bought earphones and watched the movie a moment, but could not concentrate; it had to do with children and aliens, escapist fantasy, adolescent ceremony. He gave it up and noticed it only on the edges of his vision, an erratic flicker, disconcerting. Flexing the fingers of his left hand, he felt the skin pleasantly stretch, the joints cracking, tingling, alive.

Surely Hartnett would keep his promise, he was good about those things. He and Richard had become very close. Richard had told him about his girl, what she'd been like, her verve and spirit; they had just begun to think about the future together. His last day in the hospital they had taken Richard's bandages off and they had looked at each other. Tears filled the boy's eyes, and he looked away. They were both embarrassed, seeing each other for the first time. They were not what they expected. Richard had said, How do I look? And Bill replied, Fine, and indicated the mirror over the bureau. Richard had looked at his battered face a full minute and at last had nodded, It's the same face. But I'm not the same person. He'd said to Bill, You're younger than I thought. Bill smiled, amused; he looked older than his age, always had. That meant his voice sounded older still. And to hell with chronology.

He had given Richard names and addresses. If he ever needed help —

Well, thanks, he'd said. But he didn't think he'd be in Germany any time soon.

I'll write, Bill had said.

I hope everything works out all right, Richard had replied.

You, too, Bill had said.

I won't count on it, the boy said solemnly.

I won't either, Bill said.

Then we won't be disappointed, either of us, Richard said.

They shook hands, man to man; and that was that. Except Hartnett had promised to look in on the boy, say hello, see what he needed. And what the boy needed, Hartnett couldn't provide.

All right, he thought, sleep. Sleep now. In the morning, they would be in Germany. And was it not true that all modern history begins in Germany?

He opened his eyes and looked up. The movie was flickering lamely to its damp conclusion, enough consolation to fill a cosmic silver screen, the children reunited with their befuddled parents, the aliens dispersed to other galaxies, the children so wise, goodhearted and foul-mouthed, the aliens so tolerant, a pleasant warm future for Americans to nap to. A happy glow, though to Bill it looked like a penumbra.

"Bill?" she had been sleeping in the seats across the aisle. She touched his shoulder. "You were talking in your sleep. You were in the zone, Bill."

"Sorry." He had been dreaming, and the dream slipped away; he tried to catch it, having a happy memory of it, but the images were already out of reach. "Did you have a good sleep?"

She smiled. "Airline sleep is like airline food." She was leaning over the back of his seat, her hair mussed and her eyes cloudy. He raised his head to look at her, and was struck by a sensation of utter intimacy. The sensation lasted only a moment, like the dream that had slipped away. But it left him breathless, as if his heart had stopped for a moment, leaving him suspended like an aerialist. They looked at each other a full minute, and gradually the sounds around them came into full focus, the hiss of the engines, the lift as the aircraft corrected its course, swinging east over the North Sea. He took her hand delicately, touching the pads of her fingers. Concentrating on her, he felt her reach out to him; and he felt the most unaccountable confidence in himself, in her, and in what they intended to do in Hamburg.

It was morning, a cold north light.

He said, "Are you ready for all this?"

She said, "No."

He said, "Neither am I."

She said, "I was thinking about the island."

"What about it?"

"Wouldn't it be great if we were there now, just us two."

Bill had sent word ahead that he would appreciate it if his former colleague, Harry Erickson, could meet them at the airport. He hadn't seen Harry in two years, and wanted to know how things were working out for him in the Federal Republic. When they emerged from customs he was there, his dress and manner identical with the Germans bustling around him. He was reading a German newspaper. Elinor did not recognize him at first, and when he walked up to them she thought he was a German official with unpleasant news of some kind. Then Harry smiled broadly, and she laughed. He had always seemed so tense and ill at ease in Africa, so sour and pessimistic. They went to a café for coffee, to unwind from the long journey. Bill told him they were in Hamburg for a holiday, recuperation for him, a chance to allow themselves to become reacquainted with the BRD. Harry seemed to accept that. Was there anyone he wanted to see? No one special, Bill said, it was just a private holiday. Harry was at pains to tell them how well Alice was doing, in this northern climate. The baby was now nearly a year old, a fat, happy baby, named Harry Jr. He and Alice loved Hamburg, so chilly and dry, so civilized, so commercial, so — so no-nonsense.

On Tuesday he and Elinor went to the exhibit at the Kunsthalle. The great rooms were nearly empty. The tourist season, such as it was, was long gone. Hamburgers were busy in their offices and factories. The artist on exhibit was a young Berliner, a sensation. She was not yet twenty, and she painted on a grand scale; none of the canvases was less than fifteen feet wide. Elinor stepped close up, then moved back, careful to be convincing in her role as tourist and art connoisseur. It was logical that Bill would be bored, always looking around, as if seeking a means of escape.

The Berliner worked with pen and ink, an excellent draftsman, though her figures were grotesque in the German manner. They were pictures of animals, but the animals — an ox, a crocodile, an elephant, a wolf, a bear — were not flesh and blood. She had drawn them as if they were made of building materials, steel girders, concrete, glass. Close up, they looked like structures, animals assem-

278

bled by a modern architect, not ominous or threatening, but not benign either. In black and white they presented the sterile face of a German skyscraper, Bauhaus and then some.

"She has wonderful technique," Elinor said.

Bill was noncommittal.

"I'm not so sure about the subjects," Elinor said.

Bill was standing a little behind her, looking casually around. They were alone except for a guard and a well-dressed middle-aged man with a cane. They were standing on the spacious staircase leading to the second floor. The young Berliner's works were displayed on the high stone walls.

She stood quietly; the museum seemed enveloped in a kind of hush. "They're very public, these pictures," she said, looking at them with her head cocked, her forefinger laid aside her nose. Her words echoed in the chill. "You wouldn't want them in the living room, or anywhere in your house. They belong in public places. Interesting impulse, to want to paint for a public place."

The animals had the look of public buildings, city halls, central banks, embassies, or police headquarters. The animals were transparent, the viewer could see brains, entrails, hearts. The various body parts looked like rooms, here an office, there a conference room or corridor; the tail of the immense crocodile seemed a series of cells with bars on the windows. There were no prisoners, however,

" 'Witty and unique,' " Bill read from the program. There was a picture of the artist, a buxom young woman with short black hair and one eyebrow. "These strike you as witty, El?"

"In a way," she said. "In a way, they do. They're beguiling, thrilling in a way."

" 'They demonstrate the Berliner's natural sense of isolation,' " he said, translating from the German. This was apparently the artist's estimation of her work. " 'West Berlin is a cage inside a cage.' " Not bad, he thought. In such an environment, even the animals became mechanical.

She said, "What do you think?"

"I'd rather read an essay on the subject."

She looked at him, amused, shaking her head. "Philistine." They were moving slowly up the stone steps, to the second floor.

He said, "No, I sort of like them. I like the boar." The boar was constructed with steel girders, as if the artist had drawn an assemblage from a child's erector set. The boar had a metallic face, vaguely reminiscent of a German politician — Brandt, perhaps, or Helmut Schmidt. It was hard to tell who it was, the face also bore a resemblance to the famous jowly bust of Johann Sebastian Bach. He thought it was Brandt, but the program gave no clue.

"It's fresh," Elinor said.

"Cheeky," he agreed.

"No, fresh as in *new*."

"That, also," he said.

She said, "Go along, I'll be a minute. I want to look at these some more. See what she's up to really, the girl in the cage." Elinor often preferred looking at paintings alone. He ascended the stairs, glancing casually around him. The middle-aged man with the cane had walked past them, on his way to the second-floor galleries. He had paid them scant attention, but had paused to peer at a Degas at the top of the stairs, and then had strolled on, his cane going tap-tap-tap. He had the erect bearing of a retired military officer, perhaps on his way to meet a friend for lunch; he moved around the museum as if he owned it.

The Degas was a portrait of a young dancer, and Bill looked at it, and down the staircase to the mechanical animals. No connection that he could see, though there had to be one somewhere. There was a connection between the Congress of Vienna and SALT II, so there must be a connection between the young Berliner and her animals and Degas's young dancer. No painter could fail to be influenced by Degas, as no treaty was without its shadow of Vienna; every son had a father. He looked over the railing. Elinor was still below, moving forward and back in front of the crocodile, frowning; she was examining the work, one painter to another.

He watched her a moment, then followed the taps.

The middle-aged man was standing in front of one of Max Liebermann's self-portraits. There were three of them on one ornate wall: stern, sterner, sternest. Liebermann did himself in black and white; he was his own best subject. He was his own young dancer. The middle-aged man tapped his cane impatiently, and marched on to the next room. This was the introduction to Hitler's degenerates, Nolde, Schmidt-Rottluff, Kirchner, Dix. Max Beckmann had a room all to himself. The middle-aged man seemed happier among the degenerates. He stood very still, a slight smile on his face, as if he were posing.

A sudden squeak caused Bill to turn. A line of schoolchildren entered the gallery, quiet as prisoners. They looked neither to the left nor to the right but continued through the gallery single file, turning into the hall containing the Flemish. Sneakers squeaked on the marble floors; the sound put his teeth on edge. Two male teachers, one at the head of the column, and the other at its rear, supervised the children. No doubt the children would be happier with Dutch burghers, pastoral scenes of canals, cattle, and tavern life. He felt a moment of vertigo in the large room with its creamy light.

The unnerving line of quiet children disappeared, and he and the middle-aged man were alone with the degenerates. Except he had slipped away, and was seated on the viewers' bench in the adjoining gallery, Beckmann's.

The moment of vertigo passed. He gave another look at the three Liebermanns, then stepped across the threshold. They were alone in the Beckmann room.

The middle-aged man said, "During the war, he went to Holland. And then to America."

He nodded politely. "Is that right?"

"In America, there were patrons and he was able to paint again." All this in slow, cultivated German. "In Holland he was able to do nothing, merely a few oils. But in America he regained himself. Yet his greatest period was before the war."

"A great artist," Bill said.

"I did not like the ones downstairs," the middle-aged man said. "They're trash."

"Political art," Bill said.

"All great art is political, but that was trash."

"I wouldn't say that Degas was political."

"Oh, yes," he said. He was staring at the Beckmanns on the wall fifteen feet away, and when he spoke it was to them. "I am afraid so. I am afraid that Degas is revolutionary."

Bill smiled. "The dancer has a bomb in her tutu."

"No," he said gravely. "It is not the dancer. The dancer has nothing to do with it. It is *Degas*. It is what Degas does with the dancer, how he has chosen to present her. She is his creation. The dancer is just a dancer, nothing more. Look at the lift of the chin."

It was not always successful to joke with a German, but this German was particularly solemn. Bill said, "Not the dancer, but the dance."

The middle-aged man nodded decisively. "To be sure." They were looking at one of Beckmann's triptychs, three stations of the cross; in the background was a daffy-looking snake. He gestured at the wall, sighing. "These are tormented. From his late, tormented period. Poor Max."

Bill looked at him, startled. "You knew him?"

"Slightly," he said.

"Here or in America?" He knew the other was lying. Beckmann died in 1950, and this man was about Bill's own age.

"In Berlin," the man said. He looked at his wristwatch and stood, moving his shoulders, straightening, shooting his cuffs.

Beckmann had left Berlin for good in 1937. "You must have been very young," he said.

"I used to see him in the zoo."

Bill turned, seeing Elinor; he made a little warning gesture with his hand. But when he turned back, the middle-aged man was gone. He listened for the tapping of the cane, but heard nothing. His vertigo returned, and he sat down heavily on the bench. Beckmann's Gypsy woman, with her heavy thighs and bright yellow shift, seemed to revolve in front of him. She was staring into a hand mirror, arranging her hair. Elinor said, "Are you all right? You're sweating."

He said, "Spooked."

"Max Beckmann has a bad effect on you."

"It wasn't Beckmann."

"Who, then?"

"Where did he go?"

"The gent? Who was he?"

Bill looked at her and said in English, "I think he was one of Bill Jr.'s — people. Making contact." She stared back at him but he said nothing more, for the obedient schoolchildren had returned, marching single file through the gallery. They were passing through the German Expressionists to view another period; their teacher was lecturing on the Quattrocento. The children were utterly silent, except for the squeak of their sneakers. Their discipline worried him. They were like little soldiers on parade. He rose heavily and took Elinor's hand, and they started back the way they had come. He paused in front of the Degas, looking over the balcony at the mechanical animals. The great staircase was empty. He said, "Darling, we're going to Berlin. That's where he is."

2

AND IT didn't work out," Wolf said, "any of it."

Gert was playing extended solitaire, all the cards on the table. He was speaking to her, but she did not look up. She had a choice of kings to fill the empty first file. Her hands fluttered above the cards.

"You never know what will happen there," Wolf went on. "Nothing is predictable." He turned back to the middle-aged man, who sat stolidly watching him.

The middle-aged man said, "It was an action I never understood. Why it was necessary, what it could accomplish, and what the consequences would be."

"A souvenir," Wolf said.

"Of *what?*" the middle-aged man said.

Wolf smiled. He was watching Gert, whose hands still hovered above the cards like a magician's. "It was not necessary that you understand."

The middle-aged man took out a notebook, wet his thumb, and turned pages. "I have had expenses."

Wolf continued to look at Gert. "Did you see the account in the newspaper, then?"

"No. Someone told me."

"What was in the newspaper was true." Wolf shook his head. "For once."

The middle-aged man consulted the notebook. "There was the train fare."

"At five in the morning, a man was sleeping on the bench."

"And the museum admission."

"Blown to pieces, they can't identify him."

"I think my meals should be included, also."

"A homosexual affair. That is the thinking of the American police."

"I am not interested," the middle-aged man said.

"It's important, for your understanding."

"I have no interest in the Americans. I know all I need to know."

"That is apparently how the homosexuals in America settle their differences."

"Meals, fifty Deutschmarks."

"So they have made it into an affair that interests no one, although according to the paper, the neighborhood was alarmed." He rose and stood behind Gert. "Take the king from the second file, darling. There is only one card under it, and if that plays, then you can use the other king. More than likely it will play."

"The park. It was public?"

"Of course."

"Dangerous," the middle-aged man said.

"Homosexuals. Who would have thought of homosexuals?"

"You must always know your territory."

"I have known this territory for twenty-five years. But I have not been back in a few years, so it changed. I was depending on my memory of things."

"Unwise to depend on memory."

"Yes," Wolf said.

"And the taxi here, that was fifteen Deutschmarks."

Wolf looked at him, and at the notebook, expensive, well-worn leather. The middle-aged man's expenses would be meticulously accounted for, not surprisingly. He was a professional with a clerk's mentality.

"How did they seem?"

"Who?"

"The man and the woman. Were they frightened, or nervous?"

"The woman has atrocious taste in art."

Wolf nodded, smiling.

"The man is cultivated. His German was fluent, and of course that is not usual. Americans never speak German."

"How did you know they were American?"

"It is obvious."

Wolf wondered how it was obvious, but decided not to pursue it.

"I would say the man's German is even more fluent than yours."

So it was the accent, of course, though he was wrong about the relative fluency. The ambassador's German was formal. He had no command of the vernacular.

"As to their behavior, it was normal."

Wolf nodded.

"They were not followed," the middle-aged man said.

"I told you they wouldn't be."

"I decide that for myself." He smiled and ripped the page from his notebook, and handed it across the table. "And the fee, of course. The stipend. That is at the bottom."

"You have the retainer."

"Yes, that has been subtracted."

"Naturally," Wolf said.

"The accounts must be maintained, otherwise —" He shrugged.

"There would be no order," Wolf said. It was like talking to a bank officer.

The middle-aged man consulted his watch and stood. Gert continued to study her cards. Wolf reached into his pocket, brought out a roll of bills, peeled off five, and handed them to the middle-aged man. "Something extra," he said, "for your fine work."

The middle-aged man counted the bills, and put them in the leather notebook, closing it firmly. "They took the five o'clock train to Berlin." He walked quickly to the door, opening it and looking out. "I will go now."

"*Auf Wiedersehen*," Wolf said.

"Good-bye," the middle-aged man said in English, and was gone.

Wolf sat quietly a moment, thinking. Where do they come from? he wondered. And when they finished an assignment, where did they go? How did they live, and in what circumstances? They were mercenaries in the service of rebellion, had been doing it all their

286

lives; they were underground men. Max had been one. This middle-aged professional was another. It was not a despicable life; they used the skills they had. And they were reliable because they were anonymous, fitting into any of a dozen cities in Europe, leading inconspicuous lives, wanting only to escape notice by the authorities. This one had modest habits, he did not gamble and drank only mineral water. He had done several assignments in the past month, and done them well, never any complaint; and he was never inquisitive, quite the reverse. Wolf found himself drawn to the middle-aged man, and told him more than he needed to. He was certain that the information would be filed and forgotten. He already had a memory stuffed to overflowing; he was not a man who needed *more*. He already had what he needed.

Gert had chosen the king in the second file, and it played. She was flying through the end game, slapping the cards left and right.

Wolf said, "It's time."

She looked up, smiling brilliantly.

"We're on our way now."

"Yes?"

"Berlin," he said. He watched her collect the cards and put them in her purse. She rose and did a model's turn, her skirt flaring. She stood by the door while he collected their luggage, two Brooks Brothers suitcases. Wolf was dressed in a gray herringbone suit with a striped tie. He wore polished wing-tip shoes and horn-rimmed spectacles. He looked at himself in the mirror, smiling broadly. An American businessman, an advertising specialist, traveling with his wife, who had a cold so fierce she could hardly speak. Yet they were a handsome couple, obviously fond of each other; she was so pretty, and he was unmistakably successful. Wolf carried a shoulder bag with maps and Michelin guides, a German phrasebook, a Walkman, and *Time* magazine. They looked at each other and laughed and laughed.

"Yuppies," Gert said, repeating the word she had learned from him. She executed another pirouette, admiring herself in the mirror. Her outfit was very expensive, and suited her. She knew this, and was pleased.

Crossing the border from the BRD to the DDR, the train slows, then abruptly accelerates. Guard towers flank the roadbed and there

287

are always soldiers on foot with leashed German shepherds. Concertina wire lies thick and tangled between the boundaries, no man's land. There are mines also, and sensing devices. The country is flat and uninspiring, except perhaps to the eye of a tank commander, identifying contours: here a rise, there a dip, defilade, enfilade. Of course the border is cleared of trees and underbrush. Flags snap proudly in the breeze, evidence of patriotism. A Western civilian promptly identifies a cheerless Third World country, where time decelerates, seems almost to stand still. At night there are few lights. The roads are narrow and at every crossing long lines of bicycles, a few ancient private cars, and brand-new military vehicles. The gates go down well in advance of the approach of the train.

Fifty miles beyond the border, customs officials in bottle-green uniforms enter the first-class coaches. These happen to be DDR coaches so the no smoking signs are in German, French, Italian, Arabic, and Russian. (The BRD coaches have signs in German, French, Italian, Arabic, and English — thus do the salesmen of the superpowers demand that attention must be paid.) DDR customs officials — more properly passport control officers, since the train will not stop in East Germany they are interested in identities rather than contraband — appear without warning, wordlessly extending their open hands for the traveler's papers. DDR officials carry sidearms in stubby leather holsters. Metal attaché cases hang on leather straps from their necks. The attaché cases open to become writing platforms. The officials are careful to check faces against photographs before carefully affixing the stamp in the blackest, coarsest ink. Diplomatic U.S. passports receive special attention, pages laboriously turned, inspected with raised eyebrows. The officials are brusque but efficient, often quite young. They work four to a coach, two at each end moving toward the center; no one may leave the coach during passport check. In the bad old days of the Cold War the windows were sealed and covered at the border, as if the East German terrain were too dangerous or alarming to be viewed by a foreigner. But all that is past, and now a traveler is free to gaze out the window as northern Europe rolls by, opaque and monotonous, dark as a German fairy tale.

Approaching East Berlin, the train halts briefly to discharge the DDR officials. Spandau Station, then Zoo. The lights of the Ku-damm are brilliant, lurid after the dour hills, forests, and villages of East Germany. Glittering showcase of the West, it is an over-weight bird in a gilded cage, the only city in the world to which a visit is an overt political act, a conscious decision to distress oneself, to do business with ghosts; every monument, every gallery, every street, hotel, museum, and cabaret carries political significance, though to an American diplomat the significance is deeper than politics. An American diplomat goes to Berlin as a lover goes to Venice. Berlin is not where the Cold War began — except in the sense, perhaps, that the Reformation, for example, "began" in Wittenberg — but it is where it is seen in its sharpest relief. Dry, gray East, moist, mauve West. Like Venice, the city is no longer dynamic. It is worn out, a down-at-heel philosopher who no longer thinks but gabs, the bore at the dinner table, growing more self-absorbed and orotund and cynical with each glass of wine. The guests cease to listen, but become fascinated with *him,* his appear-ance and persona — his burned-out face and flabby body, his cor-ruption, his bad teeth and trembling hands and malicious mouth, and somewhere behind that the pentimento of what he once was, muscular, magisterial, gay, potent. An American diplomat, con-scious of his own middle age, his disappointments and flagging energies and lost illusions, marvels at the endurance of the city. Illusions are better lost. Energies must be conserved. Disappoint-ment is inevitable. Middle age is the consequence of youth. The glittering showcase of the West is now an old rummy, but not dead, nor moribund, nor Communist. An American diplomat returns to Berlin as to his home room at grade school, to sit at the desk that's too small, and remember the spinster drilling arithmetic, multipli-cation tables; before arithmetic became mathematics, and mathe-matics calculus.

The Zoo Station in Berlin is always crowded, day and night. This night the Norths arrive it is less crowded. The tourist season is well past, yet there are groups of young people with backpacks and parkas, carrying radios. They are Dutch, Swedes, Canadians, and English, all young, mostly genderless, identified by the little flags sewn into their backpacks. There are no Americans, but American music is everywhere. Elvis, Willie Nelson, Prince, Madonna. To the traveler's eye, the Swedes look alert and healthy, the Canadians and English dull and wasted. The group of Dutch young-sters gather near a steel pylon, waiting for the train that will take them to Cologne or Munich or to Paris or Geneva. No one is traveling east. It is cold when the train eases into the station, and halts; a cold northern wind, bitter as steel, blows dust and bits of paper.

Alighting from the train, Bill and Elinor look around them; they pay special attention to the young Europeans, but there is no one familiar. No one seems interested in them, two well-married, well-traveled Americans. They are traveling light, each carrying a blue canvas bag, so there is no need for a porter even if there were one available, which there isn't. They stand a moment together in the chill, savoring the diesel smell of the Zoo Station; this is their sixth trip to Berlin, and they are always filled with astonishment at the sight of it, its size and its gloom, the resigned look of the women on the platform, and the heaviness of the men. She wishes, as always, that she had her sketch pad handy. Kirchner and Beckmann were always sketching on trains and buses and street corners. But of course it is too cold, and they have other business. She looks around, smiling in spite of herself; in fact, she feels the most profound sadness. All European train stations are romantic, but Berlin's Zoo Station is expecially so, if by romance one means a goad to the imagination, fire to the fuel; the mnemonics are fierce.

"To the hotel?"

"I guess so," she said.

"Shall we walk?"

She said, "It's awfully cold. The wind —"

"We walked the first time, remember? It was about this time of year, the first time we came. There wasn't a cab in sight so we walked. Remember, the train was sealed all the way from the border. Some commisar was put into the compartment with us. He had a bad leg. He *smelled*. Remember that?" They walked down the steps into the concourse. He said, "Come on, it's not that far." They had been staying at the same hotel for twenty years, a small hotel off the Ku-damm, only six blocks from the station. The rooms were large and there was a small bar off the reception. The bartender always recognized them, clicking his heels when they entered. He said, "We can check in, have a drink, and then go to Rocken-wall's. Have a good dinner."

"Well," she said, puzzled. "I don't know. What do you mean? After the zoo?"

"We're not going to the zoo tonight," he said firmly. They were standing in the middle of the concourse, not moving. He was talking to her in German, and watching the people navigate around them. "We'll go in the morning."

"Oh, Bill," she said wearily.

"It's time enough."

"I don't know if I can wait. And Rockenwall's is so far away. And what'll we do at dinner, toast our good luck?"

He took her hand and they began to walk down the concourse, and into the muddle of the lobby. In the lobby there were more young people and American music. "In the daylight," he said. "It's time enough." Two middle-aged policemen were watching the young people, who were sitting on the stone floor, giggling. Bill smiled, touching her arm. "It doesn't matter anyway, the zoo is closed. Zoo closes at night, everyone knows that. All zoos close at night."

"All right," she said. "Rockenwall's."

He nodded at the youngsters and the police. "Do you think it's a bust?"

"No," she said. "They're just looking at the girls."

They swung out of the lobby and onto the street, Berlin's bright lights, advertisements, restaurants, shops. Pedestrians walked quickly, their chins buried in coat collars. The wind was sharp. Somewhere out of sight, near the zoo's dark zone, they heard a siren's bleat. They walked for a block, then hailed a cab. The hotel was as they remembered it, but the bartender was gone. Visiting his son in South America, the young woman at the desk said; he would be back in a month, after Christmas. The bar was empty, and dark.

They left their bags at the reception desk and took a cab to Rockenwall's. They rode for miles, circling Berlin's featureless perimeter. It is a very large city, one of the largest in Europe. Elinor had been silent since the Zoo Station. He ordered a bottle of Champagne to cheer her up. But she would not cheer. He was tired of making decisions and fell into a kind of dull fatalism. Events are in the saddle, he thought; best to give yourself up, and cease to pretend that you were in control in any serious way. You were in Berlin. That was the decision, the *act;* everything else was reaction. Not acts, gestures.

He did not look at the menu, but simply told the waiter to bring him the specialty; Elinor said that was fine with her, too. So they ate a tedious meal, Kraut nouvelle cuisine, so pretty and delicate. He told her stories, and she smiled dutifully but wasn't interested — really, wasn't listening. He was trying to figure a way to declare conclusively that he would go alone to the zoo in the morning. At last, tired of his monologue, he trailed off into silence. Now they resembled the middle-aged couple you always saw in restaurants, picking at their food and not speaking, each staring in a different direction. God, you said, what an awful life they must have. And turned away because the sight of them was depressing. The waiter brought coffee and a bill. She stared into her coffee with a vacant expression. She was thinking that he had not mentioned the boy, for no reason other than there was nothing to say that had not been said and resaid. They would meet him soon enough. She wondered whether he would speak English or German. Bill would want to meet him alone, but she would not allow that. How droll after all that the rendezvous would be in Berlin, at the zoo. She looked at him, his eyes far away.

He came out of his reverie, smiled at her, and raised his glass, a toast. Our good luck, he said in German.

Our very good luck, she whispered. She scarcely looked up. She was tracing a figure on the tablecloth. She moved her fingernail in slow, precise circles.

The waiter was hovering. They were the last table. He knew they should leave. Wasn't it necessary to have a good night's sleep? Certainly he would want to be alert in the morning. But he made no move. He did not want to leave the table. The restaurant was familiar; even the dreadful food was familiar. He remembered it from the time, fifteen years ago, that they served heavy German food. Sumptuous sauces, roebuck and game, delicious North Sea sole, sautéed, not poached. Rockenwall's then was a great favorite of politicians and the diplomatic community, and the spies; spies of every race and nationality. It was noisier then, riotous in five languages. Now it was a quiet restaurant for the prosperous businessmen and bureaucrats of the New Germany, muted voices and soft laughter, the tinkle of crystal and impeccable service, very expensive. Well, it had always been expensive; and the old nervous energy had turned to exhaustion. He stared at the tablecloth, sharply cornered and white as milk except where he'd spilled Champagne. In the old days the *digestif* trolley had been superb, rolled to tableside, its inventory unrivaled in Berlin: Armagnac, framboise, marc, schnapps, a dozen others. Everyone laughing, deciding what to celebrate, a birthday or anniversary or promotion; there was always something. He remembered that they had Armagnac as old as he was and so he smiled, touching her foot with his own.

He said, "Do you want to play footsie?"

He looked across the white linen to the trolley by the window, and through the window to the dark street. He wondered if they were there; probably they were. Well, to hell with them. He sat quietly a moment, remembering the good times in Berlin. He thought he had just enough courage to overturn the water glass, and then apologize for it. Without looking at the waiter he said in a conversational voice, "Two Armagnacs, old ones, the 1936 vintage. Doubles, please."

Two balloon glasses filled with Armagnac arrived, with a second bill. The sum could feed a family of four for a month, depending on how much they drank with their meals. He drained half the glass, feeling the liquor burn and his eyes commence to water. The taste was familiar, but nothing else was. He watched the candle flicker in the glass, felt the liquor settling. By God, it was good; it would be even better if she would talk to him. The last time they were at Rockenwall's, sometime in Carter's term, they had a table by the window. Kurt Kleust had joined them, had flown in from Bonn for the occasion. Elinor had been very talkative, telling some Washington story, making everyone laugh. The story was funnier in German than it was in English. He sipped the Armagnac, thinking that it would be a terrible mistake to get drunk, definitely contraindicated.

He murmured aloud, "But I'm already drunk."

Elinor leaned across the table. "Please, Bill."

She had not touched her glass so he finished his own, and then took hers. He finished that in two swallows. His head began to thicken. He and Elinor were sitting in a little zone of silence, as if they were drugged. She looked very tired, her hair falling in ...... commas either side of her face. The long candles threw soft shadows; not a woodcut, a watercolor. This would not be a good time to have an argument, but he could see her watching him; and her expression was not encouraging. He wanted never to lie to her, never keep a secret from her, never betray her. He wanted to be better with her than he was with himself. They were two sides of the same coin, that was what she had always maintained. Except that one side was sober and the other side was drunk. A light went off in the main room. How nice it would be to spend the next two days at table, in semidarkness, drinking fifty-year-old Armagnac at quiet Rockenwall's, a kind of landlocked anonymous state like Andorra, a neutral nation, never at war, always in repose, serene behind secure borders.

"Bill?" Her voice was small and hushed. She continued to trace the figure with her fingernail, looking at it with a child's concentration. She spoke as if she were afraid of being overheard. "Can we go now?"

"Wouldn't you like to stay here forever?"

"No, Bill."

"It's a hell of a nice restaurant."

"It was nicer in the old days."

"Never mind them," he said. "You didn't drink your Armagnac. It's god damned good Armnagnac."

"There'll be other Armagnacs, Bill."

"Not at Rockenwall's."

"Why?"

"Because I don't want to come back here."

She said, "All right."

"What you said was true, it was better in the old days. Remember the night you made everybody laugh? Kurt, and those English friends of his."

She folded her napkin, nodding.

"You were talking Washington psychobabble, translating into German. You were a scream."

"It was your birthday," she said.

He had forgotten. That was why they had been drinking the

1936 Armagnac. He lifted the balloon glass, looking through it at her. "This is a 1936, an exceptional year. A hell of a lot happened in 1936, I've looked it up. The Spanish Civil War began, Trotsky was exiled, Chaplin did *Modern Times*. That's a lot to happen in one lousy year." He moved the balloon glass from side to side, distorting her features. "It's fifty years old, same's me."

She leaned across the table and took his hand, pulling at his fingers. She looked at his hand, not trusting herself to speak.

He said, "It's not numb anymore."

She smiled, squeezing his hand.

He flexed it. "See?"

"I've always liked your hands," she said.

"You know. I've been meaning to tell you. I hated the idea of Prowler Fowler fooling around with my hand."

She said, "Bill."

"Anything could've happened."

She looked at him sideways.

"He could've screwed it up, sabotaged it. Made it numb for life. Revenge, do you see what I mean? To put me out of business. He always had a thing about you."

She said, "Well."

He waited for her to say something more and when she didn't he added, "And I was afraid you had a thing about him. It worried the hell out of me."

She said, "Oh, Bill," quavering a little.

"But you didn't."

She smiled at him, her warmest smile.

"And I knew that, so it was all right. You have to act on what you know, not what you suspect." He put down the balloon glass with a thud. "I would've killed the son of a bitch, ripped his teeth out." He was squinting at her, his eyes unfocused and wavering. "Where would we have been, without each other?"

She said, "I can't imagine."

"Our belief in each other."

"Yes," she said.

"Well, I can't either. Imagine."

She said, "You were all I ever wanted."

"He dyes his damn hair, did you know that?"

She squeezed his hand again, and laughed out loud.

"Good shape, though. Jesus, he's in terrific shape."

"Not such great shape, Bill. You didn't notice his neck. He has wattles."

"Waddles?"

"Big ones," she said. "I don't know how the stewardess stands it. Definitely unsexy."

"It's a relief to know that," he said.

"A neck like a turkey." She made a carving motion below her chin.

"It would interfere, wouldn't it?"

"You have no idea," she said.

"Thing like that, screw up a relationship."

"But not a marriage," she said.

"No," he said. "That's what I mean. How could you have a marriage with a man who dyes his hair. You'd never know what was real and what wasn't. All that camouflage, you'd never *know*."

"No, you never would."

"And then you wouldn't feel good about yourself."

"Or him either," she said.

"It goes without saying, see what I'm saying," he said.

"I see what you're saying."

"I hope you're comfortable with this."

She squeezed his hand again. "You have no idea."

He looked at her face, soft in the candlelight. "Okay," he said. "Dear Bill."

"It's never how great you are in the good times, but how great you are in the bad." He was still looking at her, so blurred across the table. "That's what I've wanted to tell you."

She turned, closing her eyes.

"And it's time to go," he said.

"I don't want to."

"Me either, but it's the way things are. I've liked it here with you. And I've upset you and I'm sorry." He took out his wallet, and flipped it open on the table. He was having trouble focusing. A rustle behind him; he imagined he heard the click of heels. He had been droll, they both had; but it was a bad time and he couldn't sustain it and now she was near tears. He would be too but he was drunk; if you wanted to bawl, Armagnac was not the spirit of choice. He looked at his watch, delaying things a moment, letting the moments accumulate, thickening. "My God," he said suddenly. His voice was loud, somewhere between amused and outraged. She immediately looked up. He was staring at his watch, at the time and the date. He opened his wallet and began taking out banknotes. "Do you know what day it is? It's Thursday, and it's four in the afternoon in America. It's Thanksgiving, darling," he said.

3

BILL KNEW some spycraft, from novels and from friends; the novels were more reliable than the friends. And of course when he was ambassador he supervised the activities of the station chief. He knew what they did, not always how they did it. The station chief played his cards carefully and when he dealt the deck was often shy an ace or a trey, depending. When security became a problem, they briefed him on certain procedures. He knew, for example, that there was no way to know for certain whether you were being followed, unless you were on a desert or the open sea. But if you suspected that you were, you probably were, and there were steps to take to throw the shadow or confuse him. There were ways to lose shadows, even five or six shadows. If you didn't want to lose them there were ways to do that, too. All this sounded simple enough, surrounded as it was by an air of unreality. It depended on how much paranoia you could summon, or how little.

They were loitering now, in the Berlin Zoo, having separated at the hotel and gone in different directions. This was Bill's bright idea. They had gone first by cab, then on foot, by bus, by cab again, by subway, and then, reunited in front of the Café Einstein, on foot to the zoo. His fatalism had not left him, was, if anything, deeper. He could imagine no good outcome, no happy ending. But he wanted to make his best attempt. Without any evidence for it, he believed that he and Elinor had been traced from Hamburg. Duer's people had been on the train, had followed them to the hotel, and to Rockenwall's. Had followed them back from Rockenwall's as well, though he had seen no sign of a shadow. But of course that didn't mean anything. He had thought briefly of leading them into the East Zone and losing them there. They wanted Bill Jr. very badly but not badly enough to enter the East Zone, which presented a danger to him and Elinor as well, because what would he say to the Vopos when fifteen minutes later they came out again —

My goodness, this isn't East Berlin, *Communist* Berlin? We've taken the wrong subway, we only wanted to go shopping, Swiss watches, furs, and electronic gadgetry, pharmaceuticals. Gosh, sorry.

And then there was his black passport, which would raise other questions. Possibly they would think he was defecting, joining the moles of the West German security services who were flying over the wall like swallows returning to Capistrano. Thinking about the East Zone he had concluded, *I am at a disadvantage.*

Now, loitering in the zoo, he believed them alone and unwatched, at least by Duer or Duer's people. There were two suspicious *herren*, sharing a bench (suspicious because when he and Elinor strolled by, one of them tipped his hat), but in the gloomy atmosphere everything was suspicious, even the animals. It was a gray northern morning, more winter than autumn, trees bare of leaves, snow in the air, a few old people here and there, many of them with small nasty dogs on long leather leashes. There were no children about, and no vendors. The animals clustered sullenly together in their cages.

Bill and Elinor walked for an hour, then hailed a cab and went for lunch in a restaurant off the Ku-damm. They had been seated not ten minutes when she asked him, irritably, please not to look at every face as if he expected a ghost, or Herr Duer. *Please,* she said. If they're here, they're here. If they're not here, they're not here. You're driving me crazy, she said.

He looked up from his beer, surprised. He was not looking for ghosts or for Herr Duer. He was looking for their son, or the girl. That was obvious. He knew in his bones that an approach would be made that day. He explained this to her, the feeling in his bones, and she nodded wearily. But perhaps she was right. He was altogether too eager and conspicuous. They were both on edge, however. And she was becoming as sour and pessimistic as he was.

After lunch, they took a cab back to the zoo.

The zoo had always seemed to him a jungle, undefined and lacking in order. The wide paths and bushes, and trees without leaves, the damp soil and animal smell; all this was threatening, a female's dark uncontrolled energy. Dark and green in summer, and in the autumn and winter merely dark, the zoo was an unpredictable frontier. Yet there was a wonderful serenity, a hush as profound as the interior of a church or a cavern; in the ancient clammy air one waited for the blast of an organ or the drip of water. One waited for an echo. Wolf's senses stretched, tingling, as he clenched his teeth, smiling, anticipating Gert. She was due any moment; any moment she would come swinging through the zoo entrance, looking neither to the left nor to the right; dependable Gert, a disciplined soldier. He stepped forward into the shadows, thinking of himself as a fearless explorer — Cortez, Columbus — pressing to the edge of the future's precipice.

I am the last of my line, he thought. *I am the last echo.* The last North. They had made their way through the centuries, surviving war, plague, famine, poverty; a tough family, though stingy with their genes. And now he was the last of them, and the judge of them. The idea elated him: the only son of an only son of an only son, and the most *American* of the three, the least rooted, the least restrained, the boldest, the most individual, the freest spirit, the captive of his deepest self; and the one most removed from Europe and the chains of the past, dead history, discredited faith. He thought, I will be the one to control events, like any good American. Spit in history's eye. And I will respond, never fear. How symmetrical that Europe would be his theater of operations, the place where he would realize his life and liberty, and sound his own echo. He would reverberate, and the nation that believed itself under God would come to understand that a death was a death after all; a death in Beirut or in Kabul or in Washington or in Berlin, it was the same death. The names changed, the identities of the mourners changed, the consequences changed, the circumstances changed; a life was a life, whether extinguished by a bullet, a bomb, the thrust of a knife, or the unexpected cessation of a heart. By one's own hand or by another hand, premeditated or at random, natural or unnatural. Call it God's will, the roll of the dice. The ambassador would understand soon enough. And the ambassador's wife? Yes, she too. The only daughter of an only daughter; her line would also come to an end, though through different means. She who was so mordant and sarcastic, memorizer of box scores, accomplice; she who was so secure within herself, so *certain* in the fashion of bourgeois American women, holding things together; she would have ample opportunity to muse over the events, to extract what meaning there was; to reprise her own life, and the ambassador's; to think, and to paint her pictures while she thought. And wonder if one day his fate would be hers also. In that way she would be introduced to the modern world.

He watched Gert move to the gate, and pause; she paid at the window, and swept through, eyes straight ahead. She had told him she was frightened always of the zoo, for there was no place to hide; she liked glass and concrete, city streets and electric lights and the noise of automobiles and amplified music. The zoo was so still. She moved to the bench, sat, and took out her pad and pencil.

Look at the buffalo, he whispered.

And she did.

He whispered, You are a bourgeois housewife.

She primly arranged her skirt, and crossed her legs.

He smiled happily; they were telepathic, had always been telepathic. He watched her lean forward, concentrating, beginning to sketch the motionless Cape buffalo, her pencil skimming over the page in swift, decisive strokes. Or so it seemed from thirty feet away. Huge beasts, they were frightening. They were not limber. They never moved, and were explicitly unforgiving. He watched her turn on the bench, uncomfortable, ill at ease in her clothes, wearing a smart suit of French manufacture, her hair long and gathered at the neck. A black pullover completed her ensemble. She had concentrated on her role. She was supposed to walk casually but look sharply, as always. Notice everything. She reached down to touch her ankle, grimacing a little; her feet hurt. The shoes were expensive, low-heeled shoes of the *haute bourgeoisie*. Also, the pantyhose were unfamiliar. He had looked at her in her pantyhose and American bra and said, "Sexy." He had told her who she had to be, a bored housewife sketching in the zoo; so bored she thought nothing of sketching in the cold; so bored she moved about, now sketching on this bench, now on that. A bored housewife, uncomfortable in her own skin. Watching her, he believed in her, in the role he had created for her. An observer could be forgiven for thinking she was waiting for her lover; but such a thought would be false.

He told her what to think about, so her face would have the correct look. She would want to go deep into her imagination, her sense of things in the bourgeois life. It would be a look that would discourage familiarity even as it disarmed. Think about what you're going to have for dinner, Gert dear. Thinking about what a son of a bitch your husband is, how thick, how insensitive, how cruel, how mediocre. How ungrateful your children are. How routine and unfulfilled your life. Look at the other women in the park, and decide whether they are alluring, and attractive. And if they are attractive, why they are attractive; and then decide whether what they are wearing would look good on you. And how much it would cost, out of pocket. He gave her money to put into her purse so that she would feel like a prosperous housewife. And when you sketch, look beneath the skin of things, the animals and the vegetation, to the essence. Not the top, he said, the *spin*.

He handed her a little red tam and said, When you see them, make no sign of recognition. Pass by. Do not look at them. You do not know them, so there is no reason to recognize them. (He cocked the red tam on the side of her head, jaunty, just so.) Look at the animals, then circle back. When you encounter them the third or fourth time, smile briefly, as you would acknowledge any stranger in a public place.

How will you know them? Remember. Remember the time in Hamburg.

No, she said.

Gert! Remember the woman who cried, and the sarcasm of the man? Remember how tall he is, how he stoops, and how the woman always holds her chin just so? Remember them later, when they had drunk too much? You will recognize them because of me.

What?

The family resemblance. He kissed and fondled her, whispering something into her teeth. She laughed and hugged him. He said, They may say something to you.

She looked at him.

You smile, and you do not reply. Pass by, and walk quickly out of the zoo. When you see that you have excited their interest, turn and walk quickly out of the zoo. You know the route. Keep walking, no matter what. Do not run, but hurry. And return here, and wait.

Will they know me?

No, he said. Because you have already decided to be someone else. We have talked about your new identity. You will be someone you have been before, when you were modeling in Paris. Remember? You will have Paris expressions and your physical characteristics will be French. You are a young matron, the wife of a businessman. *Comme ça?* So they will not recognize you. No one will.

Except you, she said, and he nodded and kissed her again.

I will be close by, he agreed.

All the elements had come together at last. Things fit. A late afternoon in late autumn, the Berlin Zoo, no surprises. And still the uncertainty, no one could know how the cards would fall. It was enough that he had put them in play, Gert and the ambassador and his wife. It was a game of chance on a green baize table, an abrupt zone of insecurity, as arbitrary as the headlines of tomorrow's newspaper. And so much depended on Gert, Germany's child. He watched her now, as the ambassador and his wife came through the turnstile and hesitated, alert as animals in the wild, but without energy. The energy was Gert's.

She did not expect her feet to hurt so. She was not used to walking, or taking exercise. She had a servant to clean, and on the weekends she and her husband went to the racecourse or watched television. He was an older man — a businessman! At night he liked to watch vulgar films on television. Often she went to the zoo to sit

303

and sketch amateurishly, and consider her days as a businessman's bored and frivolous wife.

When she saw them, she did not immediately register the fact. She was sketching a Cape buffalo, ugly creature, wide, thick horns, brutally curved. She was working on the horns, more interesting than the beast's face or body. She saw them stroll by, the man looking around, seeing her, pausing, his hand on the woman's arm — the woman who held her chin just so, she would be his wife — and walking on. She said something to his wife, but she did not turn. Gert concentrated on the buffalo, and when she next looked up they were gone. She completed the sketch and moved off down the path. She walked with determination, as if she were following the lines of a script. She thought of this part of the afternoon as a ballet. The wind was sharp but she was not uncomfortable. The wind fluttered her skirt, and she felt a few drops of rain. She put her sketch pad under the pullover. Then she saw them again, standing in front of the elephant house.

She veered off onto another path that would take her around in a loop. She had looked carefully at the man, at his broad back; he did not look well. He stooped, and walked slowly; his head was bent. She wondered if he were ill, the weather was so raw.

When she came around again, they were facing her. The woman was looking into her eyes. The woman smiled warmly, and Gert returned the smile, a fleeting smile, the casual, distracted smile that strangers exchange to be polite. But he was right, there was a family resemblance.

The woman said in German, "Are you Bill's friend?"

Not Bill, *Wolf.*

The woman said, "You look so familiar."

Gert said, "I am just a bourgeois housewife."

The man smiled, and put his arm around his wife's waist. Gert knew it was a signal of some kind. She looked into the man's face, and was startled by his expression, so sympathetic yet intense. His gray eyes were cold, and he looked frightened. It was an expression she often saw on the faces of people that she met for the first time. It signaled confusion. She smiled at him openly, without guile, wanting to appear friendly. She expected him to speak, but he said nothing.

The woman stepped forward, saying again, "I believe we have met somewhere, perhaps in the past." She grinned. "I, too, am a bourgeois housewife, with a desire to sketch. But I have never gone to the zoo to sketch. It's so cold and raw today. Don't you think?"

Gert did not reply.

"We, my husband and I, are here to meet our son."

The man said quietly, "El, it's not her."

"We were to meet him here in the park, some time today, or perhaps tomorrow."

Gert smiled, and moved to pass by them.

The woman said, "You are a very pretty young girl. May I see what you've sketched? What is your name?"

Gert said, *"Bitte,"* and walked off. She hoped that this was the right thing to say. It hardly ever failed, a simple *"bitte."* But the woman seemed to recognize her, though of course that was impossible. She had never met the woman before. However, her face was familiar; the eyes, and the set of the mouth. She forced herself to remember that this was only the second encounter and she had been told, quite specifically, at the *third* or *fourth* encounter she was to leave the zoo, and go straight home.

Gert heard the woman call after her. She heard their footsteps coming up behind her.

Gert had one encounter to go. But she did not mind being in the zoo, she knew it so well. The rain had stopped and the sun was trying to break through the belt of clouds, low and layered on the horizon. It was late now, almost four. All they would see would be a sunset, the last rays of light before dusk. November in northern Europe was very gloomy, always.

She moved quickly left, then right through the shrubbery to the narrow path that led back to the entrance. It was likely she would encounter them again there, for the third time; and then she could leave the zoo grounds. Her new shoes squeaked, clicking on the path. She heard something behind her and turned again, this time right. She knew exactly where she was, though there were no landmarks. She was deep in the park, where Berlin's rooftops were not visible, and the street noise muffled. It seemed to her unnaturally quiet. She slowed, listening carefully; she heard no footsteps behind her, but she knew also that she was not alone.

Gert wondered what the woman had meant, that they had met before "in the past." She said it as if the past were a location, like a house or restaurant in Berlin or Leipzig, a specific place existing perhaps only in the memory. But they had never met, she was certain of that. Blood pounded in her temples, and she stopped a moment to allow the blood to subside.

Gert was at a crossroads.

She felt the presence of the woman before she saw her. She smelled expensive perfume, and felt the atmosphere change. Her head cleared and she waited, poised. The voice at her side said, "We do not mean you harm."

Gert did not turn, but continued to stare straight ahead, every sense alert. They were familiar words, she had heard them many times; and they were always false.

"But we must know. Are you Bill's friend?"

The voice was soft and seductive, but others had been. People used words like weapons, the more seductive, the more lethal.

"Do you want to take us to him?"

Gert said, "I don't know you, I'm afraid."

The woman said, "There is no need to be afraid."

Gert smiled.

"I'm Bill's mother. I'm Elinor North." The woman touched her on the elbow, but Gert did not return the gesture or react in any way, so the woman removed her hand. Gert turned her head, and the woman smiled encouragingly. Gert did not know what kind of woman she was, but believed that she was strong, like the statue in the square. Perhaps even heroic. She wondered where the man was. They have taken different paths.

"May I see your sketch pad?"

Gert shook her head, and made as if to go.

"Tell us what to do, and we will do it. My husband and I are exhausted. Do you understand?" The woman was no longer smiling. "We don't know what he wants of us. Where he wants to meet. We are willing to meet with him, wherever. But it must be now. So if you want to walk away, do so. Tell him that we are here. We will stay another hour. No longer. Do you understand me?" The woman stepped back, Gert watching her. The woman's German was grammatically perfect, but the accent was faulty. Gert knew that the woman was trying to prepare her for — something. She felt tremendous danger. "I know you are Bill's friend. It's hard for me to talk."

Without knowing why, Gert wanted to delay a moment. On impulse she handed the woman her sketch pad.

"This is quite good," the woman said. "The Cape buffalo, and Bill and me. I like the horns." She handed the sketch pad back. "We will be here another hour. Tell him that. Tell him there is no one with us. We are alone." Gert began to move away, but the woman followed. Gert turned, reaching into her handbag, and the woman stopped dead. They stood staring at each other, five feet apart.

Gert thought the woman did not know what she was saying. She did not know where she was. This was not the past, but the present. She said she was Bill's mother; perhaps that was true and perhaps it wasn't. Gert hated her soft words, and full sentences. She talked too much. Now and then her hand went to her left ear, to touch a gold earring; a nervous gesture. She was not moving now. Gert's hand gripped the little .25 in her purse. She was waiting for an impulse. It began to rain again, little drops, barely more than a heavy gray mist. She heard a voice behind her, "Gert," so soft no one else could hear it, though the woman seemed to react. Gert withdrew her hand from her purse and let the purse swing from her shoulder. She moved back calmly, a step at a time. She stood with her sketchbook in her hand, feeling the thick cardboard and the soft sheets in between. The woman had said, *Quite good.* She liked the horns. Now her face seemed to soften, her mouth moving, her fingers touching her lips. The woman was looking over Gert's shoulder, rising on the balls of her feet, concentrating, staring as if Gert weren't there. She made a sudden movement and then Gert was running, and in a moment was out of sight, left and right and left again down the narrow paths. She knew she was free to go home, and wait for him there. Then they would be together again, all business concluded, free at last. A bitter day, Gert thought as she ran, the purse banging against her hip; the day left an acid taste on the tongue. These people had no business here. They were foreigners, intruders in Berlin. She accelerated, flying around a curve in the path, then slowed to a walk. She thought, What will I do if he leaves me, goes away back to America?

4

E LINOR SAID, "Hello, Bill."
"Where is he?"
She looked at him. He was standing behind a hedge. The
hedge was waist-high and in his green loden coat he looked to be
part of the scenery, a motionless green man. He seemed bigger,
thicker around the shoulders, but perhaps that was only the coat.
His hair was longer than it had been the last time, in Hamburg,
neatly combed, the color more natural. He was clean-shaven, the
skin drawn tight over the bones; the planes of his forehead were
straight as rulers. She took a step forward but he shook his head.
His face carried authority. It was a hard male face. Not a Washington face or a Boston face or a Lake Forest face, God knows; not an
American face.

"Where is he?" Again, in rapid German, as if he couldn't get the
words out fast enough. Perhaps that was it, Bill Jr. speaking to her
in German, his lips curling around the words; it was easy to sneer
in German. She noticed that his shirt collar was frayed, and missing its top button. She replied in English, "He's here, somewhere
in the zoo. Or are we in the Tiergarten now? He'll be back in a
moment, you know Dad. He took another path, perhaps he's lost

308

his way." Then, smiling, her tone still conversational: "I spoke to your friend, and looked at the sketches she made. She showed them to me. She's good, she's a talented girl. And very pretty. Lovely dark eyes, we noticed her at the entrance, and knew right away that she was your friend. It was not difficult. We've always known your tastes, Bill." He said nothing, nor did his expression change. She thought it was like talking to a sardonic tree. She said, "Dad was here a minute ago."

"How many are with you?"

"No one's with us, we're alone."

He raised his eyebrows. "No security?"

She said in German, "Do we need security?"

He nodded slowly. "Listen. I want you to get him, and bring him here."

"What is her name, your friend? Or is she your wife? You've been together so long, are you married?" She wanted him to know that he was not a total mystery to them. She thought that if he once spoke familiarly, the mask might fall. Or break. She was obliged to believe that he wore a mask, had taken a role, because he spoke to her as though she were a casual acquaintance, or a servant. The laundress, someone to patch his collar and replace the button. She was no more than five feet from him but the space between them was charged, a magnetic field. She could feel it. They spoke across a great chasm.

"Get him now, and tell him to return here."

"Then what?"

He said, "You leave. Tell him to return here alone."

She said, very slowly, in English, "We travel together, your father and I. We always have." His face seemed to flush, but in the drizzle and the gathering dusk it was hard to tell. She said, "We are inseparable, as you know." Except right now. She had no idea where he was, and she wasn't sure where she was. The Landwehrkanal separated the zoo from the Tiergarten, and she could not remember if they'd crossed the little bridge. He had gone one direction, she another. Wherever she was, *he* wasn't there. And she wanted him near her. She wanted them together. She wanted him to talk to the boy, he had always been more successful at it. She said, "We used to be inseparable as a family, your father and I, and you. All the odd places we lived, do you remember Africa at all, when you were very little? The time your father was hurt, and I burst into tears over the telephone when I heard the news. You were right there beside me, and reached over to touch my arm, but I couldn't stop crying. We didn't know whether he was dead or alive. Do you remember that?" She leaned forward, feeling the drizzle on her cheeks, trying to recognize him as a part of her. She said, "I liked meeting your friend. She must have a name, what is it?" He lifted his chin, as if about to speak; but he said nothing. "And I have a name, too. Why don't you use it? Or don't you need names? In the new order, will names be eliminated, like private property? A nation of nameless citizens, parents, sons, all nameless. Interchangeable parts, everyone anonymous, like the modern art I hate so. White on white on white." She hesitated as her voice rose, her temper nearly out of control. His eyes moved left and right, and it occurred to her suddenly that he was not listening to her. It was as if he had the ability to suspend his hearing. Her words moved around him, like rushing water around a boulder. She felt herself growing lightheaded under his erratic gaze, opaque as marble.

He said, "Get him."

"Don't use that tone of voice with me." Her mouth went dry. She had never allowed herself to be bullied.

He said, "So?"

"You want him, you get him."

"Yes," he said.

"What is it that you want from him, Bill? Or from me."

"I remember Africa," he said in English. "The rains, the heat, the little Ford car, the market, the houseboys. The boy who cooked. The boy who cleaned. The boy who mowed the lawn and tended the flowers. The boy who mixed the drinks. And what was he then, a second secretary? Lowest rung of the ladder."

"You were very young," she said. She tried on a smile, but it didn't fit. "You were only a little boy. You have a remarkable memory, Bill. We worried so about taking you to Africa."

"Why were you so worried?"

She shrugged, it was so long ago.

"There must be a reason."

He seemed genuinely interested, and when she replied that they were worried about the insecurity of the countryside — the government's authority did not extend much beyond the capital military district, and its hold even there was fragile—and disease in general, he smiled thinly. She added that they had wanted very badly to see the African continent, not that they had much choice. The Department's postings were to suit the Department's convenience, not the convenience of a Foreign Service officer. Certainly not second secretaries, or their wives or children. "We were given all the shots," she said, "except you were so young. There were one or two shots they refused to give you, fearing a reaction. It worried us because Africa was Africa." She said, "But no one got sick, and your father and I and you, too, loved Africa."

He said, "Remember, a year later, when I began to have nightmares?" He was speaking German again, so softly she had to lean forward to hear him. "I had them every night, for a long time. What was I? Five years old?"

"I don't remember," she said truthfully. "I don't remember that you had nightmares. Why? Do you remember them?"

"No," he said. "But they were frightening. Of course so much is frightening to a five-year-old. Yet at that age, a child is resilient. I have forgotten the plot of the nightmares, but I remember the effect. I remember what it was like, alone in the bed."

"Yes," she said doubtfully. "You had the room closest to the flower garden, at night with the windows open . . ." Her memory stirred, then lay still, disclosing nothing. She did not remember the nightmares. Both she and Bill were heavy sleepers, and Bill Jr. was a very heavy sleeper. "The garden outside your window, remember how sweet-smelling it was? We were very happy there."

"We were? I don't remember."

"How strange. You, with your good memory. The rains, the heat, the little Ford car . . . the houseboys."

"I remember very well the call that night. When, as you say, you burst into tears over the telephone. The houseboy came to get me, to take me back to bed. They were all whispering, 'the boys,' back in their 'quarters,' the two rooms they were allotted. We were waiting dinner. I remember the black skins of the boys, and my skin so white. I laid my forearm across the forearm of the houseboy, an X in black and white. My arm so small, his so thick. I remember thinking that he could snap my arm like a twig, though of course he would never do such a thing; not then. He told me a story, putting me to bed. You were on the telephone with the embassy." He looked at her standing in the drizzle; they forgot everything that wasn't convenient, that would not contribute to their good opinion of themselves. He thought she had aged in the four years since he'd seen her, thick around the hips, her hands crabbed. She was clasping and unclasping her hands, moving her wedding ring around her finger; and her voice had thickened, too. It was a voice comfortable with fatalism and confusion. He thought she was just this side of sullen, protecting what was hers. "And the next day, the drive to the airport, and then to the hospital in the airplane. I wanted to stay with the houseboy, but you insisted. *He wants to see you,* you said. *Don't you want to see your father?*" He let the thought hang, watching her flustered reaction. "It was a small airplane, I suppose it was an asset of the CIA. Everything is, in that part of the world. Your escort let me touch the barrel of his Browning, his 'piece,' black as the forearm of our houseboy. Shall I call the houseboy by name? You called him Charles, though of course that was not his real name. It was the name you gave him, for your convenience. A name you could pronounce. *Charles, fetch the drinks. Charles, see to the dishes. Charles,* always willing."

"It was his name," she said.

"His *Christian* name," he said. "But he was not a Christian."

You should have heard the buzz of conversation in the houseboys' rooms, when they learned what had happened. The *baas* had been attacked and injured, upcountry where the government's writ did not run. The *baas* had shown his white skin, the passport of the ruling classes, and it was not magic after all. The *baas* had lost his juju. His blood had been spilled. Things were never the same after that, were they? That day, our boys entered the twentieth century. Remember when they saw us off at the door, waving as we left for the airport in an embassy car, driven by your escort? So subdued, they averted their eyes; they knew they were the enemy. It was the beginning of reality for them. The *baas* had raised their consciousness, wouldn't you say? Charles had packed something for the *baas,* some fruit I think it was, and your escort sent it sailing out the window, back at their feet; you didn't even notice. Then we were in the plane, but the airstrip where we were to land was insecure, so we circled and circled, until assured that a landing was safe. You never said a word, just sat and looked out the window, as we circled. We were told to put down, there were no rebels in the area. Remember that shantytown, the rain forest all around us, so green? We landed in a shower, your escort so handy with an umbrella. He was out of his mind with fear, he had the umbrella in one hand and the Browning in the other. You held my hand as we ran to the car, your escort very nervous because the driver was a black. And the short drive to the hospital — the streets were empty except for government troops on every corner. We assumed they were government troops because they were in uniform; but they wore the other uniform, too, faces black as night. You couldn't wait to get to him. You ran down the corridor, I remember the sound your wet shoes made. You were crying then, too. And ran to him in the bed. I tried to keep up but you were faster. You just flew down the corridor, you were so anxious to see him. From the doorway I watched you bend over him, climbing on the bed, your skirt hiked up over your thighs. He was laughing, so happy to see you. I see your ringed hand, his face on the pillow. He was bandaged, and there was blood on some of the bandages. Blood on the doctor, blood on that Kraut friend of his. Blood on the sheets. I stood in the doorway, waiting. No one saw me. But as the poet said, Who cares for the roses when the forest is burning?

He was conscious of his voice, low and guttural, and her wide eyes. She drew back, and he could see the whites of her eyes. He was looking for some flicker of recognition, but he did not see it. So he took another step into the past, speaking still in German. "It was strange then. And even stranger in retrospect, though I remember everything. Every single thing. You were very angry, do you remember how angry you were? Spitting nails, you said later, when you could talk about it. Such an injustice, him wounded and in bed, in pain, almost killed. For what? you said." He raised his voice to a falsetto, mocking her. *Who do you think you are, you two, Jack Armstrong and Siegfried? I have been worried to death.* " He watched her closely now as he turned the screw. "You looked up from the bed, your hair mussed, your face wet. I had never seen an expres-

313

sion such as that. Certainly I had never expected to see you with such an expression, you who were so composed and even-tempered, so well-bred. You said something to that fascist friend of his, the one who works for the Bonn administration. You were sitting on the bed with his head in your lap, looking at him but talking to the fascist. Saying how *foolish,* how *reckless,* they had been. Challenging the savages. But thank God, no one was killed, meaning that *they* had not been killed. The fascist was grinning. You were spitting nails at the fascist, but he kept shaking his head. He had his arm in a sling and was leaning against the wall, smoking; so self-satisfied. He looked as if he'd stepped off a yacht, so debonair, expurgated. Then the fascist commenced his explanation, everyone quiet and attentive while he talked. The important work that they were doing, the bad luck that followed. The fascist said something in German, a quotation of some sort, and everyone laughed. Then the Kraut doctor pulled out a bottle of Champagne, popped the cork; the cork hit the ceiling. Smiles all around. After all, things could have turned out — differently. Worse than they did turn out. The white men were alive. The white men had survived. After a while, I went outside. There were boys playing ball, it must have been soccer. They were older than me, playing with a ragged soccer ball, dodging puddles. When they saw me, my white skin and blue eyes, they ran. So I was alone in the courtyard, wondering why they had run away. Were they afraid? What power did I have that they would be afraid of me, a five-year-old boy. Or was I someone necessary to avoid? I stood outside his room. I heard you laugh, once, and I looked inside. His face was gray as ashes but he was grinning as you fed him a sip of Champagne. One sip only, the doctor said. You fed him as you might have fed an infant. A thin line of Champagne dribbled down his chin, and you wiped it away with a cloth. I heard a noise then and looked behind me. Your embassy escort was standing outside the door, swinging the Browning by its grip; he was an enormous man, very muscular, very frightened. Perhaps it was the first time he had ventured outside embassy ghetto. The boys were well away by this time, standing across the road; they were standing quite still, looking at the glowering white man with the Browning. He had been watching me all this time, but when he saw me look at him he went inside. He stood just inside the door, his shadow visible; his shadow, and the shadow of the Browning. I wanted to go across the street with the others, but I dared not. I was afraid that if I crossed the street, he would shoot me. So I stepped into the middle of the courtyard and kicked the soccer ball, a feeble kick in their direction. It was their ball, and they were entitled to it. It bounced across the road and hit a tree. They made no move to fetch it. I was ashamed of my cowardice, I knew I had let them down; and I knew that we were on the same side. I turned my back on your escort and walked away, around the side of the building, trying to lose myself; low windows, the sills were eye-level. The rooms were empty and dark, with their doors open; I could hear your noise, laughter and commotion down the long hall. All the rooms were empty, except the last one. Three blacks, a man in bed, two young nurses attending. His rifle lay beside the bed, old and not at all lethal-looking; not like the Browning. The nurses were doing something to his stomach, but he neither moved nor cried out. His face was opaque, almost featureless but filled with life, as life teems under the skin of the ocean. I knew that somehow he was connected to the ambassador, and what had happened in the bush. He turned suddenly and our eyes met. I could feel the ignition. What must he have thought, a white boy outside his window? The nurses were oblivious, whispering, applying a dressing to his stomach. We stared at each other, and he made no move. We communicated by other means. Perhaps he saw under my skin what I had seen under his. When one of the nurses turned and caught sight of me, she gave a little gasp, turning toward the man in the bed. His eyes never left mine, but he nodded his head curtly. The two nurses conferred, then one of them left his side and came to the window, and pulled down the shade. But not before he had put his forefinger to his mouth, the universal signal; not that I needed to be told. Not that I needed to be reminded to keep silent about the wounded black man in the dark room. Not that I needed to be threatened, either. I walked back the way I had come, stopping again at the ambassador's window. The laughter was quieter now. Someone suggested that you leave, he needed rest. I saw you rise and walk to the door. You were holding a cup of Champagne. When you got to the door you did a dance, a kind of boogie. Then the fascist German said, Where's Bill Jr.? And you said, I don't know. I think he went outside. He's so young and Bill's so tired and beaten up. . . . Hearing that, I left the window and walked across the street, retrieved the soccer ball, and gave it a good kick. The boys were still there. One of them caught it, and they ran away. The sun was so hot, the puddles were already evaporating. I stood in the courtyard, watching the man with the Browning, and remembering the wounded man in the bed: one of the nurses had dipped her hands into a cup of water, and patted his mouth, moistening his lips. They had been so silent and efficient, and clandestine. It occurred to me that they loved him, whoever he was. It was some time after that, the nightmares began." At the end his voice was so low it was almost a whisper.

He watched her shake her head. She raised her arms, and then let them fall, a gesture of exhaustion. She said, "No," shaking her head vigorously, a denial.

"Oh, yes," he said. "All of it's true. It is very vivid. It is vivid still."

"My God —" she began.

He smiled. It always came as such a surprise, the subplot, the thing taking place offstage, in the wings. So disconcerting, when you applied theory to memory, meaning when you applied a theory of history to history itself. When you rejected the benign interpretation, a belief in good will or ill luck or the purest chance in the way the facts cavorted. There were those with power and those without power and the powerless would not be liberated until the powerful were eliminated, shot dead. No middle ground. Either you had a Browning or you didn't. So now he had given her another Africa, a seething, burning Africa, and it seemed not to agree with her Africa of fragrant gardens and willing, childlike servants, nicknamed like household pets; or Jack Armstrong and Siegfried on the prowl. She lived in a Western dream world. *We were very happy there. Your father and I and you, too, loved Africa.* Loving it most when they were destroying Africans. *We used to be inseparable as a family, your father and I, and you, too.*

He watched her put her hand to her temples. He said, "Later that night, back in the capital, back home, embassy ghetto, you called your father in Illinois. On the telephone with your father you were very stiff upper lip, British memsahib. You described to him the kind of day you'd had. And you told him what you had not bothered to tell me. You said, *We almost lost him.* Can you imagine what I thought, hearing that? But I had my secrets, too."

"It was not my father," she said. "It was your father's father. It was Grandfather North I called that night."

He shrugged. "Then he went away again, back to the United States, with you. He had to make his report. I was left alone with Charles, and the other . . . boys. You'll be surprised to learn that Charles was trying to educate himself. He was trying to learn to read English. I was five years old, and I could read better than he could. So I tutored him. At *five.* And he told me about the village he came from, the life there; the political life of the village, what the people believed in, and what brought him to the capital. He was the sixth son of a chief, did you know that? Your Charles, head boy. That would be the sort of thing you'd appreciate, a fine old county family. Someone came by every afternoon to see how I was getting on, those weeks when he was at the State Department and CIA reporting on his misadventures, and the state of play on the Dark Continent. Sometimes it was the fascist German, sometimes one of the embassy people. How're things, Billy. Have everything you need? Heard from your folks today, they're fine, be home soon. By then, of course, the coup was over. The government had prevailed, and the streets were quiet. When I asked Charles about it, he was not communicative. The time was not right, he said. There had been a mistake. We had been reading from *Huckleberry Finn,* a child's version, one of my books. Too many Nigger Jims, he said. He did not know the embassy's role. But now there are quite a few documents available from that time, and it's no mystery what the embassy tried to do. What *he* tried to do. His role in aborting the revolution. Naturally it did not stay aborted for long, Africa being Africa . . ."

"I knew who Charles was," she said, exasperated, her voice rising. "I knew where he came from, what his aspirations were."

"Because the embassy ran a check, right?"

"He told me," she said.

"You can't remember the nightmares, but you remember that."

"My God, Bill."

"Every night," he said.

She sighed, a long, drawn-out sigh. She seemed to diminish, her shoulders slumping.

He thought, Almost there now. "That's only one slice of history from my magnificent childhood."

She said, "It's fiction."

"No," he said. "It's real enough."

She said, "I didn't say it wasn't real. I said it was fiction."

How they loved to conceal their own duplicity, and the evil consequences of their actions. Americans with their myriad instruments of surveillance, cameras, wires, sensors, satellites, aircraft. The countries of the West were wired for sound, no conversation so casual that it would escape the electronic monitor. But still they knew nothing. They could not put what they knew into context, because they did not believe in history. They said, It's fiction. Meaning: Oh, it's real enough to you, but it isn't the truth. They wanted things to be nice so that they could sleep soundly at night. He looked at her now, so defeated. They accepted their mediocrity, reveled in it. No accident that he was who he was, a man to put things right. To redress the balance. To indict them for their crimes, though looking at her now, so pathetic, it hardly seemed worth the trouble. Still, there was a debt owed. He would require full payment. It was his pleasure and obligation to do so. They, he and Gert, had risked so much, focusing their lives at a single point. They had neglected nothing, forgotten nothing. His inspiration was Gert. She was a great hero, like La Pasionaria or Emma Goldman or Rosa Luxemburg. He had restored her to life, had replaced that which they had stolen from her; she would be his forever. He loved her with all his soul, and even now he grew heavy, thinking of her. He could feel her urgent breath on his neck, commanding him. He did not need to love anyone else, for his love must not be diluted. He wanted purity of heart, purity of action. And must do nothing to betray her. Her trust was absolute, and he would leave nothing undone to guarantee it. He and Gert and their compatriots, so intimate, close as lovers, so harmonious with their single vision of justice — they had agreed long ago: no compromise, no clemency. No peace. Let the game be played on German soil. They would pursue their enemies to the ends of the earth and they had to be lucky only once. They had taken an oath on it, in the names of all the revolutionary dead, in this century and the stupendous last century, and all the centuries of struggle and sacrifice. They acted in the name of humanity. Now they would realize their great vision, and set the clock ticking. A single act calculated to outrage and bewilder their enemies, to exhaust their patience and comprehension, and introduce to them this brainstorm: that anything was possible, that there were no exclusions, no forbearance, no compassion, no limit. He said in English, "You must take responsibility."

"Responsibility," she said dully, looking at him. What did he mean? Responsibility for what?

He said, "Find him. Bring him here."

She shook her head, not trusting herself to speak.

"Get him now."

"I'm here," the ambassador said, emerging suddenly from the dusk.

He had watched them from the beginning, watched Elinor and the girl, Elinor looking at the sketches, the girl's sweet smile. He himself could not be seen, and did not want to interfere. He watched the girl hurry away, then his wife and son together, talking. The boy appeared as if by magic, no more than ten feet from him. Bill watched Elinor's face come alight, a smile any mother would give a returning son, even a prodigal; most particularly a prodigal. *I don't care where you've been, or what you've done, you're mine, and I forgive you.* He believed that somehow Elinor could connect. He had not thought beyond that — only connect, and then see what would follow. Odd how one ignored the experience of a lifetime. It was the amateur's approach to any summit meeting. Anything could follow if only they got to know each other again, talked across a table, had a drink together and located common ground. Surely there would be common ground. Listening to them, he wondered what it was he hoped for. A tearful reconciliation? Expressions of love? Perhaps a mutual acknowledgment of past error, dignified apologies. A sentence or two of atonement, with a promise to forget the past.

The truth was, the time for connection was long past — and, in fact, there was a connection. But it was not a "connection." It was not vivifying. He hated her. He hated them both. And it was not theoretical, it was personal. It was *them*. Listening to his son, he closed his eyes. The boy was talking about Africa, their common life together; he closed his eyes and tried to imagine the five-year-old with tousled hair and solemn expression, the bright boy who always seemed older than his years. The boy who knew too much. The boy who demanded that a picture be removed from the wall of his room before he could go to sleep at night. It didn't matter which picture: one had to go. It was a cute ritual, a family joke, his grave insistence, his pudgy finger moving, then stopping: *There, that one!* Except that all of them were Elinor's, drawn with her own hand. His eyes squeezed shut, the ambassador tried to make something of that. It was an obvious technique of the diplomatic craft, what you want and what they want, and trying to find consequence in an unconscious or trivial act, fooling with language. Anything to get an agreement, some common ground on which all parties could stand without shame. When you dealt from strength you always wanted agreement because agreement proposed stability: a predictable future, meaning a future much like the past. And that was precisely what the opposition did not want. So you watched the *which* clauses and where the commas went, and you understood that it was all a dance in fulfillment of the natural cycle, eat or be eaten. Perhaps his demand that a picture be removed from his bedroom wall was an undeclared wish to destroy his mother's fertility. Or perhaps he didn't like the view.

He stepped from behind the tree and went to Elinor's side. He and the boy looked at each other. He felt his son's vitality, his nervous energy, his resolve and elation. It all came down to this. Never had he felt more a bankrupt, an old nation opposing a young one; and the young one was of his own making. He said, "We're here. What do you want?"

"She can go. You stay."

Elinor linked her arm through Bill's, smiling at him. Then she turned back to her son. "Why me?" she asked. "And as I told you before, don't speak to us in that tone of voice." She thought, A little bit prim in the circumstances. Mom as headmistress. And as she spoke she heard her own mother's flat midwestern voice, and that caused her to smile.

Perhaps Bill Jr. heard it too, for he said, petulantly, "You're not in charge here."

Bill thought, *Grübelei*. The shape of the table, square, rectangular, round, oblong; coffin-shaped, dumbbell-shaped, Z-shaped, T-shaped. It had been months and months, working that one out. The opposition knew we were tired, and that gave them an advantage; unfortunately, the reverse was not also true. They were not tired, and our knowledge of that was no help at all. Those talks, it was like listening to Pachelbel's Canon for six months, no relief. He had made that remark to Elinor long ago and Bill Jr. had looked up and said, Who's Papa Bell?

He put his arm around Elinor, realizing as he did so that his hand had gone numb. Fowler and the hospital room, Richard and the nurses, came back to mind, in and out of his memory. He wondered if they had missed a fragment, or whether the numbness was psychosomatic. His mind was numb, along with the hand. Papa Bell: They had laughed and laughed, and couldn't explain the joke to Bill Jr., he was so young. He caught his breath, feeling Elinor's warmth. Her scent filled his nostrils, and he drew closer to her. He kissed her on the cheek, feeling her soft warmth, and feeling furtive also, as if the affection between them was forbidden, and would be taken as a sign of weakness.

The boy said, "So here we are at last."

"Speak English," Bill said.

"This is normal," the boy said, continuing in German. So that was the way it would go, they speaking in English, the boy in German.

"We met your girl," Bill said.

"My girl," Bill Jr. said. "She's not *my girl*. What do you think she is, a servant?"

"Your girl," Bill said. "She's very pretty."

"She was dressed up for you to" — he sought the word — "admire."

Bill said, "Besides the girl, how many are you?"

"Many," he said.

"They hate Americans," Bill said. "Why do they trust you?"

"I hate Americans even more than they do. Isn't that what you always said? It takes one to know one. Isn't that one of your —"

"Clichés, yes," Bill said.

"We haven't much time. You have no idea, the effort. And the luck."

Bill said, "Congratulations, then."

"Get on with it," Elinor said. "Whatever it is."

"They were with you this morning, your shadows."

"Who was with us?"

"Duer's people, three of them. Not at all difficult to spot, Herr Duer's storm troopers. He must be losing his touch. You lost them somehow because when you came back here they were gone."

"They're not Duer's," Bill said. "Probably they were somebody else's, my people maybe." He knew the boy was lying, and the knowledge chilled him; the fact that he knew absolutely. His tone of voice, even in German; the way his mouth moved. The connection between them was direct. He wondered if the boy had the same ability.

"No, they were Duer's. We know who they are. We have photographs of them, and identities."

He said, "We were not followed. Your mother wouldn't allow it."

"So? And you, Ambassador?"

"She didn't ask me."

"Clumsy, Ambassador. Very clumsy."

Bill listened to him. He imagined he could hear his son's heartbeat, and trace his brain waves. And his son could surely do the same. But none of this would have any effect, except on his own emotions; he was shaken, realizing now the blood tie, and the reciprocity, between them.

"Get on with it," Elinor said again.

"It would be best if she goes."

"No, it wouldn't be best," Elinor said. "I told you before. Your father and I, we're inseparable. Always have been." She hesitated, sighing, as if she were suddenly out of breath. "Oh, Billy," she said, her voice falling, the child's name false-sounding. The boy had brought his hands slowly to the level of the hedge so that they could see what he carried. They knew it was there, but seeing it and knowing it were separate facts; he wanted to frighten them. Pretty, sleek, heavy weapon, the quintessence of the gunsmith's art. He handled it knowledgeably, as if he knew what he was doing.

Ugly piece, Bill thought, a weapon that had no sporting purpose whatever.

His son said, "Have you thought about it at all, these past few days, your career in the government? What you did and why, and the consequences."

"Not much," Bill said.

"You never thought you'd be called to account."

"Not by you," Bill said. His words made no impression. It was as if he was hurling words at a wall, the word rebounding, misshapen, taking odd bounces.

"Now you know," he said. Then, "I've been told you didn't tell them much about me."

"That's right," Bill said.

"I'm interested why not. I'm the enemy, isn't that so? You took an oath to defend your Constitution against people like me. Enemies foreign and domestic. Enemies without and within. I'm both. What happened to your oath?"

"Stop it," Elinor said.

"You look old, Ambassador."

He did not reply. He supposed it was true.

"Sick, you look washed up."

"I had an idea that this was between us," Bill said. "And that it can end right here. If you have me, then you won't need anyone else. Do you understand?" He watched the boy shift position, cradling the weapon, dipping his shoulder characteristically, his expression suddenly igniting. The boy wanted what everyone wanted, freedom, liberation from whatever demons haunted him. A clean bed, enough to eat, good health, however one defined well-being; a fully-booked Lubyanka, a bottle of fifty-year-old Armagnac, a country club membership. An end to the noise in one's own head, a sense that the conditions of the present moment were intolerable; to secure the future, kill the past. He waited for a reaction and when there was none, Bill added, "And there isn't anything in the oath about informing on my son. If I'm the target."

Elinor said, *"Stop it!"*

"I thought about it a lot, though. Elinor and I decided that you were our responsibility." He watched his son for the signal he knew would come but the boy only nodded.

"A sentimental position," he said.

"Call it whatever you like. But it isn't sentimental. And you haven't answered my question."

"Well, it won't end right here. That's the point." He swung the weapon around so that it was pointed at his father's chest. "What do you suppose the consequences of this will be?"

Elinor said, "I will hate you for the rest of my days."

He looked past her as if she were not present. "Ambassador? What do you suppose the consequences will be?"

He thought that Elinor's promise was sufficient. She would make a formidable enemy. But he tried once more to concentrate, to see things clearly. The trouble was, the entire world was present; nothing existed beyond this obscure place, a zoo in a divided city. House rules, he thought; but he did not know what they were. He said, "It could end right here. That could be one consequence. But that's up to you."

"Yes," he said. "It is. But there'll be more. There's always *more*. There'll be a great commotion, won't there? And fear, fear everywhere, and anger and embarrassment, and despair, at what the world's coming to. And then we'll be just a little bit closer to our objective."

"I'm that important?"

"To me you are," he said.

Bill shook his head, clearing it. He had heard the words, and tried to think carefully about a reply. Just then he was certain he was going to die. No power on earth could prevent it. He was thinking about the value of life, his own; but it was difficult, with the entire world present. He was an American ambassador but he could be anyone, of any sex, nationality, age, or position. It would be a life given in vain, one more private soldier fallen on an anonymous battlefield. And who would remember, a month or a year or five years from this day? Elinor would. And of course the boy, and it was only a feature of the circumstances that their memories would not agree. He moved to separate himself from her. He took his arm from around her shoulder, searching instead for her hand, finding it, squeezing. The boy was talking but he wasn't listening. He was trying to think, though there was a great roaring in his head; difficult to think, looking down the barrel of a gun. But of course that was the idea. It was one of the great ideas of Western man. Unlike his father, he would not have time to struggle, except for these few moments. The truth was, he had not expected to be "called to account" by his son or by anyone else. He did not know if that was pride or humility. He knew that with Elinor he was the happiest he'd been, and was not ashamed of his life inside the government. He whispered that to her, and she froze. He turned toward her, concentrating. If he concentrated hard enough she would understand why he must not resist. Resistance was not the point here. The point was not to run away, or to have fear. There was a natural last act to everything, and this was the natural last act for him. He remembered the swollen crocodile, turning on the surface of the African lake, blown by the wind. And that had not been how it looked from afar. As for the consequences — his question, and his son's — they would be unforeseen. They would be in the turbulent future, and they would have nothing to do with this place, where they, a family after all, now stood. New security arrangements, no doubt. Editorials. A statement from the secretary.

Elinor took a step forward, letting go of Bill's rigid hand, gesturing sharply. She uttered a rapid sentence, filled with contempt. She held nothing back. She moved toward the hedge that separated them, trying to penetrate the opacity of his eyes. It was darkening, already deep dusk. From somewhere nearby an animal coughed. She could not see his eyes, so she could not judge his intentions. Bill had moved to one side, but she had no intention of standing quietly in the darkness, listening and waiting.

This is what happened. The boy fired two shots, both of them hitting the ambassador in the chest. The power of the charge drove him back. He was flat on his back, arms raised as if to ward off further blows. He made no sound. She screamed, and lunged forward. If she could reach him, she would kill him with her hands. She blundered into the hedge, then stopped. There was a fence concealed in the hedge. She pressed into it, arms flailing. The wire bit into her stomach. She could hear her own voice, an animal's moan. She reached and kept reaching but she could not advance. Then she stepped back, shocked. The girl had come up behind her son and now stood beside him, much as she had stood beside

Bill. The girl linked her arm through the boy's and they stood a moment, their arms linked, not speaking. They looked so young. The girl's red tam was bright and jaunty. They took a look around, and then a step backward, and in a moment were gone. She heard their footsteps, running away. She was alone. When it was quiet again she bent down to comfort the dying man.